Customer Communications 1999–2000

The Chartered Institute of Marketing/Butterworth-Heinemann Marketing Series is the most comprehensive, widely used and important collection of books in marketing and sales currently available worldwide.

As the CIM's official publisher, Butterworth-Heinemann develops, produces and publishes the complete series in association with the CIM. We aim to provide definitive marketing books for students and practitioners that promote excellence in marketing education and practice.

The series titles are written by CIM senior examiners and leading marketing educators for professionals, students and those studying the CIM's Certificate, Advanced Certificate and Postgraduate Diploma courses. Now firmly established, these titles provide practical study support to CIM and other marketing students and to practitioners at all levels.

The Chartered
Institute of Marketing

Formed in 1911, The Chartered Institute of Marketing is now the largest professional marketing management body in the world with over 60,000 members located worldwide. Its primary objectives are focused on the development of awareness and understanding of marketing throughout UK industry and commerce and in the raising of standards of professionalism in the education, training and practice of this key business discipline.

Customer Communications 1999–2000

Gill Wood

Published on behalf of
The Chartered Institute of Marketing

OXFORD AUCKLAND BOSTON JOHANNESBURG MELBOURNE NEW DELHI

For Alexander

Butterworth-Heinemann
Linacre House, Jordan Hill, Oxford OX2 8DP
225 Wildwood Avenue, Woburn, MA 01801-2041
A division of Reed Educational and Professional Publishing Ltd

℞ A member of the Reed Elsevier plc group

First published 1999

British Library Cataloguing in Publication Data
A catalogue record for this book is available from the British Library

ISBN 0 7506 4367 6

Composition by Genesis Typesetting, Laser Quay, Rochester, Kent
Printed and bound in Italy

Contents

A quick word from the Chief Examiner

I am delighted to recommend to you the new series of CIM workbooks. All of these have been written by authors involved with examining and marking for the CIM.

Preparing for the CIM Exams is hard work. These workbooks are designed to make that work as interesting and illuminating as possible, as well as providing you with the knowledge you need to pass. I wish you success.

Trevor Watkins
CIM Chief Examiner,
Deputy Vice Chancellor,
South Bank University

Preface

The new Customer Communications syllabus has replaced the Business Communications syllabus in a bid to reflect the changes taking place in the world of marketing. This book is written specifically for students who are studying the updated syllabus.

The book provides candidates with easy-to-digest syllabus coverage and a clear focus on the examination in the form of useful study hints, tips for examination success and question practice, with full answer guidelines to help with self-assessment and revision.

The intention of the book is to improve the reader's understanding of communications and to maximize personal communication skills. These topics make essential reading for all marketing professionals. For now, more than ever before, communication skills are an essential prerequisite in all areas of business and none more so than in the competitive world of marketing.

Thank you to all those who helped in the preparation of this workbook.

Gill Wood

How to use your CIM workbook

The authors have been careful to structure your book with the exams in mind. Each unit, therefore, covers an essential part of the syllabus. You need to work through the complete workbook systematically to ensure that you have covered everything you need to know.

This workbook is divided into eleven units. Each unit contains the following standard elements:

Objectives tell you what part of the syllabus you will be covering and what you will be expected to know having read the unit.

Study guides tell you how long the unit is and how long its activities take to do.

Study tips are designed to help you extend your knowledge. It is not possible for the workbook to cover everything you need to know to pass. What you read in the workbook needs to be supplemented by practical experience at work, day-to-day reading and discussion in class.

Questions are designed to give you practice – they will be similar to those you get in the exam.

Answers give you a suggested format for answering exam questions. *Remember* there is no such thing as a model answer – you should use these examples only as guidelines.

Activities give you the chance to put what you have learnt into practice.

Exam tips are hints from the senior examiner or examiner which are designed to help you avoid common mistakes made by previous candidates.

Definitions are used for words you must know to pass the exam.

Summaries cover what you should have picked up from reading the unit.

A glossary is provided at the back of the book to help define and underpin understanding of the key terms used in each unit.

Introduction

As very few people live or work in isolation, communication with others is a fundamental part of one's life. Most jobs can only be achieved through communication, whether that involves giving/receiving instructions, sharing ideas with colleagues or giving information to external customers or suppliers. Away from work, the ability to communicate can affect the quality of personal relationships. In addition to this, communication is integral to marketing, involving, as it does, communication initiatives that range from persuasive sales calls and presentations to clients to the production of simple brochures and leaflets and the creation of sophisticated packaging, logos and advertising.

Communication is, therefore, a core skill which marketing professionals need to use daily. Consequently, the module Customer Communications forms the bedrock of the CIM qualification and the foundation to the other subjects you will study.

The Customer Communications syllabus is a new subject introduced as part of Syllabus 2000 and replaces the Business Communications syllabus. Its development is in response to feedback received from employers, tutors and students. It not only takes account of the changes taking place in the world of marketing but also reflects the evolution of the Business Communication examination paper which has, since its introduction in 1994, increasingly tested candidates' communication skills in a variety of marketing situations.

Thus the focus of the Customer Communications syllabus is on business communications from a marketing perspective. Much of the original syllabus content, such as the communication process, oral communication, written communication and the interpretation and presentation of statistical information, continue to be featured in the new syllabus.

One of the main changes to the syllabus has involved updating the indicative content to reflect the impact of technological innovation on communications. Another change relates to the increasing emphasis placed on the customer and how this has affected customer communications. The breadth of the syllabus has also been extended not only to include the role of marketing research in determining appropriate customer communications but also to incorporate the wide range of promotional activities used by organizations in communicating with customers.

The Customer Communications syllabus

Whether you are studying this module as part of a taught course at a local college or via a course of self-study, it is useful to have an overview of the subject at the beginning. The aims and objectives clearly indicate the breadth of the syllabus and what you will be able to do by the time you have finished studying this module. In planning your study time, the percentage weighting against each indicative content or topic area indicates how much of your total study time should be spent on each area and also reflects the composition of the examination. Thus you can expect that questions relating to the topic 'Finding out about the customer' will only make up 10 per cent of an examination paper.

If you are undertaking this module through the continuous assessment route read Appendix A at the start of your course.

The syllabus for Customer Communications is provided in Appendix B.

Tutor guidance notes

The following notes are provided for tutors to assist them in determining a scheme of work and with lesson planning. However, candidates, especially those embarking on a course of self-study, may be interested to read what the senior examiner considers should be the breadth and depth of indicative content coverage and how candidates can expect to be assessed on these topic areas.

Introduction to tutor guidance notes

This module provides a basic introduction to customer communications for candidates who are working in junior marketing positions or are considering moving into the field of marketing. At foundation level, the module leads on to The Marketing Customer Interface at operational level and on to Integrated Marketing Communications at strategic level. The module has strong links with both Marketing Fundamentals and Marketing in Practice at Certificate level. It also provides students with an introduction to areas that feature in the Marketing Operations and Effective Management for Marketing modules at Advanced Certificate level.

Whilst the content of the module bears many similarities to its predecessor, Business Communications, it has been updated to reflect the following aspects of customer communications: the importance of customer focus; the role of marketing research; using the promotional mix; and the impact of new media developments. The revised module also reflects the evolution of the Business Communications unit, in which communications tasks were placed in a marketing context. Marketing application will therefore be a key feature in the examination, where students will be asked to perform a variety of tasks in a range of marketing contexts, roles and business sectors.

It is intended that students will be tested in an examination in which they will answer a compulsory mini case study and three further questions from a choice of six.

The importance of the customer (25 per cent)

The key message that needs to be communicated to students is the importance of customer-centred organizations. Tutors need to differentiate between the different types of 'customers' that marketing students will communicate with. The differences between internal and external customers should be reinforced and the differences between customers and consumers should be emphasized. The concepts of the decision-making unit and the role of stakeholders should be introduced in relation to the communication process. At a basic level, students should be able to identify the needs of different target audiences in relation to customer communications.

Tutors should highlight the change in customer expectations. Areas to cover include the move to 'customer charters', the rise of the aspirational customer, ethical concerns and the growth in litigation.

This area should also introduce the important role played by relationship marketing, the use of loyalty schemes and the efforts made to measure customer satisfaction. Other points to be highlighted here are the role of front line staff in dealing with customers and customer complaints.

Finding out about the customer (10 per cent)

For this section tutors should provide a basic introduction to various research techniques, types and sources of data and show how information gathered can assist the formulation of effective customer communications. For example, candidates should be able to interpret information from questionnaires and focus groups to help formulate messages to specific audiences.

The process of effective communication (25 per cent)

The key point here is that students should be aware of basic theories about the communication process and customer behaviour so that students can design effective customer communications. Consequently it would be appropriate to introduce the encoding/decoding process of communication. In addition, it would be appropriate to introduce students to a simplified black box model of consumer behaviour and combine it with the various influences on consumer behaviour. Other relevant theory that should be covered includes barriers to communication and the role of body language.

Students need to have an underlying knowledge and understanding about the role of oral communication; in particular, they should be clear about what makes an effective presentation, interview or meeting.

A substantial amount of time should be spent enabling students to practise interpreting, analysing and summarizing written and graphical information so that it can be condensed into a report or other communication format.

Communication formats and media (25 per cent)

The examination paper will reflect how marketing communication tasks are undertaken in a variety of organizations, industry sectors and markets. Students should therefore be comfortable undertaking communication tasks in a variety of roles in a range of contexts: the private and public sectors; the manufacturing and service sectors; the retail sector; professional services; the not-for-profit sector; and in an international context.

Tutors need to provide students with practice in drafting the following types of internal and external communications: letters; memoranda; notices; reports; e-mails; meetings documentation; press releases; press articles; newsletters; briefs; mailshots; telemarketing scripts; and advertisements.

Tutors should provide students with a basic understanding of the following in relation to customer communications: branding; corporate identity; sales promotions; corporate entertainment; events; packaging; point of sale; corporate literature; and websites.

A basic knowledge about consumer behaviour can be applied in this area of the syllabus so that students are capable of drafting a variety of internal and external communications that contain appropriate messages, in the correct tone and produced in a suitable format that would elicit a favourable response.

Technological developments and trends in communications (15 per cent)

Students will be expected to be aware of developments in this area through reading appropriate marketing magazines and the quality press. Students are not expected to have technological expertise in this area. Consequently there will be no questions on how computers work or how to use a mobile phone to access e-mail. The emphasis should be on preparing candidates to answer questions that are set in the context of new media and being able to demonstrate how technological changes impact on the way organizations communicate and do business.

The key points to cover here are how the internet has enabled faster communication, opened up a new global distribution channel, effected business re-engineering and enhanced relationships between suppliers. Other key points are the process of selling on-line, how digital technology will impact upon media decisions, how digital technology will improve communication with, for example, interactive catalogues, newsletters, distance learning and video conferencing, and how improved databases will assist relationship marketing.

Candidates will be expected to know about e-mail in the workplace and to be able to differentiate between an effective and an ineffective website.

Reading list

To guide you in further reading and study, here is the recommended reading list.

Essential reading
Blundel, R. (1998). *Effective Business Communication*, Prentice Hall.
Wood, G. (1999). *Customer Communications*, Butterworth-Heinemann.

Additional reading
McMillan, S. (1997). *How to be a Better Communicator*, Kogan Page/Industrial Society.
Stanton, N. (1996). *Mastering Communication*, Macmillan Press.

Optional reading
Conrad Levinson, J. and Rubin, C. (1996). *Guerrilla Marketing Online Attack*, Piatkus.
Foster, J. (1998). *Effective Writing Skills for Public Relations*, Kogan Page.
Oliver P. (1997). *Teach Yourself Research*, Hodder & Stoughton.
Simons, C. and Naylor Stables, B. (1997). *Effective Communication for Managers*, Cassell.

Unit 1 ■ The importance of the customer

Objectives

In this unit you will:

❏ Look at the different types of customers that you and your organization deal with.

❏ Examine the various ways you and your organization communicate with customers.

By the end of the unit you should be able to:

❏ Understand the importance of effective customer communications in marketing.

❏ Identify the internal and external customers in a given situation.

❏ Be aware of what is meant by the terms *stakeholder* and *decision making unit.*

❏ Appreciate how communication methods and messages alter depending on the context and the customer.

Study Guide

This unit provides an overview of the relationship between people and organizations and their customers. It covers indicative content areas 2.1.1 and 2.1.2 of the syllabus. Some of the unit is revisited in Units 7, 8 and 9 where there is further information about the various communication formats.

You should take one hour to read the unit and a further hour to complete the activities in the unit.

Study Tip

After reading this unit you could develop your understanding of this area by selecting two different organizations that you are familiar with. Compare and contrast the organizations in terms of size, objectives, industry sector (or whether public or private sector) and the type of customers they have to communicate with. Then consider the various ways that these organizations communicate with their internal and external customers and consider how their communications could be improved.

Why are customers important to you?

In studying customer communications within a marketing context, the importance of the customer cannot be underestimated. If you define a

1

customer as 'a person one has dealings with', then clearly everyone, irrespective of job role, organization or industry sector, is affected by the issues arising from this subject.

Definition of customer communications

Customer communication in business is the process by which information is transferred and received from one individual or group to another both within and outside the organization. The communication can take place verbally or non-verbally and may be transmitted through a variety of communication methods, such as reports, presentations, letters, advertising or in meetings.

Why do people communicate in business?

The main reasons for people to communicate in business organizations, internally and externally, are as follows:

- To *build relationships* internally and externally with individuals and groups.
- To give *specific instructions* to others on a range of business matters, both procedural and strategic.
- To *disseminate information* on a range of corporate matters such as the mission statement, policy issues or, in the case of the external market, on price changes or new promotional initiatives.
- To *share ideas and values* on general organizational issues, possibly to maintain or subtly change the corporate culture.
- To share ideas and values on work-specific issues or procedural tasks.
- To *negotiate* matters of policy such as a joint venture or merger.
- To *discuss* or negotiate on personal or professional matters such as remuneration and other higher- and lower-level hygiene factors.
- To *motivate, interest and stimulate* employees for commitment and loyalty to the firm.
- To create an awareness of the organization, its products or services and *persuade* the external market, for example to make a purchase decision or to request further information.
- To receive feedback in order to monitor whether the communication was understood and the reaction of the recipient to the message.

Activity 1.1

Consider who you communicate with, why and how. Remember to consider not only who you send information to but also from whom you receive information.

If, for instance, you are working in a marketing department of a firm that makes and sells garden furniture and you have responsibility for the organization's marketing communications, then in an average working day you may communicate with a large number of people in a variety of ways . . .

You may receive information by post from potential suppliers informing you about advertising opportunities. You may send a mailshot to customers on the company's database to encourage them to order products from a new brochure. You may fax a press release to a gardening magazine to raise the firm's profile. You may telephone a designer to change the layout of a brochure before it goes to print. Your line manager may e-mail you, asking you to organize a corporate event for an important business client. You may meet with a colleague to discuss how a project should be progressed. You may deliver a presentation to colleagues showing sales revenue figures in a graph. Or you may draft a report for the senior management team based on research that you have carried out.

So who are your customers?

All the people you communicate with are your customers – not just the people who buy your employer's goods and services. And while your customers may be different to those described on page 2, you will no doubt find that you have been involved in communicating with people both inside and outside of your organization. You will have sent and received information to and from colleagues, suppliers and your firm's paying customers for a variety of reasons and in a variety of communication formats.

Who are an organization's customers?

In the traditional sense of the word, *customers* are the people who buy a firm's products. To communicate with them effectively, an organization needs to know who they are, what they want from the firm's products or services, where they are located and the most cost-effective methods of communicating with them. By doing this, it will be easier to develop effective communications, such as advertising, sales literature, packaging and product instructions, that appeal to and are understood by the customer.

The consumer/user

However, the person who pays for the product may not be the user or the consumer of the product. For example, a manufacturer of toys needs to communicate with the children who will play with the product, so they will exert pressure on parents (the purchaser/decision maker in this example) to make the purchase.

The decision making unit

In business to business marketing, it may be relevant for an organization to communicate not only with the purchaser, but also with others who could be involved in the decision to purchase. The other people involved in the purchase decision are often referred to as the *decision making unit*.

For example, a firm that supplies computer systems to other businesses needs to communicate with a variety of people who may not be customers but who may influence the decision to buy or not and therefore need to be communicated with.

The purchaser

The purchasing official may have sourced a new computer system and may ultimately place the order. As far as customer communications are concerned, it is important to make the purchaser's job easy, ensuring that up-to-date product, contact and after-sales information is easy to digest and that the ordering process is easy.

The initiator

The initiator or the specifier could be a member of staff or senior manager or even an external consultant, who sees the possibilities for new equipment to improve efficiency. The computer company must consider who these people might be and raise their awareness about its products, possibly via relevant trade press advertising, sales promotional material, exhibitions or public relations activities.

The user

The users in this example would be the staff who would use the computer system. These people may not influence the decision at the outset of the process but may be invited along to test equipment as part of a task group before the purchase decision is finalized. After the decision to purchase has been made, the good opinion of these people is vital if repeat business is to be transacted. The computer company could ensure good customer communications by providing clear user manuals and by providing training and helplines.

The influencer

Influencers could be the technical staff who affect the purchase decision by supplying information about a variety of suppliers or by setting buying specifications. Or they could be staff in the finance department who could block the purchase decision with financial constraints. Similar to the situation with initiators, these *customers* need to be supplied with sufficient information about the product/service via whatever channels are considered suitable.

The decision maker

These people are the most influential in terms of making the purchase decision. They may be a senior manager or the managing director. It is vital to identify who these people are within a firm. The computer company's message could be communicated directly by a sales representative who might use some form of corporate entertaining to influence the purchase decision.

The gatekeeper

Gatekeepers control the flow of information through an organization and may be switchboard operators or secretaries who are responsible for dealing with incoming calls, mailshots and trade journals that arrive by post. The computer company should communicate effectively with this *customer* in order to be able to reach others in the decision making unit. Sales representatives need to be able to talk persuasively to the gatekeeper to obtain appointments or pass on information to the decision makers or influencers.

The stakeholders/publics

Most organizations also have a mix of stakeholders or publics, i.e. internal and external individuals or groups who come into contact with an organization or who affect or are affected by its activities. From a communications point of view they can be considered as important customers or target audiences with whom the organization must communicate.

An organization may choose to communicate with these publics, such as the media or the local community, because it is good for its public relations image and ultimately good for business. Or it may be a legal requirement to produce an annual report for shareholders or it may be essential to a close relationship with suppliers or distributors. In addition, most organizations wish to communicate effectively with current and potential employees to attract and retain the best staff in the marketplace. An organization's stakeholders might comprise the following (see Figure 1.1).

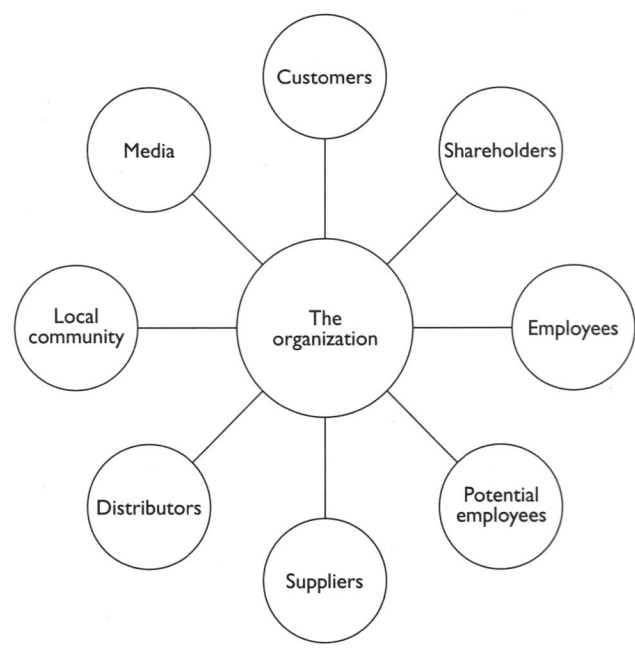

Figure 1.1
An organization's stakeholders

Internal marketing and internal communications

From your perspective, sometimes you are the customer and someone else is the service provider. For example, when you receive your payslip from the finance department, you are the customer and expect it to be correct, be delivered on time and the salary payment actually paid into your bank account. If there is a problem, you expect to be dealt with courteously and promptly. You do not expect to have to engage in lengthy correspondence to rectify a mistake. If you do receive information from the finance department, say, for example, about a new profit related pay scheme, you expect it to be clearly written and well presented.

At other times you could be the service provider to your colleagues or line manager, for instance, when you are asked to find out the costings of producing a sales promotion item as part of a future promotional campaign. Your internal customers will expect you to have completed the task on time, accurately, and to present it clearly at the next planning meeting.

So internal marketing is about working together with colleagues and providing them with a good service so that, as a team, your organization achieves its goals.

An organization's internal communications

Just as individuals have internal customers, such as colleagues and line managers, that they have to deal with, organizations have internal customers in the form of their staff.

From an organization's perspective, internal communication is vital to internal marketing and the maintenance of employee motivation and company competitiveness. Without a culture of internal marketing and effective internal customer communications, the employees within an organization face the following problems:

- Communication problems.
- Frustration and non-cooperation.
- Time-wasting and inefficiency.
- Stress and lack of job satisfaction.
- Poor quality of work.

All of these problems eventually lead to poor service to the external customer, which eventually leads to reduced profit in the long term.

As Kevin Thomson, in a recent *Marketing Business* article, said:

> The internal customer has become one of the top priorities for marketers today. It's increasingly being recognised that building strong relationships with the people inside the organisation allows them to build profitable relationships with those outside. Staff – or internal customers – are the company's most important asset for external marketing.

To foster strong relationships and an atmosphere of shared values, communication and information should flow two ways. Information will obviously flow downwards from senior management to employees, but mechanisms should be put in place to ensure that it also flows upwards from employees to senior managers.

Two-way communications
To encourage a two-way flow of information organizations can choose from a variety of methods to enable managers to hear the views and opinions of employees:

- Regular staff meetings and team briefings.
- Meetings with senior managers where the overall performance of the firm and future developments are discussed.

- Performance reviews/appraisal systems that enable staff to suggest how they could be empowered to do their jobs better.
- Suggestion schemes where employees are rewarded if they suggest ideas that are implemented.
- Works councils where staff can get involved in the running of the organization.

Future challenges for internal communications

The changing environment in which organizations operate means that it may be difficult to communicate with staff in the traditional way, and pressures upon staff may mean that they are less inclined to be committed to the organization's values and culture.

Factors influencing change

- The combination of downsized organizations and flatter management structures has removed layers of management and this means employees are nearer to the decision makers and the communication process is speeded up. However, staff who are less secure in their jobs and more pressurized to work faster and harder are less likely to communicate openly with their colleagues and managers.
- The trend to teleworking, with more people working away from the office, means it is more difficult to create a corporate culture and sense of belonging where people feel happy to communicate on an informal basis.
- The merging of companies across the UK and elsewhere in the world is creating global organizations that do not have local identities and which cross over different cultures, languages and operating systems. This can make it difficult for senior managers to communicate effectively with employees.

The internal communications mix

Internal customer communications involve the effective use of memos, letters, reports, notices, e-mails, meetings, team briefings, telephone calls and presentations. Obviously some of these communication methods can be used to communicate externally. In this workbook we are making the distinction that external communications are those that are used to promote and sell the organization's goods and services, which we will refer to as the *external communications mix*. For guidance on using internal customer communication methods, see Unit 6 and 8.

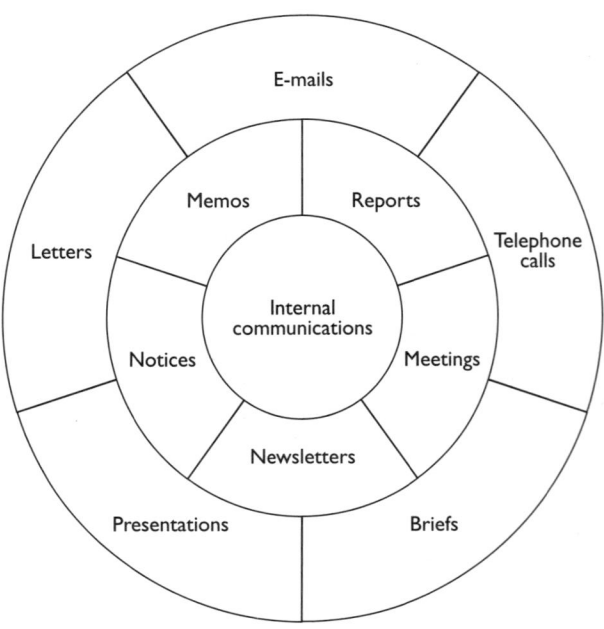

Figure 1.2
Internal communications

The external communications mix

To communicate with external customers, organizations use a range of activities that can be described as the *external communications mix*. These activities range from advertising, direct marketing and selling to public relations and the creation of a strong corporate identity. These activities are used to create brands, to inform customers about product improvements and to promote sales, and because most organizations are not interested in a one-off sale, communications are used to build an ongoing relationship with the customer. For guidance on how to use these communication activities, see Unit 9.

Figure 1.3
The external communications mix

Activity 1.2

Identify the stakeholders that a car manufacturer would communicate with. Use the list of stakeholders mentioned in Figure 1.1 and add to them if you can. Briefly explain what methods of communication might be used, what messages might be communicated and why it is important for the organization to communicate with these stakeholders.

(**See** Activity debrief at the end of the unit.)

Exam/Revision Hints

Be prepared to answer questions where you have to identify the stakeholders or customers in a given situation. See Question 7(a) on the specimen paper in Unit 11. Ensure that you are able to distinguish between internal and external customers and able to determine the appropriate communication method and message that might be relevant in a given situation. Avoid attempting to rote learn the contents of this unit. Instead, familiarize yourself with the material so that the knowledge you have gained will give you an overview of the whole subject before you cover other topics in the book.

Summary

In this unit you will have developed your understanding of the term *customer* and used this to appreciate the range of internal and external communications that individuals and organizations use to communicate with their *customers*.

You will also have gained an insight into the role internal communications plays in internal marketing and the importance of two-way communications in achieving a customer-focused and successful organization.

Activity debrief

Activity 1.2

Stakeholder	Message	Method	Why
Consumers – these would be broken down into various target groups in the consumer and business to business markets	Information about products, persuasive messages to brand the cars and persuade customers to buy.	All the promotional mix: advertising, branding, sponsorship, sales literature, direct marketing, public relations and a trained sales force.	To raise awareness. To increase sales.
Shareholders	Performance, dividend payout, future developments.	Annual general meeting. Annual report. PR to financial press.	Need shareholder support and need to promote correct image. Legal obligation to set out performance information.
Employees	Company performance. Future plans. Training information. Improvements in staff facilities. Staff news.	Internal newsletter. Memos, meetings, staff notice-board.	To maintain good industrial relations and staff motivation.
Potential employees	What the company does. What job opportunities are available.	Recruitment advertising. Corporate image.	To recruit from the biggest pool of available staff so will have better selection.
Suppliers	Company production plans and requirements.	Meetings. Tender documents. Contracts.	To help firms supply best components at the right time and to ensure that the organization and its suppliers work together in partnership.
Distributors	Product and technical information.	Point of sale material, sales literature and promotional items for branding purposes.	To assist dealerships in selling cars.
Local community – could be residents who live near factories, or local charities	That the firm cares for the local community.	PR activities. Sponsorship.	Good PR which could help, for example, if the firm applies for planning permission to extend factory premises.
The media	Product information and information about company performance.	Press releases. Events.	To raise the company profile. To promote its image.
Government, local, national and international	They are an ethical firm and a good employer.	Via senior management on a personal level.	To establish good relations so can put pressure to bear regarding legislation that might affect the industry.

Stakeholder	Message	Method	Why
Pressure groups	They are an ethical firm that cares about the environment.	PR.	To negate effect of conflicting messages from environmental pressure groups.
Competitors	To develop strategic alliances.	Via senior management on a personal level.	To rationalize operations, cut costs and expand into other markets.

Specimen examination question

You have been shortlisted for the post of Communications Manager at a privatized electricity company. As part of the selection process you have been asked to do a presentation on the importance of effective internal marketing and internal communications to the success of the organization. Draw on your experience to explain how some organizations improve their internal communication systems. Draft the notes that will form the basis of your presentation.

Specimen answer

PRESENTATION NOTES
INTERNAL MARKETING AND INTERNAL COMMUNICATIONS

Introduction

I have been asked to deliver a short presentation on the importance of effective internal marketing and internal communications. I will explain what is meant by these terms and how they contribute to the success of a company and then will draw on my experience within other organizations to describe how they have improved their internal communication systems.

Key points

Internal marketing

Internal marketing means creating a culture where staff work together as a team, seeing each other as internal customers, who require good service. With internal marketing the contribution of all staff is recognized and valued as helping to achieve the goals set by the organization.

For example, in my experience at a successful packaging firm where all the staff know what is expected of them and how their individual contribution affects whether a job is completed well and on time, they know this affects whether the client is retained. Contrast this example with that of a building firm where staff have to alter work that has been carried out badly by colleagues and time is wasted because builders are not given the correct information about work that needs to be undertaken.

Benefits of internal marketing culture:

- Shared values.
- Co-operation.
- Efficiency.
- Job satisfaction.
- High-quality work.
- Loyalty.
- Effective communications.

Internal communications

The organization's internal communications system is vital in the creation and maintenance of an effective marketing culture among staff. This approach should transcend all petty differences and encompass both staff within a department and staff in different departments, on different sites and even in different countries.

Improving internal communications

Establish a two-way flow of information so that managers hear staff views and opinions as well as staff hearing about management objectives, views and plans by:

- Regular staff meetings and team briefings to discuss plans, work and how to get around difficulties.
- Meetings with senior managers regarding current performance, future objectives, plans and how they affect staff.
- Empower staff to become involved in improving quality, facilities, systems and procedures.
- Performance reviews to tell staff how they are doing, what could be improved and to identify what training is needed to improve individual performance.
- Feedback to managers on their performance.
- Suggestion schemes.
- Establish a culture where people are not afraid to air their views or grievances.
- Use the staff notice-board effectively to inform of events, training and even to quash rumours.
- Establish an internal newsletter.
- Train managers to run effective team briefings.
- Train staff to hold effective meetings.
- Establish a house style for letters, memos and reports.
- Encourage staff not to resort to sending an e-mail to everyone and anyone.
- Remind staff how to use the internal telephone system effectively.
- Establish effective recording systems, whether for taking messages, informing other staff of your whereabouts, recording sales visits or job instructions.
- Introduce staff manuals and policy documents so that staff are clear about systems and procedures in the firm.

Summary
A culture of internal marketing and an effective internal communications system is vital to the success of an organization. If staff are well informed, empowered and listened to, they are more likely to know and share the aims of the company and work together to play their part in achieving them.

Unit 2 Managing the customer relationship

Objectives

In this unit you will:

❑ Examine the changing context of customer needs.

❑ Appreciate the role of communications in implementing customer care.

❑ See how customer communications help build customer relationships.

❑ Look at why customer care systems sometimes fail.

By the end of this unit you should be able to:

❑ Use communication skills to establish good customer care.

❑ Handle customer complaints effectively.

❑ Identify how customer care could be improved in a given situation.

❑ Devise appropriate customer communications as part of a customer care programme.

Study Guide

This unit develops the customer theme from Unit 1 and focuses on how customer communications are a vital part of good customer care and customer service. The section on telephone skills, verbal and non-verbal communication will be further developed in Unit 5.

The unit covers indicative content areas 2.1.3, 2.1.4, 2.1.5 and 2.1.6 of the syllabus.

It will take you a minimum of three hours to work through this unit.

Study Tip

At the end of this unit you could check whether your place of work has specific policies or procedures for dealing with quality or customer care issues. Consider how these are implemented.

In addition, you could undertake an audit of the various ways that customers are communicated with and check whether they comply with stated customer care standards.

For example, if you work in a doctor's surgery you could look at the following:

● How patients' telephone queries are dealt with.
● How patients are dealt with when they visit the surgery.
● The appearance and content of any documentation that is given to patients, such as appointment cards, patients' booklets or notices that are displayed in the surgery.

Relations with customers

Customer care, customer service, customer satisfaction. Are these merely buzzwords that organizations pay lip service to, or have we really entered a new age of customer focus? Customer focus, or putting the customer at the centre of the organization's operations, has always been central to marketing philosophy. But for a time it seemed that many firms in various industry sectors had forgotten the customer in their bid to maximize profits and minimize costs. However, in a bid to meet the growing demands of customers and having to keep up with more innovative customer-focused competition, many firms have been forced to re-examine carefully how their customers are really treated. And even firms operating in markets that traditionally compete on price are faced with the fact that it only needs one competitor to break rank and raise customer expectations and all are faced with a compelling need to jump on the customer care bandwagon.

The changing context of customer needs

UK consumers are more demanding than ever before. The idea of the stiff upper-lipped British consumer who prefers to suffer in silence is an outdated stereotype. According to a Henley Centre research survey (*Marketing*, November 1998), 56 per cent of people say they have complained in person about poor services or faulty goods over the past year, a massive leap from 39 per cent in 1997.

The Henley Centre survey showed that consumers are more assertive and willing to take action against companies. This may range from complaining about faulty goods or inadequate service, warning friends and family away from a company, to stopping purchasing from a company because it is viewed as unhealthy, unethical or environmentally unsound.

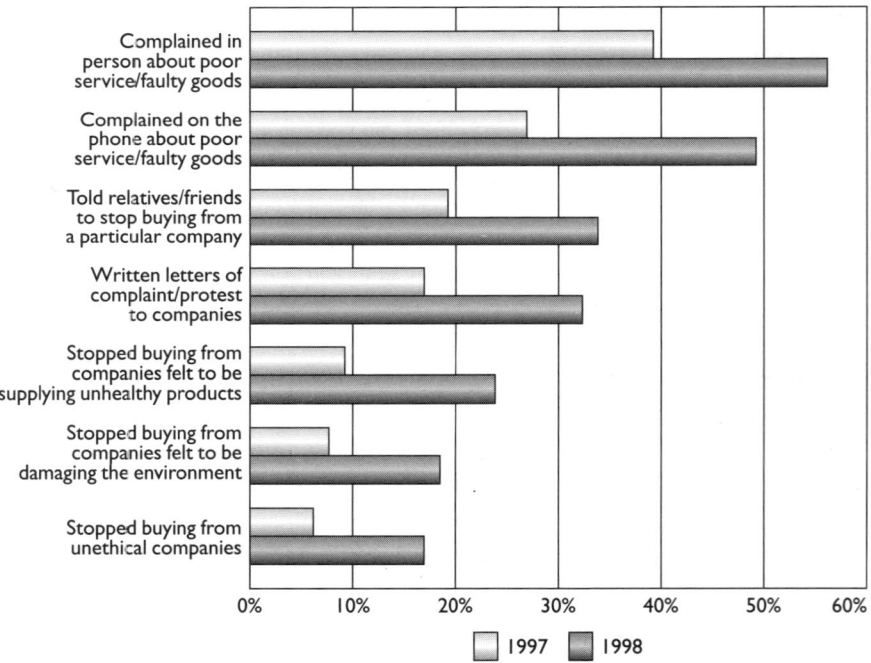

Figure 2.1
The rise of the assertive customer. Reproduced with kind permission from *Marketing* magazine.

Reasons for the changing customer environment

UK consumers are more likely to complain nowadays because they are more educated, have more sophisticated tastes and are more widely travelled. In particular, travel to countries like the USA, where consumers have long demanded superior service standards and are much more likely to seek compensation and sue, has been a powerful influence on UK consumers.

In addition, British firms and their staff have tried to emulate the Japanese approach to continuous product and service improvement in a bid to repeat their spectacular successes in the motor, technology and other industry sectors.

The impact of customer focus

UK consumers are now less tolerant and demand high service standards. This attitude transcends industry sectors, with consumers unwilling to accept shoddy workmanship from builders, or lame excuses about unsatisfactory hotels from holiday companies, or poor service from shop assistants, or overcomplicated application forms from mortgage companies, or overbearing attitudes from health professionals.

The result is that organizations operate in a more competitive and litigious environment where consumer demands have to be responded to. Most organizations realize that it is far easier and cheaper to retain current customers than it is to cultivate new ones. Moreover, research shows that dissatisfied customers tend to spread news of their bad experiences very quickly – something that not only affects an organization's image but also affects the bottom line in the long run.

As a consequence, a whole industry has grown up to deal with customer care issues. There are now many jobs with a focus on customer care that may involve anything from drafting customer charters to dealing with customer complaints. There are a myriad of training courses designed to improve employees' customer service and a multitude of consultants who will analyse a firm's customer service levels. Bringing firms under the spotlight there are *Which?* reports that compare the pros and cons of rival brands and even television programmes which name and shame companies where products or services do not stand up to public scrutiny.

Figure 2.2
Example of a customer charter. (Taken from The NHS Patient's Charter and is reproduced with the kind permission of the Department of Health.)

Rights and standards throughout the NHS

Access to services

You have the *right* to:

- receive health care on the basis of your clinical need, not on your ability to pay, your lifestyle or any other factor;
- be registered with a GP and be able to change your GP easily and quickly if you want to;
- get emergency medical treatment at any time through your GP, the emergency ambulance service and hospital accident and emergency departments; and
- be referred to a consultant acceptable to you, when your GP thinks it is necessary, and to be referred for a second opinion if you and your GP agree this is desirable.

The impact of consumerism

For many years pressure groups have sought to influence organizations to change their products, prices, packaging, advertising and ways of doing business in many different ways. Firms that have been customer-focused have seized upon these 'complaints' and turned them into opportunities to provide products and services that are more in tune with the market and have used their customer communications effectively to promote the product/service strengths either via packaging, advertising or PR. An example of this is the number of different organizations that have made 'green' claims in recent years.

However, it is important that if a firm gives in to public pressure, it should then manage its communications with customers to get the best PR out of its changed stance.

The Bank of Scotland's customer communications

An example where this did not happen was when the Bank of Scotland outraged many sections of its customer base when it announced a deal with a US television evangelist. In the face of angry customers it scrapped the plan to provide a telephone bank service for millions of his US followers, after he made outspoken attacks on gays, feminists, Muslims, Hindus and effectively insulted the whole of Scotland.

Initially the bank stood its ground even as many customers closed accounts, local authorities, charities and trade unions threatened to take their trade elsewhere and protestors handcuffed themselves to its headquarters.

Then, after senior management realized their blunder, they authorized an extensive media campaign of damage limitation.

However, during the campaign at an annual shareholders' meeting, the Bank's Governor appeared to only begrudgingly apologize for the fiasco, apparently seeming not to regret what the bank had done but appearing more to regret that people did not like what it had done. Thus an extensive media campaign to apologize and acknowledge public pressure was wasted because the people at the top of the company lacked a customer focus in communicating with an important group of stakeholders.

Consider an issue of public concern that might affect a firm of your choice. Explain how stakeholders might communicate their objections about the issue to the firm. Suggest how the firm might react and what it could do to ensure that customer relations were not damaged.

(**See** Activity debrief at the end of the unit.)

Ethical marketing

Ethical businesses are those who recognize that they have a social responsibility, i.e. that they cannot conduct their business without due regard to broader social concerns. They may go one stage further than obeying the law or may even set themselves a voluntary code of practice where no law exists.

Lands' End

Lands' End supplies casual clothing by mail order. They use their catalogue to communicate with customers about their customer focus. They feature endorsements from satisfied customers, for example:

When I tore my trousers on a railway carriage door I asked if you could repair them. Instead you replaced them immediately. You really do push the boundary of customer service further than anyone could reasonably expect.

They also feature a statement about their business ethics:

We contract only with suppliers who produce products of high quality and value, who ensure their employees are of legal age, work under safe and healthy conditions, are paid fairly and are not discriminated against.

They also provide a free copy of their Standards of Business Conduct via a freephone number.

In the UK, strict employment law protects workers from exploitation but there is no law that prevents firms from sourcing supplies from countries where workers are exploited. An ethical business might respond to consumer pressure as part of its customer focus and only contract with suppliers that do not exploit their workers.

Relationship marketing

The main idea behind relationship marketing is to build strong relationships with customers in order to retain them instead of concentrating efforts on recruiting new ones.

There are several factors which influence customer retention:

- High-quality products to encourage repeat purchase.
- Customers need to feel valued to be loyal, and this can only be created by excellent customer service.
- Taking long-term marketing decisions, for example continuous improvement or innovation to keep ahead of customer needs.
- Frequent customer contact to establish customer profiles in order to ensure accurate customer targeting of goods, services and information.

Consequently relationship marketing is closely aligned with both customer care principles and the basic tenets of consumerism. From a customer communications perspective, the most important factor in relationship marketing is the creation of a dialogue between the organization and the consumer. This results in the consumer getting what they want and at the same time becoming a loyal customer who recommends others to the firm.

A good illustration of relationship marketing is the way supermarkets have established loyalty cards to encourage customers to collect reward points when they shop at stores. The advantage to customers is that after collecting so many reward points these are converted into money-off coupons. The advantage to the store is that when customers register for a loyalty card they provide the store with valuable customer information. This information is used to build up profiles of customers who use a particular store in a particular area. This can help individual stores to stock the products wanted by their particular clientele. So, for example, a store in a location with a large Jewish community would know to stock a range of kosher products.

Each time a customer uses the card to collect points from shopping, the customer's purchase history is added to. The value of this information is that past purchase history is the best indicator of future purchase behaviour. This helps stores with many marketing decisions, including, for example, planning appropriate targeted customer communications such as direct marketing and advertising campaigns.

Activity 2.2

Consider a loyalty scheme that you are familiar with and describe how it works to the advantage of the customer and the organization.

(**See** Activity debrief at the end of the unit.)

Quality and customer care

Customer care and its close relation, quality, are not new ideas, only old ones that have been brushed down and spruced up. They help to remind organizations that they should not rest on their laurels in an increasingly competitive and unforgiving world.

Customer care and quality are linked in that both are concerned with getting things right first time. Quality management is usually associated more with production issues whilst customer care is more concerned with the organization's relationship with its customers and customer service issues.

Quality management is basically concerned with: establishing standards for a product or service; establishing procedures, production methods and service criteria to ensure that standards are met; the monitoring of actual quality; and taking action when quality falls below standard.

With customer care, the aim is to close the gap between customers' expectations and their experience. This is often achieved by finding out what the customer thinks and what they want in terms of product/service quality, packaging, delivery and after-sales service.

For some large service delivery organizations, such as banks, it has been a case of realizing that customers need to be treated as people who *matter* and they have had to concentrate on delivering a personal service that makes people feel welcome.

For Lloyds Bank in the early 1990s, it was a case of laying down a service challenge to staff that set out a number of minimum standards. These included:

- Not letting the telephone ring more than four times before it is answered.
- The person answering should introduce themselves by name.
- Queues at tills should not have more than five people in them.
- Establishing various levels of product knowledge that staff should have.

Some organizations have considered the total product concept and have looked to add value. An example of this is the toy car manufacturer that packs the product in a box which folds into a toy garage.

Other organizations have gone further and have gone through a process of business process re-engineering. In these cases firms have looked at the whole transaction process a customer goes through from the customer's point of view in order to simplify it and make it easier. In the insurance industry this has revolutionized the way some firms operate so that services are no longer sold through intermediaries but delivered direct and therefore more cheaply to the consumer.

Delighting the customer

Some companies have gone to great lengths to get the detail right. For example, when Nissan dealerships take a car in for a service they provide a replacement courtesy car, check the car over and undertake repairs, clean it and leave a free air freshener inside. A few days later they telephone the customer to find out if there are any problems and to check whether the customer is happy with their treatment.

However, the most innovative companies have gone even further to exceed customer expectations. In many cases these organizations consider that most jobs have two parts – the mechanics of what needs to be done, and the people part. Maws, manufacturers of baby feeding products, established a customer care line to answer new mothers' queries. When one anxious mother called the number to ask about stockists for a product to soothe a crying baby, a highly trained member of staff manning the care line not only provided clear information about stockists and how the product should be used but also felt empowered to send out a complimentary pack of the product. Good business practice indeed, because these relatively inexpensive items have to be replaced every six weeks and of course, by exceeding customer expectations, they won a loyal customer who is also prepared to sing the company's praises to other potential customers.

Customer delight will ratchet up standards – it is not a static relationship. If the customer is delighted by something for the first time, they eventually get used to the extra service. For example, delivering a fresh bowl of fruit to a hotel room as part of the service soon becomes expected and customer expectations rise even further.

Managing the customer relationship

Customer relations should not concentrate on handling complaints, i.e. putting wrong things right, it should be about quality issues and customer service improvements.

Steps involved in establishing quality

- Establish standards of quality for a product or service.
- Establish procedures to ensure that quality standards are met.
- Monitor quality.
- Take control action when quality falls below standard.

Steps involved in improving customer service

- Measure standards by finding out levels of customer satisfaction.
- Analyse the feedback.
- Act upon the information and develop what people want, for example customer-friendly systems or getting the detail right.
- Consider how much further you could go in terms of exceeding customer expectation.

What do customers want?

In analysing customer feedback it appears that the majority of feedback and complaints are not about actual products but seemingly peripheral issues, such as late delivery, the way the product does not pour easily from the carton, the way the customer was spoken to or given the wrong information. There are four key characteristics of good customer service.

A positive/proactive attitude
Customers do not want to be faced with apathetic staff who have to be asked the right question before they will be helpful and suggest a solution to a customer problem.

Customer-friendly systems
Customers need payment to be made easy, user-friendly application forms and store layouts or computer programs to be designed with the user in mind.

Knowledgeable staff
Customers want to be dealt with by trained staff who have a satisfactory level of technical knowledge.

Product/service reliability
Products that work consistently. Services that turn up on time – every time.

Rules of good customer service

- Getting it right first time.
- Listening to customers to find out what they actually want.
- Communicating clearly and positively with customers.
- Making it easy for staff to help customers.
- Employing staff who are genuinely courteous.
- Encouraging staff to be fair, understanding and flexible in their response.
- Handling complaints in a constructive way.
- Investigating mistakes and learning from them.

1	Smile; be polite, helpful and friendly.
2	Listen and show interest.
3	Satisfy queries positively.
4	Do not guess, find out.
5	Work tidily and safely.

Figure 2.3
An extract from Asda's customer care policy

Managing customer care communications

Customer comunications as a part of customer care

Good customer communications are a vital part of customer care. The communication may be face to face with a customer, in writing or on the telephone – whatever the method, it is essential that the communication is clear, concise, courteous, creates the right impression and conveys the correct message.

First impressions

You can create a good first impression with customers through positive action, such as:

- Good personal grooming.
- Smart clothes or uniform.
- Punctuality.
- A tidy and well-organized work environment.
- Smart reception areas.
- Establishing a consistent method for greeting people when they enter the organization.
- An overall positive image in all documentation such as invoices, application forms, instruction manuals, leaflets, posters, signs, company vans and shop windows.

Verbal communication

When speaking with customers, whether face to face or on the telephone, it is important that what you say to the customer is perceived as helpful, welcoming and appropriate to the situation.

It is easy for a culture of internal orientation to become established in an organization. This is evident when staff become so focused on internal procedures that they do not respond appropriately to customer queries or requests. They may answer customers in such a way as to irritate or annoy customers because they feel that their custom is not valued.

Sentences that drive customers away

- 'I'm in the middle of something' or 'x's busy – could you call back?'
- 'There's nothing we can do – it's company policy.'
- 'We're closing – you'll have to come back tomorrow.'
- 'You'll have to give me your account number before I can help you.'

Change the following phrases so that they demonstrate customer care.

1 'I don't know.'
2 'That's not *my* job.'
3 'I don't think we have that in stock.'
4 'You'll have to call back.'

(**See** Activity debrief at the end of the unit.)

Tone – how you say things

The tone that you use can be either intentionally or unintentionally inappropriate and can infuriate customers. An apathetic, droning or listless tone of voice can convey the message that you don't care or are not interested in the customer and their problem/query. A rushed tone can make you sound impatient with the customer. In fact different tones of voice can change the meaning of the same words. By changing the inflection in your voice, you can say the words 'Your statement is ready now' in an angry way, sarcastically, apologetically, shyly and even in a humorous way.

Customers obviously want to be greeted or spoken to by someone whose tone of voice sounds interested, helpful and patient and, if appropriate, sounds apologetic and sincere if they have been treated unfairly or a mistake has been made.

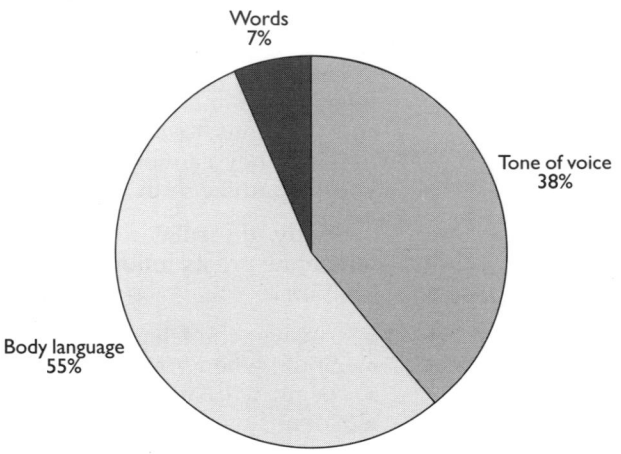

Figure 2.4
How we receive messages

Non-verbal communication

Negative body language

By using inappropriate body language you can make your customers angry. For example, if you give a customer a blank stare because you are preoccupied with a personal matter, the customer will probably feel that you are intentionally making them feel uncomfortable or that you are not interested in what the customer wants.

By holding your head down and avoiding eye contact or being busy talking with colleagues, you will also convey the message that you are not interested in the customer.

Similarly, if you are talking with a customer and fidget in a distracted way, such as drumming your fingers on a desk or playing with a pen, this could also give the impression that you are not interested in dealing with the customer.

If a customer asks you a question and you shrug your shoulders, this could indicate that you do not know the answer and that you do not care either.

Positive body language

You can also use body language in a positive way. Simply by making eye contact with customers you show interest in them and what they have to say. A friendly smile can make you seem approachable, and simply by moving in the direction of a customer with a slight inclination of the head you can indicate that you are available to help, without actually saying anything.

Listening skills

Listening skills are a vital part of customer care. By using effective listening skills you can obtain all the necessary and relevant information you need to find out what customers want or what they are not happy with. Listening is an active, not a passive activity. By checking what a customer has said and paraphrasing it, you can check that you have understood exactly what they mean. This avoids confusion and time being wasted.

In many situations where you are dealing with unhappy customers, listening skills are very important to understand the problem. Often customers will go into great detail about a number of things that they are not happy with. However, it is usually one thing in particular that they want rectified. A good listener can select the most relevant information and decide what can be done about the situation.

Telephone skills and customer care

Because so much communication with customers is by telephone it is important to briefly mention this area here, although it will be developed in more detail in Unit 5.

The same rules of good customer communications apply in terms of what is said and how it is said. However, it is more important in telephone conversations to pay special attention to the tone used with customers because they cannot see your reaction and therefore cannot tell whether you empathize with them or understand what they are saying.

Briefly, the rules for good customer communications when using the telephone are as follows:

- Answer the telephone promptly.
- Smile when you first pick up the telephone.
- Begin with an appropriate greeting.
- Identify yourself/your department or the organization.
- Establish the caller's needs.
- Speak clearly.
- Speak slowly.
- Avoid jargon.
- Be courteous.
- Be concise.
- Take messages accurately and pass them to the appropriate person where necessary.
- Listen carefully and do not interrupt the customer.
- Show empathy and understanding.
- If dealing with an angry customer, do not argue with the caller or offer lame excuses.
- If you undertake to do something for a customer during a telephone conversation, do it, don't just hope they won't come back.
- Give the caller a name, department or extension number to enable them to pursue the matter if they need to call back at a later date/time.
- End the call effectively so that the caller knows what action is to be taken, what has been agreed or when someone will come back to them.
- Close the call politely with an appropriate greeting and thank the caller for calling.

Why do customer care systems sometimes fail?

There is no doubt that thousands of organizations providing products and services implement customer care programmes and yet still have customers who receive poor service and complain about it.

The problem often lies in allocating a specific department for customer care instead of training and empowering all staff to deal with customer care issues.

A common problem is that companies impose customer care programmes on staff without explaining the reasons behind them, or do not allow staff who deal with customers every day to influence how customer care is implemented.

Other problems occur where firms have organized supposedly customer-centred systems and processes designed to enable staff to help customers but prospective customers are asked so many personal questions which have no relevance to the actual query that they are put off from doing business with the organization.

In other cases organizations move from a localized branch network where staff may know customers quite well, to a round-the-clock service provision supported by centralized telephone services in a bid to give customers improved access to services. Unfortunately, customers may then find that they spend a long time explaining a particular problem or enquiry to an anonymous person and if they have to call again they are faced with another anonymous voice to whom they have to explain the whole thing all over again.

Customer service can also fail if it is commoditized through call centres with staff on short-term contracts. Often these staff fail to see the company's goals as they are often more concerned about their job security. It is also difficult to see how staff could be encouraged to take customer care seriously if senior managers do not treat their internal customers/staff appropriately.

Many staff feel that customer care is something that senior managers pay lip service to because they do not allocate adequate resources to it or establish any reward or recognition system aimed at customer care standards. Some companies persist in thinking that technology is the answer to tackling customer care issues. There needs to be a balance between using telephone technology to speed up response and put customers through to the right department without trapping them in *voice-mail jail*. Technology on its own does not improve customer service if there are no humans available to help solve customers' problems.

In the final analysis, if the product breaks or does not work or the service does not arrive or does not do the job it was asked to do, no amount of apologies, discounts or gestures will change the situation, so quality still remains a key aspect of any customer care programme.

Complaints

Benefits of complaints

Most organizations that supply products and services find that there are occasions when customers are not satisfied and have need to complain. As part of their approach to customer care issues, some organizations have established customer service departments or introduced policies to handle complaints so that complaints are dealt with in a consistent and appropriate way.

The advantage of recognizing that things do go wrong and that customers do complain is that instead of seeing complaints as an unfortunate occurrence, it means that complaints can be examined to help identify how to improve products and services.

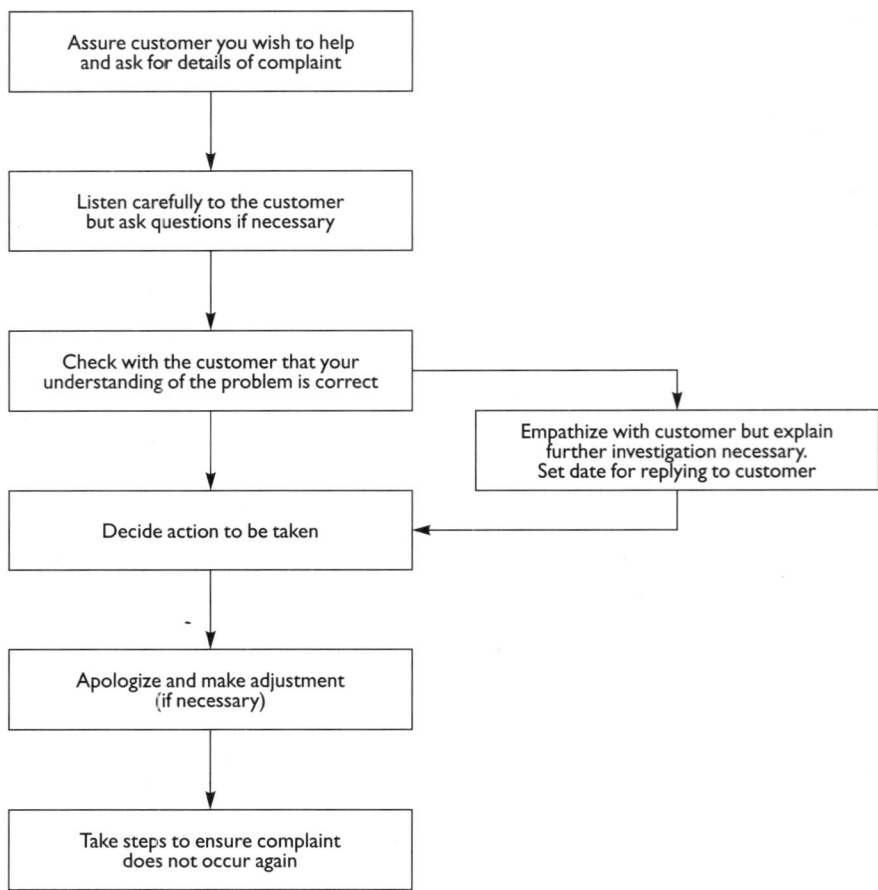

```
┌─────────────────────────────────┐
│   Assure customer you wish to help │
│   and ask for details of complaint │
└─────────────────────────────────┘
                │
                ▼
┌─────────────────────────────────┐
│   Listen carefully to the customer │
│    but ask questions if necessary  │
└─────────────────────────────────┘
                │
                ▼
┌─────────────────────────────────┐        ┌──────────────────────────────┐
│   Check with the customer that your│───────│  Empathize with customer but explain│
│   understanding of the problem is  │        │  further investigation necessary.  │
│   correct                          │        │  Set date for replying to customer │
└─────────────────────────────────┘        └──────────────────────────────┘
                │                                          │
                ▼                                          │
┌─────────────────────────────────┐◄──────────────────────┘
│        Decide action to be taken   │
└─────────────────────────────────┘
                │
                ▼
┌─────────────────────────────────┐
│   Apologize and make adjustment    │
│          (if necessary)            │
└─────────────────────────────────┘
                │
                ▼
┌─────────────────────────────────┐
│   Take steps to ensure complaint   │
│        does not occur again        │
└─────────────────────────────────┘
```

Figure 2.5
A complaints procedure

Resolving complaints satisfactorily usually means that customers become more loyal in the long term because they appreciate that they have been listened to.

Organizations that recognize that it is useful to encourage customers to complain because it provides valuable feedback usually take active steps to obtain this feedback. (See Unit 3 for more guidance in this area.)

Handling complaints

There is obviously no one way to deal with complaints as the approach must be tailored to the circumstances. However, there are a number of general approaches that can be adapted to help deal with difficult situations where customers are dissatisfied and a complaint needs to be handled in a sensitive way. Here is a list of helpful approaches:

- Use appropriate body language to show empathy with the customer.
- Use diplomatic phrases to calm angry customers, for example, 'This is obviously an unsatisfactory situation' or 'I'm sorry you're upset about this situation'.
- Apologize for the fact that there has been a problem – this does not mean you are accepting full blame.
- Do not interrupt the customer and use effective listening skills to get an overview of the problem and show that you are taking the customer seriously.
- Clarify the problem by checking details and making notes so that you can fully investigate the complaint.
- Be positive, not defensive. So, for instance, you could thank the customer for telling you about the situation because you need to know about the problem if it is to be rectified.
- Tell the customer what steps you are going to take so that they know they have not just sounded off and wasted their time.
- In cases of serious allegations you may need to explain that you cannot take the matter at face value and that you must investigate to verify the allegations.

Read the scenario below and identify the areas where Orange could improve their customer service and explain how they might improve their customer communications.

A customer purchases an Orange mobile telephone and is promised connection to the service later that day. Unfortunately the customer is unable to follow the complicated instructions in the user manual and rings the helpline telephone number. The customer tries to get through to the helpline number for three consecutive days but finds that it is constantly engaged. She eventually contacts the head office but there are no staff available to help because it is a weekend. However, the switchboard operator transfers her to the customer helpline. A call centre operator answers her call but he is unable to help because the customer was not allocated a security code number when she bought the telephone. However, the call centre operator promises to pass on the matter to head office to be dealt with after the weekend.

After the weekend the customer has not been contacted by anyone from the head office so she decides to contact them again. She complains bitterly to a person in the customer service department about the overcomplicated manual and the service she has received. The member of staff provides a lengthy explanation about how a shortage of staff means the helpline is constantly engaged. The customer becomes irate and says that she is not interested in Orange's staffing problems. She demands help with using her telephone, an apology for the way she has been treated and a discount on her bill to make up for the number of telephone calls she has made. The member of staff refuses to apologize, stating that it is not his fault that there have been problems. He explains that he has no authority to agree a discount on her bill and that it is not the company's policy to give discounts. However, he is able to give her the security code to enable her to use the telephone and clarifies the misleading instructions in the user manual. At the end of the call the customer can use her mobile telephone but she is still angry about the way she has been treated.

(**See** Activity debrief at the end of the unit.)

How to encourage customers to complain

- Make it easy for people to complain by publicizing your complaints procedure.
- Stay close to your customers – regularly find out what customers think by asking them.
- Put yourself in your customers' shoes by mystery shopping to find out what customers think.
- Don't deflect complaints, find out what the customer expected and what can be done to put something right.

Be prepared to describe how and why customer expectations have changed. See Question 7(b) on the specimen paper in Unit 11 for an example of the kind of question you could be asked.

Familiarize yourself with what constitutes customer care and how to handle complaints. See Questons 4(a) and 4(b) in Unit 11.

Ensure that your understanding of the material in this unit can be applied to any given situation where you might be asked to suggest ways in which customer care or customer communications could be improved.

Summary

In this unit you will have considered how and why customer expectations have changed in recent years.

You will have studied what customer care, quality and good customer service are.

You will also have developed a general understanding of the vital role that customer communications play in establishing and maintaining good relations with customers.

Activity debrief

Activity 2.1

For this answer the assumption made is that the issue is genetically modified foods and the company is a manufacturer of baby food. The stakeholders might be customers who purchase the products and a pressure group such as the National Childbirth Trust (NCT). Customers might communicate their objection to the use of genetically modified components in baby food by telephoning and writing to the company and boycotting its products. The NCT might undertake a media campaign using print and broadcast media.

The firm could deal with the objections by trying to assure consumers that the genetically modified products are safe via an extensive PR campaign. This would be unlikely to succeed against an intensive lobbying campaign. Ultimately the manufacturer may have to give in to consumer demands to ban genetically modified foods from the production cycle.

If they did give in to public pressure, it would then be advisable to publicize the fact to maintain good relations with stakeholders. The changed stance could be publicized through a PR campaign, changing product labels to announce the change and via advertising. They would also need to set up a customer care line and communicate the news to all concerned callers. They might also get involved in a joint campaign with the pressure group, to promote the banning of genetically modified products in all other baby foods.

Activity 2.2

Tesco Baby Club Card

Pregnant women are encouraged to apply for a club card and the reward is money-off coupons for baby products. The mother-to-be completes an application form, providing information such as name, address, information about the family and the baby's birth date.

The money-off coupons encourage repeat purchase at Tesco's stores. The card means the company can record each customer transaction and establish a customer profile. The company can then target the customer with information about relevant products and services. The organization can also sell this information to other organizations wishing to communicate with customers of a certain age, living in a certain area, who have a particular purchase history.

The baby club card scheme also features a frequent customer contact programme. Mothers receive a magazine with hints and advice which is sent to coincide with the various developmental stages that babies go through. So, for example, when the baby is aged four months old, the mother is sent a magazine which gives advice on how to wean babies onto solid food and contains advertising and money-off coupons relating to first-stage baby food products.

In this way both the organization and the customer receive benefits from the relationship that is established between the two parties.

Activity 2.3

Experiences where customers are delighted will be as varied as the people reading this workbook. You could have gone to the local supermarket, asked for help with packing your bags and been pleasantly surprised when you were also helped to your car with the bags. You may have wanted to buy certain items that were out of stock at the chemist and been surprised that the manager not only arranged to order them but arranged next-day delivery too. You may have asked for the balance of your bank account and been surprised that it was overdrawn. If the bank clerk cancelled the interest charges and arranged for you to have your bank statements sent out more frequently so that you could keep a better check on your account, you would have been delighted. Or you may have been travelling by plane on business and needed something to read but not had time to buy a newspaper. You may have been pleased to find that a free newspaper had been provided and been delighted that there was a complete selection of all the daily newspapers to choose from.

In estimating the cost of improving a service, you could, for example, calculate the cost of sending out a bank statement every week to a customer in comparison to the cost of attracting a new customer. If a weekly bank statement cost £15 over a year to produce and post, it would be likely to be much cheaper than the annual cost of marketing and advertising divided by the number of new customers gained each year.

Activity 2.4

1 'I'm not sure what we can do about that but if you give me your details I will make sure that someone gets back to you – when would it be convenient for them to contact you?'
2 'I don't actually handle the payments but if you hold on . . .' *either* 'I will transfer you to x in y department who will help you' *or* 'I will ask x in y department to come down to speak to you if you could just wait for a few minutes.'
3 'I don't think we have that in stock but I'll just go and check for you.'
4 'X is not at their desk at the moment but if you give me your telephone number I will ask them to call you back.'

Activity 2.5

To improve customer communications, Orange would have to improve their instruction manual so that customers find it easy to operate their telephones. They need to provide adequate staffing so that the system they have established to provide customer service actually works and customers can get through to the helpline. They need to rethink the process involving the allocation of security code numbers so that dealerships always allocate a security code and/or that call centre operators can still help customers who do not know their code.

Internal communications need to be improved to ensure that if staff in one department take a message it is always logged and passed on to relevant staff in another department. Staff need to be trained to deal with customer complaints. The member of the customer service team should have apologized on behalf of Orange about the service the customer has received. He should have concentrated on helping her use the telephone, not wasted the customer's time explaining internal staffing problems.

The company should also empower its staff to use reasonable judgement in giving a discount on a bill where a customer has good reason to be unhappy about the product or service they have received.

Specimen examination question

1(a)

You are the manager of an estate agents' responsible for a team of six negotiators who regularly deal with customers buying and selling houses. The team deals with customers on the telephone and those who visit the estate agency office.

To improve standards of customer care you decide to involve staff in determining best practice for dealing with customers.

To assist staff in formulating a protocol for best practice, draft five minimum standards you would expect to achieve when dealing with telephone calls from customers.

1(b)

You overhear a customer complaining to one of the negotiators that the property details sheet for his house contains incorrect room measurements, incorrect room descriptions and a number of spelling mistakes.

The member of staff's response to the customer is that he is not responsible for preparing the property information sheet and that prospective buyers will find out what the house is really like when they view it.

In advising the member of staff how to provide good customer service, outline five main points that you would make to him about the above situation.

Specimen answer

1(a)

Minimum standards for dealing with customer telephone calls:

- Answer the telephone within six rings.
- Introduce yourself by name and state the name of the firm.
- Smile when you answer the telephone.
- When taking messages for colleagues, always use company message pads and ensure that all details are taken down correctly..
- When dealing with telephone messages, return all calls the same day.

1(b)

Main points about how the member of staff's customer service could be improved:

- He should appreciate that all documentation and communications with customers should be right first time, as mistakes give a bad impression that the firm is careless in all its dealings with customers.
- He should have apologized to the customer on behalf of the company about the mistakes, not tried to minimize the importance of the mistakes made.
- He should not have been defensive with the customer about the mistakes made. It is not relevant to the customer whether he or someone else prepared the property details sheet and made the mistakes.
- He should have arranged for the mistakes to be rectified and a new sheet sent out to the customer immediately.
- He should have spoken to the person responsible for the mistakes and made sure that it did not happen again.

Finding out about customer communications

Objectives

In this unit you will:

❑ Explore the role of marketing research in communications.

❑ Examine various research methods and sources of data.

❑ See how data can be used to improve customer communications.

By the end of this unit you should be able to:

❑ Determine the type of research that could help improve customer communications in a given situation.

❑ Describe various marketing research methods.

❑ Devise a questionnaire.

❑ Evaluate research data to make customer communication decisions.

Study Guide

This unit covers indicative content areas 2.2.1, 2.2.2 and 2.2.3 of the syllabus and develops your understanding of how marketing research can be used to determine customer communication decisions. It should take you two hours to work through this unit.

Study Tip

Think about any occasions when your opinions/views have been canvassed by an organization and consider the methods used to collect the information. In addition, collect samples of any questionnaires that you have been sent and assess their design and effectiveness.

Finding out how best to communicate with customers

Marketing research helps organizations supply the correct marketing mix. This unit concentrates on how marketing research can be useful in determining one aspect of the marketing mix. It focuses on finding out the best way to communicate with customers.

As you have already identified in Units 1 and 2, customer communications can involve communicating with internal and external target audiences and can include a wide range of customer communications. These may include advertising, direct marketing, sales literature, face to face selling, telephone ordering, meetings, team briefings, sales conferences or staff newsletters.

How promotion and communication research can help

Below are a number of different situations that illustrate how marketing research can help determine the most appropriate customer communications.

Example 1 The business to business situation
Assume you are the marketing manager in a firm about to launch a new service. You have decided to appoint a marketing communications consultancy to produce promotional material. You shortlist a number of consultancies to pitch for the work. After the pitch presentations you appoint one of the consultancies.

One of the unsuccessful firms then contacts you for feedback to find out why they did not get the job. This firm would, in fact, be conducting marketing research with the aim of improving their performance when pitching for future work. As the potential customer, you could provide valuable feedback about the way the firm could improve how staff answer the telephone, how well their staff deliver client presentations and how effective their promotional brochure is.

Example 2 The new media situation
Assume you are the Marketing Manager of a chain of cinemas. You have just run an advertising campaign to promote the introduction of a website where cinema-goers can find out about forthcoming films and can book seats online. You could use marketing research to evaluate the success of the campaign by finding out how many people accessed the site after the advertising campaign finished. You could then use the website to find out from customers if the contents of the website were relevant and its design appealing. You could also monitor the number of on-line registrations and bookings to see if it was a viable form of customer communications.

Example 3 The internal communications problem
Assume you are the Chief Executive of a manufacturing firm with several factories in different locations. Reduced orders last year meant that several hundred redundancies were made. Staff were angry that they were not informed about the redundancies and initially heard about them through the local media.

You now intend to re-organize a number of departments and restructure supervisory and management positions within the firm. You believe you need to implement a structured communications programme and you are also considering introducing a staff newsletter but are unsure what it should contain. Within this context you decide to undertake some in-depth interviews with a random selection of staff to find out how best to improve internal communications.

Activity 3.1

You work in the marketing department of a mail order company that sells fashion items via off-the-page advertising in various national newspapers and magazines. How would you find out which of the newspapers or magazines generates most orders.

(**See** Activity debrief at the end of the unit.)

You are the manager of a city centre hotel that caters for people staying overnight on business. How would you find out about the quality of your hotel's customer communications, such as how people are treated when they telephone to make a reservation, how they are greeted at the front desk when they arrive and how staff deal with complaints.

(**See** Activity debrief at the end of the unit.)

Types of research

Marketing research methods can produce qualitative and quantitative information.

Quantitative research

Quantitative research seeks to measure or quantify information for statistical analysis. It involves asking a sufficiently large number (sample) of people a number of questions in order to draw general conclusions.

For example, you may design a questionnaire in which there is a question that asks if the packaging on a product provides them with sufficient information. This question would elicit a simple yes, no or don't know answer. If you questioned 500 people and 400 people answered no, there would be an overwhelming 80 per cent majority who feel that the customer communications need to be improved as far as packaging/ labelling information is concerned.

Qualitative research

Qualitative research explores attitudes, perceptions and ideas. As it asks for opinions it is difficult to obtain the information from simple closed style questions, so it usually involves face to face interviews with individuals or small groups. However, qualitative information can be elicited from open style questioning on surveys, though this is hard to collate and quantify when surveying large numbers of people.

For example, with qualitative research you may ask people 'In what way do you think the labelling on the packaging should be improved?' With this style of question, you could get as many different answers as the number of people you asked. Although you would build up a picture of what the labelling should say, it would be difficult to collate the information because each answer would be expressed differently.

However, you can use a combination of closed questioning to find out if there is a majority in favour of the labelling being changed and an open question which asks how it should be changed but limits people to choosing one of four different ways in which it could be changed. For example, you could ask them to select from options which might include: larger print; more information about additives; full explanations about environmentally friendly claims; or clearer information about storage and sell by dates.

Data collection methods

Data collection methods depend on the type of information required. Two distinct categories of data exist:

- *Primary data* is new data specifically collected for a project through field research. Field research is actively involved in the marketplace, usually involving direct contact with groups of consumers.
- *Secondary data* is data which already exists and can be collected by desk research. Desk research may already exist within the firm and has to be accessed through reports and figures, or it may be more general information published by external sources.

Secondary data sources

This type of data can be collected from internal sources such as sales reports, financial data and internal marketing data. Information on response rates to a mailshot, coupon redemption figures or the previous year's results of testing one copy approach against another for advertising or direct marketing can be valuable sources of information when evaluating customer communications and promotional activity. In addition, sales staff out in the field may file reports on customer perceptions of the latest advertising campaign or the new brochure, and these are also relatively low cost methods and immediate sources of information.

Internal databases with customer purchase history can also be invaluable in determining the type of promotional material that should be sent to customers.

Secondary data can be collected from competitors. Looking at the way the competition communicates with its market from press articles, advertising campaigns, in-house newsletters and annual reports can be a very rich source of information on what is happening in the market you operate in.

External secondary sources such as published government information are unlikely to be of use in relation to customer communications. However, research published by Mintel, Jordans, Key Note Publications and directories for certain industry sectors can be useful when looking at overall trends in, say, media spend and promotional activity. However, any new published research is already slightly out of date and is unlikely to be specific enough to help you identify how you can measure or improve the way your organization communicates internally and externally.

Primary data sources

This type of data can be obtained through various methods, including observation, experimentation, in-depth interviews and surveys.

Observation

Observation can help organizations find out about customer communications by looking at competitor promotional material or exhibition stands or using mystery shoppers to monitor the way that staff deal with customers. Similarly, mystery shoppers can be used on a firm's own staff to monitor customer communications. For example, after a period of training residential care home managers in customer care skills, on such topics as how to greet prospective residents and what to say when showing people round, the senior management of a company decided to send a number of mystery shoppers to the homes to find out how each home manager communicated with prospective customers.

Experimentation

Experimentation can help assess the impact of variation in any promotional activity that is undertaken. For example, an animal protection charity wanted to assess whether it should use a 'shock approach'. It sent a fundraising mailshot to one half of the customer database together with a shocking photograph of animal cruelty and to the other half just sent the letter to assess which approach was most successful. Similarly, copy variations can be tested in advertising and direct marketing activity.

In-depth interviews

In-depth interviews can be used to probe people's attitudes and motivations about any aspect of the marketing mix offering. They can be used to find out customers' views on a wide range of communication issues, such as sales promotions, advertising concepts, product names, packaging, brand images and corporate identities.

Individual interviews or in-depth interviews are informal and more conversational than questionnaires and allow respondents to talk in an unconstrained way. Techniques can be used to find out respondents' deeper attitudes by using projective techniques such as word association and sentence completion tests. For example, when the Midland Bank recently changed its name to HSBC, it was likely that they used this method to find out how the new name would be perceived and if it would work in the marketplace.

Focus groups are usually led by a trained discussion leader or moderator and will contain about five to eight people from the target audience. These discussion groups can be shown draft storyboards which show the draft stages of a 30-second television commercial. This is a useful way to check that the advertising proposition and message is appropriate and appealing before entailing the expense of actually shooting a commercial.

The idea behind getting a group of people together in a focus group as opposed to interviewing individuals is that the discussion is likely to become more wide-ranging as people make comments and others in the group either agree or disagree. Sometimes the discussion can appear to go off at a tangent, and that is where the moderator brings the group back on track. This approach can be very useful in determining customer attitudes to the way that an organization communicates with them. For example, a fashion mail order company asked a discussion group about their reaction to the spring/summer catalogue. They found out that the customers thought that the photographs of cheaper dresses made the items look much better than they were in reality. As a consequence, customers were often very disappointed when they received their orders and this explained the high rate of returns of cheaper items photographed in exotic locations.

Activity 3.3

The head teacher at a school is under pressure to attract more pupils in the next academic year. He would like to produce a brochure about the school that contains information he imagines prospective schoolchildren and their parents would be interested in, such as examination results, sporting successes, information about school trips and concerts as well as information about the staff and class sizes. He wants to find out if the contents of the brochure are relevant and interesting to his target audience before it is printed and distributed. Suggest how he might find out this information.

(**See** Activity debrief at the end of the unit.)

Surveys

Surveys, which collect data through the use of questionnaires, are the most common method of primary research. They can be used to collect both quantitative and qualitative data depending on the structure of the questionnaire and the contact methods chosen.

A survey asks questions of a number of respondents selected to represent the target market. Below is a selection of factors that can be measured through a questionnaire:

- Finding out which media customers are exposed to in order to plan media buying.
- Measuring pre-advertising or PR campaign awareness of products/ services.
- Measuring post-campaign awareness to assess the effectiveness of advertising or PR campaigns.
- Finding out attitudes to brand names, promotional campaigns, sales promotions and other incentives.
- Rating your organization's performance against the competition.
- Finding out about customer expectations of customer service and what kind of information they require from the organization.
- Finding out whether customer service and customer communications, such as speed of delivery, helpfulness of staff and waiting times when customers telephone, are satisfactory.

Contact methods

Surveys can be conducted by contacting respondents by telephone, mail or face to face.

Telephone surveys

These are a fast, convenient way to access a large number of respondents. Computer-assisted telephone interviewing can be used to guide the interviewer through a sequence of questions which appear on a screen and answers are then keyed directly into the computer for analysis. Nissan dealerships contact a selection of customers who have had their cars serviced. When they contact the customer they ask about the level of satisfaction with the car's condition and also ask about how quickly staff contacted the customer with a price quotation and how helpful the staff were on the telephone and in face to face encounters in the dealership.

Postal questionnaires

These can be inexpensive and reach geographically dispersed samples but can result in low response rates. Customers may be encouraged to respond if there is some incentive to do so. In business to business situations customers may be very pleased to respond because they feel that their feedback may improve the product/service offering and the way the organization communicates with them.

Face to face contact

Personal interviewing is a popular method of collecting information and if sales staff do it as part of their sales job in business to business sales situations it can elicit valuable customer feedback. However, it can be time-consuming and expensive for an organization in the consumer market to employ staff to ask questions of passers-by.

Questionnaire design

If you are producing a questionnaire that respondents will read and complete on their own, it is important to consider the design and layout of the questionnaire.

When designing a questionnaire, some attention should be paid to the layout so that there is plenty of white space and clear type to make it easy to read. Simple tick box options should be used where possible, although where relevant you can include a 'if other please specify' category so that you do not miss crucial alternative customer information. By paying careful attention to layout and restricting it to one page in length, you can make a questionnaire seem quicker to complete than it really is.

When designing questionnaires, it is useful if there is an introductory statement that outlines the objectives of the survey. Response rates can be improved if there is some incentive to encourage the customer to hand in a completed questionnaire. This could be as simple as a discount voucher, a free sample or entry into a prize draw. However, incentives alone will not encourage respondents to complete a questionnaire if it is not designed to be brief and easy to complete.

Respondents should be thanked for taking the time to complete the questionnaire and you should make it easy for them to return it, possibly using a Freepost address.

Questions should be sequenced in a logical order and grouped by subject, for example, under headings such as About you, About your family, Media habits, etc. It is advisable to ask personal questions at the end of the questionnaire so that the respondent is not put off by an initial personal question asking about earnings and age.

You should be careful to ask only absolutely necessary questions, otherwise you run the risk of the respondent getting bored answering unnecessary questions.

Questions should usually follow from the general to the specific. If you are designing a questionnaire for mortgage customers, it is likely that you would first ask if the respondent has a mortgage, then proceed perhaps to ask for how long and then to ask more relevant detailed questions about their understanding of company information about mortgages and buildings insurance. This approach is particularly important if you are conducting face to face surveys where, for instance, you may only want to question people living in rented accommodation and who do not have mortgages, in which case you need to ask questions about this at the beginning.

Types of questions

You can ask *open* questions that invite an opinion and leave the respondent free to choose how to answer. For example, you could ask, 'What do you think of our delivery times?' but you will find that these answers are hard to collate and quantify.

You can ask *closed* questions that warrant a yes or no response or a rating on a scale, for example, 'Have you ever had any goods delivered late?' Or you could ask the respondent, 'How would you rate our delivery service – excellent, satisfactory or poor?'

Multiple choice questions are closed in the sense that answers are predetermined but they introduce choice from a list of responses. For example, you could ask the question, 'How did you hear about us?' You could then offer a selection of options with a tick box beside them. The respondents could tick one or more boxes to indicate how they heard about your organization. These options might include: through a friend, through an advertisement or through a leaflet that was posted to me.

Rating scales help to quantify opinions and attitudes. These take several forms:

1 How did you feel the brochure description compared to the hotel accommodation you stayed in during your holiday?

Accurate   ❏ ❏ ❏ ❏ ❏   Misleading

2 Indicate in order of importance (1 being most important) the additional features you would like to be part of your holiday package:

(a) Free 24-hour emergency health care line.
(b) Free breakdown service with your car hire.
(c) Free sports facilities.
(d) Free childminding service.
(e) Free guidebook and map of the resort.
(f) Any other feature (please specify and denote order of importance).

Questions to be avoided

Avoid wording that could cause confusion or bias in the response. Avoid leading questions, such as 'Does inhaling other people's harmful smoke in cinemas concern you?', as this question predisposes the respondent to answer yes. Avoid ambiguous questions, such as 'Do you like eating in expensive restaurants?', as different people would have different views about what is expensive. Avoid confusing two-part questions, such as 'Do you like eating out and drinking wine in restaurants?', as the respondent may like eating out in restaurants but may not drink wine and will be unsure how to answer the question.

Pilot questionnaires

It is advisable to pilot test a questionnaire first within your department and then among a representative target audience to ensure that your questionnaire is easy to complete and elicits valuable information. At this stage you may realize that some questions are not vital and identify others that need to be asked.

A bank manager has set her staff certain standards relating to product knowledge. She expects staff to be familiar with all the bank's financial services. How can she find out if staff can deal satisfactorily with customer enquiries about a new mortgage product that has been introduced?

(**See** Activity debrief at the end of the unit.)

One-off or continuous research

All the types of research that have been described so far can be undertaken on a one-off basis to find out specific information at any one time. Some research is conducted on an ongoing basis and can be useful to monitor trends.

Panels of people representing certain customer groups can be set up and regularly asked for information about such things as their media exposure and what advertising they have seen. Some organizations, such as service providers or computer firms, set up user groups to discuss issues and obtain feedback from customers on a regular basis.

Combining primary and secondary sources of data

Case example

Mothercare

Mothercare cardholders are sent a short one-page questionnaire with their monthly account statement. At the top of the questionnaire a brief letter states that Mothercare have many special promotions and in-store events and that they would like cardholders to be the first to know about these so that they can benefit from cardholder discounts and offers. The letter then asks cardholders to complete a brief questionnaire with questions about contact details (this includes asking for the customer's e-mail address) and about the children the person has living with them.

Through this field research the company is collecting valuable customer information. This primary data can then be added to secondary data that Mothercare already holds about the cardholder's transactions. This enables the company to utilize research data in order to target appropriate communications to customers.

Using research data to improve customer communications

Having undertaken research, it is important that the information is used to inform decision making and make improvements as indicated by the feedback.

On a simple level, informal feedback in a social situation with a client can provide you with valuable information. Assume you are an account director in an advertising agency and line manage an account manager who is responsible for the brand x account. If you hear from the client that he is sometimes unhappy with how often the account manager contacts him with updates on the progress of the account, you would use this information to rectify the situation immediately. This identification of a potential complaint stops dissatisfaction setting in and probably means the agency has retained a happy client.

If, however, you receive a serious customer complaint, you would need to investigate the situation and then, if the complaint was warranted, you would have to make sure that the situation did not occur again.

In another context, you may receive a large amount of marketing research data on a regular basis that needs to be analysed carefully to help you make decisions about customer service and customer communications.

You are the Marketing Manager of a group of residential care homes for elderly people. You wish to plan a client communications strategy for next year. You already distribute leaflets to people you believe influence the purchase decision and also undertake various advertising strategies/ campagins. To help you decide what promotion and communications activity you need to organize, you have asked homes' managers to note how people making enquiries heard about the home. Based on the feedback below which you have received in the last six months, how would you communicate with prospective clients in the next year?

Source of information	Number of enquiries
Advertisement in the telephone directory	258
Advertisements in the local newspaper	3
Posters displayed in GPs' surgeries	6
Entry in the residential care home directory	0
Leaflets distributed to district nurses	241
Leaflets distributed to social workers	300
Posters displayed in local libraries	25
Information on the company website	1

(**See** Activity debrief at the end of the unit.)

For the examination, be prepared to use your general understanding of how marketing research methods can help an organization develop or improve its customer communications in a range of situations rather than simply rote learning the various research methods.

Practise questionnaire design techniques and see Question 2 on the specimen paper in Unit 11 for an example of the kind of question that could be asked on the examination paper.

In this unit you have developed an understanding of how research can help develop and improve an organization's customer communications and promotional activity.

You will have looked at various research methods and practised using marketing research data to make decisions about customer communications.

Activity debrief

Activity 3.1

You could give each advertisement a reference number which identifies the newspaper or magazine it appears in. When orders are taken you could ask customers to quote the relevant reference number and this would give you the information you require. In this example, you are using marketing research to identify the best media to communicate your message.

Activity 3.2

You could do this by leaving a questionnaire in people's rooms which focuses on these areas. You could provide some incentive to reward people for completing the questionnaire, either a free bottle of wine with dinner or entry into a prize draw.

Activity 3.3

Although he would probably not refer to what he is doing as primary research and he would be unlikely to consider that he is undertaking in-depth interviews or organizing focus groups, he would probably ask parents of prospective schoolchildren what they want to know when they first visit a school. He would also probably discuss his ideas for the brochure with parents and teachers at the PTA (parent teacher association) meeting and at a school governors' meeting. He may even ask children in his school what they would be interested in reading about in a brochure.

Activity 3.4

She could use mystery shoppers to enquire at the branch or by telephone to find out if customer enquiries were dealt with satisfactorily.

Activity 3.5

The main focus of communications activity would be to continue to produce leaflets about the homes and distribute these to social workers and district nurses, as these people obviously influence prospective customers.

The display advertisement in the telephone directory would be repeated again next year despite its high cost. In addition, posters would still be produced and displayed in local libraries and any other suitable buildings used by the local community.

Past examination question (June 1995)

(a) Using the information presented in Figure 1, explain how Castleford x is perceived by consumers in contrast to the consumers' ideal beer and discuss the characteristics of the competing brands in relation to Castleford x.

(10 marks)

(b) Use appropriate graphical/visual communication to illustrate Castleford x's sales data and market share information.

(10 marks)

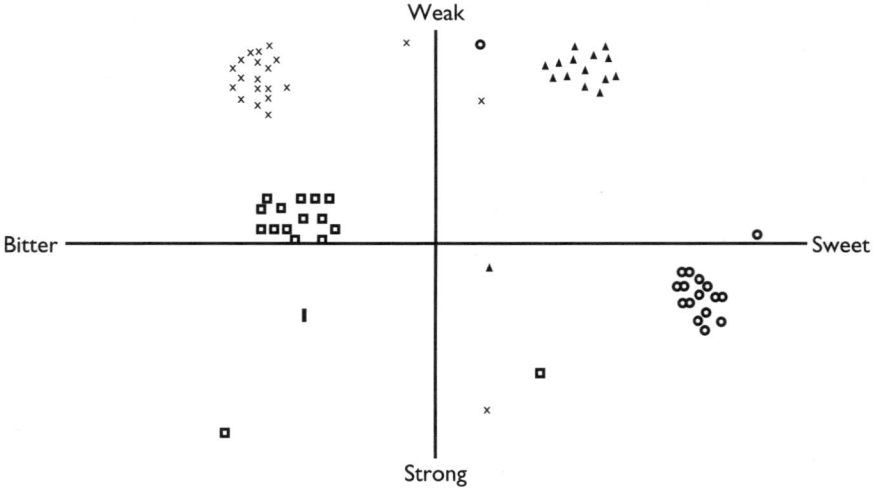

Figure 1
Scatter diagram showing research conducted into consumer perception of a range of competing lager beers

Key:

Ideal	=	ǀ
Castleford x	=	▫
Heinelad	=	×
Harper	=	▲
Millben Light	=	○

Sales data and market share information

1993–94 market share figures were as follows: Harper 16 per cent; Millben Light 10 per cent; Castleford x 34 per cent; Heinelad 27 per cent; with several other smaller brands standing at 13 per cent.

UK sales of Castleford x have increased in recent years. Sales of cans in the take-out market reached £98m in 1993–94 and the previous year stood at £91.4m. Although there was a serious low point in 1990–91 with only 65.7 m cans sold, this was preceded by high sales of £80m. The problems with distribution to off-licences and supermarkets reached crisis point in 1990. Although delisting by Bettabuys came as a crucial blow to the owners of the Castleford x brand, major changes in the senior management team and distribution strategy meant that sales were once more on target at £84.7m by 1991–92. Since then the brewers of Castleford x have had to face stiff opposition from Heinelad whose owners spent £2.5m on a particularly creative campaign last year. Castleford x's marketing director said: 'Despite the slow recovery in general economic terms we remain the brand leader in the carry-out lager market and trends indicate can sales of over £100m in the year ahead.'

Specimen answer

Castleford x is perceived by consumers to have the right kind of bitter taste that an ideal brand would have, but is considered to be weaker than an ideal beer would be.

1993/4 Market share figures

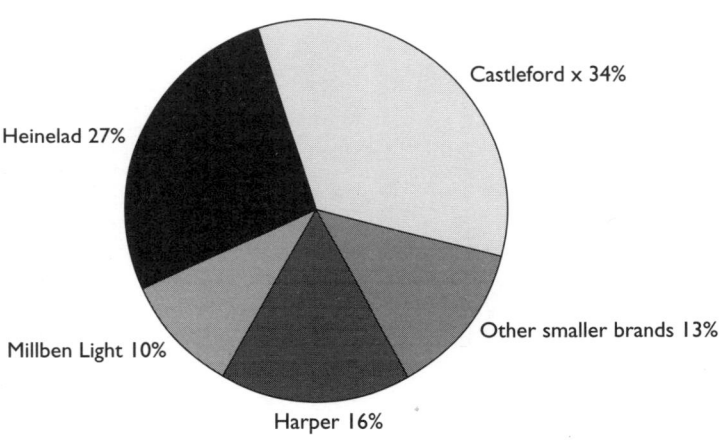

UK sales of Castleford x

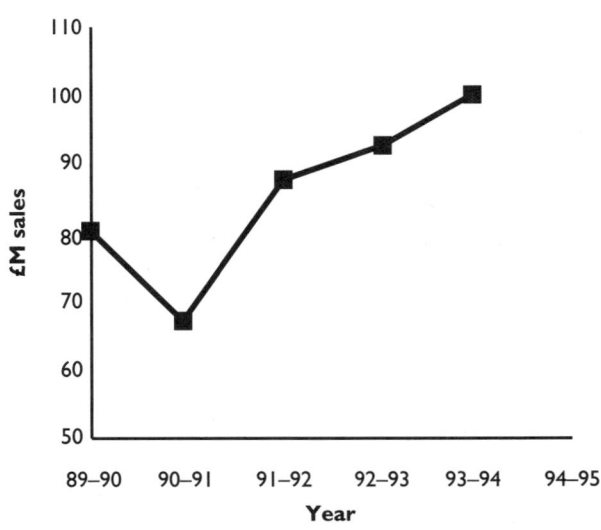

Other brands were perceived to have a range of different characteristics. Heinelad was considered to be the same if not slightly more bitter in taste to Castleford x but much weaker. Harper was considered not only to be much weaker but to also have a much sweeter taste than Castleford x. Consumers felt that Millben Light was stronger than Castleford x but too sweet.

The communication process

Objectives

In this unit you will:

❑ Examine the process of communication.

❑ Recognize the barriers to successful communication.

❑ See how an understanding of customer behaviour can help in the development of customer communications.

❑ Relate communications theory to the buying process.

By the end of this unit you should be able to:

❑ Produce a simple model of the communications process.

❑ Identify how and where barriers to communication occur.

❑ Use a planning framework in the development of customer communications.

❑ Apply communications theory to the development of customer communications.

Study Guide

This unit provides an overview of the communication process and an insight into how to be an effective communicator. It covers indicative content areas 2.3.1, 2.3.2, and 2.3.4 of the syllabus. It should take you about one hour to read through this unit and a further hour to work through the activities.

Study Tip

After reading this chapter you could identify a major item that you have purchased recently. Think about the steps you took before actually making the purchase decision and why you chose that product in favour of others in the market. Consider how you found out about the product and any other information that you obtained about it in the period prior to buying it.

The purpose of communication

In marketing, you communicate with others for the following reasons:

● To inform or persuade.
● To obtain a decision or request action.
● To get something done.
● To maintain relationships or respond to a previous communication.

39

The pressures of modern-day living mean that when you communicate in business it must be clear, accurate and efficient so that time, effort and money are not wasted. Successful communications occur when the person communicating has a clear purpose or objective which is achieved as a result of the communication.

To help you understand what actually happens when you communicate, here is a simple model of the communication process.

The communication chain

Communication is a *chain* of events which has *five* distinct dimensions (see Figure 4.1).

1 The sender has the need to communicate.
2 The need is translated into a message (encoding).
3 The message is transmitted.
4 The receiver gets the message (decoding).
5 The receiver interprets the message and provides feedback.

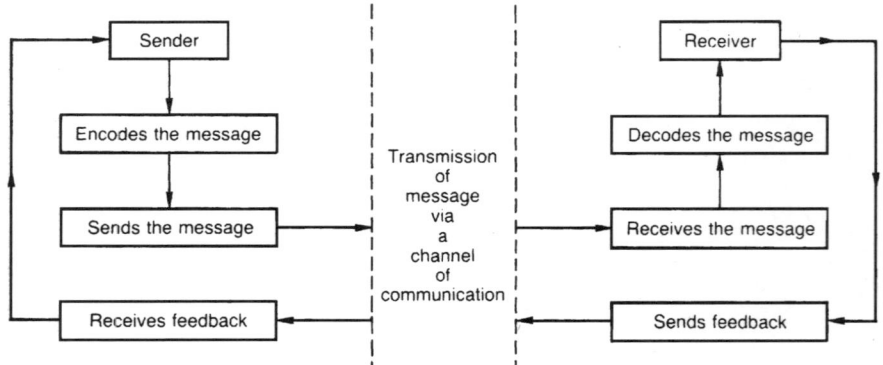

Figure 4.1
The process of communication

1 The need to communicate is *intrinsic*, but the *perception* of a message will be unique, therefore in the process of *conceiving* an idea, you will inevitably make assumptions and leave out details that seem unimportant. However, others will not perceive in the same way, therefore you must appreciate the *needs* of your recipient, their possible interpretation(s) and *plan* your message accordingly.
2 Messages may be *expressed* in a number of different ways depending on the purpose of the communication, subject or topic to be related, the needs of the recipient and your own personal skills in communication. In the process of *encoding* you will select bits of information and organize them for transmission. The first step is to decide what and how much to say; if a message contains too much information it is difficult to absorb, but if you do not include enough, it will not meet with the expectation of the recipient and may leave room for misinterpretation.
3 The *medium* you chose for transmission will depend on the message to be conveyed, location of the recipient, speed, convenience and degree of formality required. The usual internal methods are memo, report, telephone and face-to-face interaction.

   Technological advances in electronic office equipment such as computer-based systems for sending electronic mail copies of documentation have made it possible to send communications from one location to another quickly and effectively.
4 *Decoding* is in the interpretation of the message that has been received and will have been successful if the recipient has absorbed the message and assigned to it the meaning which the sender intended.

5 *Feedback* (or lack of) is the response that the recipient sends back to the sender and is a key element in the communication process because it enables the sender to *evaluate* the effectiveness of the message. Feedback may take the form of verbal (telephone call, face to face interaction, etc.), non-verbal communication or action (body language, etc.) or written messages.

Feedback is the key element that creates a *cycle* in the communication chain, enabling the information that is sent to be *reviewed* when it is received back and on this basis further communication initiatives or corrective action can be taken as necessary.

Barriers to successful communication

Distortion
It is possible to lose the meaning of a message during the communication process. This can occur at the *encoding* stage, where the sender puts their thoughts into a message. It can also occur at the *decoding* stage, where the recipient attempts to grasp the meaning of the message. This breakdown in communication can be caused by the sender not translating his message into appropriate language, with the result that the wrong message is sent or it is not understood by the recipient.

Although there may be instances where people deliberately choose to distort the message and understand only what they want the message to say, the most common reasons for the meaning being lost in the 'handling' of the message are as follows:

- Using the wrong words.
- Using jargon or technical words that are not understood.
- Using a foreign language or an accent that is not understood.
- Using words or pictures that have more than one meaning.

Noise
Noise, such as distractions or the interference that occurs as the communication is being encoded, transmitted and decoded, can obstruct the transmission of the message. There are many different types of noise that can render the message inaccurate, unclear or even mean that it is not received at all.

Technical noise
Technical noise can occur while the message is being transmitted; for example, when a poor telephone connection means the caller's voice cannot be heard or a fax machine breaks down.

Physical noise
Physical noise can occur while the message is being transmitted; for example, people talking, traffic or noisy machinery could render a speaker's voice inaudible during a presentation.

Social noise
Social noise creates interference in the transmission and decoding of messages. It is caused when people are prejudiced against others because they are of a different age, gender or social class. For example, a young woman delivering a presentation on corporate funding to older business-men may be perceived to lack credibility by some of the audience who are prejudiced because of her age and gender.

Psychological noise
A person's emotional state or attitude could interfere with message transmission. A person's anger or hostile attitude can create psychological

noise. For example, a customer whose goods have not been delivered may be unable to hear the reason why the goods have been delayed because he is so angry about the situation.

Other barriers

Perceptual bias can occur where the recipient of a message makes assumptions and selects what they want to hear. This can result in the wrong message being received. For example, if a doctor has told a patient that their condition is not serious as long as they change their diet, the patient might choose to hear only part of the message and not take in the message about changing their diet.

Information overload can occur if the recipient of the message receives too much information or information that is too technical. The result is that the key messages are not conveyed or understood. For example, when a new member of staff is given a very detailed demonstration of how several pieces of equipment work in a short space of time, it is likely that they may become confused and remember very little about what was actually said.

Contradictory non-verbal messages can occur if the person encoding a message says one thing but their body language says something else. For example, if a person wears casual clothes and a baseball cap to a job interview in a formal business environment and says that they think they would fit into the organization, they are conveying mixed messages to the interviewer.

Problems caused by communication barriers

In the workplace barriers to communication can cause misunderstandings which can lead to:

- Mistakes.
- Conflict.
- Irritation.

Activity 4.1

Read the following case study and identify the barriers to communication and the problems they are causing in the workplace.

Sally Strict, the office manager at XYZ, is nearing retirement and considers herself to be 'of the old school'. She likes the girls on her administration team to appear neat and tidy and to do as they are told without question.

One day they are short-staffed and the recruitment agency agrees to send a temporary administrative assistant to work for a week. Sally had asked the agency to send someone for two weeks but the telephone line had been so crackly that the message had not got through.

When Peter Patel, a young business studies student who liked to get work experience during his vacations, was sent by the agency to the XYZ office, Sally was shocked by his appearance. She wondered how a young man with dyed hair and earrings would ever be able to cope with the work done in her department.

She spoke to him in a sarcastic tone and said: 'You'd better make yourself busy – that is if you know anything about office work.'

Peter was very irritated by her hostile attitude. However, he knew that she and the rest of the department were under a lot of pressure to get work completed. He was sure the office manager would appreciate his hard work and he decided that if she did not, then he would just walk out and leave them in the middle of all the work they had to complete.

Later in the day the department received a large number of orders that had to be processed immediately and this would involve all the team staying late.

During the afternoon tea break, Sally, who had by now realized that Peter was an efficient and hard-working member of the team, said: 'So how are you getting on now?'

Peter immediately assumed that she was being sarcastic and 'having a go' at him. He smiled politely and said: 'Fine, thanks.'

Sally was relieved that he had not taken offence at their initial meeting and was glad to see him settling into the office.

A few minutes later, Peter put on his jacket and walked out of the office. He was determined that he was not going to stay at XYZ to be insulted by the office manager.

(**See** Activity debrief at the end of the unit.)

Effective communicators

Successful business communicators have the ability to transfer and receive information using the most appropriate channel. They eliminate barriers to communication and proceed without prejudice, bias and unsuitable language in line with the needs of the recipient. They possess the following attributes:

- *Credibility*, i.e. they are highly believable and trustworthy in terms of the content of their communication/message with which you, as a recipient, feel completely comfortable. Indeed, this is vital for successful managers and those involved in the leadership of others.
- *Precision*, this is linked to the first point and relates not just to the ability to articulate words, sentences and phrases into a meaningful communication but also helps to create a communication experience whereby the recipient(s) share the same 'mental picture' as that of the sender.
- *Perception* – a successful communicator will be able to anticipate and predict how their message will be received and therefore shape it accordingly. The reponse of the recipient(s) (which may be presented in written format, verbally or non-verbally) will then be assessed by the sender and if necessary further communication will take place to adjust for misunderstandings.
- *Control* – linked to the point above about perception is the feeling that you should now be getting, which is that successful communicators are able to control their message to a great extent and also to generate (mostly) the required response, if appropriate.
- Finally, one of the most important (natural) skills possessed by successful communicators is that of congeniality, in other words the ability to be pleasant and friendly, either in written, verbal or non-verbal communication, even if the message is serious and possibly very bad news.

Planning the business message

Professional communicators decide the purpose of their communication at the outset. By being clear about their intention, they then know if they have achieved their objective at the end of their communication.

Business communications tend to be planned, formal, impersonal and succinct. The degree of planning involved in the communication depends on the purpose and context of the communication. For example, you may carefully plan a sales call to a prospect, since you may need to deal with any objections that the customer may raise. However, you are unlikely to do this when you want to arrange lunch with a colleague, even though there may be several important matters you wish to discuss with him. In this situation you may not make detailed notes of the issues but your planning may extend to making a mental note of them.

A planning framework

- *Purpose* – identify the objective or intention of the communication.
- *Audience* – identify who you want to communicate with, their position/status, where they are located. This will assist you in considering what their perception and understanding of the message might be.
- *Structure* – identify the content of the message and the order in which the material should appear.
- *Style* – identify the appropriate type of vocabulary, the degree of formality and the tone of voice.

The PASS framework is an easy to remember mnemonic that you may be familiar with. To assist you in the planning of messages you should also consider the communication *mode* you intend to use, as the communication format and media you use will be important in determining the structure and style you adopt.

Identifying the purpose

There are an infinite number of reasons why you might communicate in business. Generally, in internal communication situations, you will be informing colleagues, line managers or subordinates about something, responding to a previous communication, obtaining a decision or requesting action. In external markets you may be trying to raise awareness in the media, persuading customers to buy or stimulating some other response, such as ordering a catalogue or ringing for more information.

Acknowledging the audience

For internal communications the position of the person you are communicating with and how well you know them will determine the style of communication you adopt in terms of the detail, complexity and words used. In addition, the purpose of the communication and the urgency of the matter will determine which communication format and media you will use.

In order to tell a colleague that you will not be available for lunch for another hour, you may just call into their office or telephone them. In contrast to this, you may write a memo or send an e-mail to inform staff about a change in the time and place of the weekly sales meeting.

In writing a press release to announce some important news about the company you work for, you may draft two versions of the press release. One may be tailored for the national press and one may be targeted at the trade press. However, if you had a particular contact in the broadcast media who you wanted to inform, you may consider using the personal touch and actually telephoning the contact with the information.

In developing advertising to your target market, you will need to consider the characteristics of the target audience in terms of their age, gender, education, social background and lifestyle when composing the words and deciding on the visual approach and the media you will use.

Structure

Having identified why you are communicating and with whom, you need then to consider what you are going to say and how you are going to organize the content of the message.

Business communications should be succinct, so you should be selective with the content you choose to include. Use relevant, accurate information and make sure that you do not overload the recipient with too much information.

Having selected the material for your message, you need to decide how you will organize it. The way you group material together and how you sequence it determines the shape of the message.

It may help you to structure the message if you identify the most important point and then follow with the supplementary information you need to include. If you are dealing with particularly complex material it may be helpful to present the simple information first and build up to the more complex argument or points you wish to make. You may feel it is important to present information in a chronological order, particularly if you are dealing with a series of events or a complaint about a number of issues.

Whatever structure you adopt, you should note that it is easier to read an argument that follows a logical progression and quicker for people to absorb information that is grouped together in chunks with relevant headings.

Style

The style you adopt in any message is governed by the words you use, the way you structure sentences and the tone of voice you adopt.

The way you use vocabulary is a personal choice. The English language is very rich and you may often have several words to choose from that will convey the same meaning. However, you should consider your audience and their familiarity with the words you use. It is not always appropriate to avoid jargon or technical words, especially when you know your audience is familiar with them and where it is important for you to establish credibility and common ground with your audience.

By changing the structure of sentences you can place emphasis on certain words and by altering the order of words you can produce greater fluency or flow.

The tone of any communication conveys the overall effect. You can create an overall impression of friendliness and informality with the greeting you use, simple wording and colloquial expressions. For example, the following sentence has a friendly, informal tone: 'Thanks for lunch yesterday. It was useful to go through the client list and I will make appointments to see each of them a.s.a.p.'

Alternatively, you can convey a formal tone by giving instructions, using technical wording and an impersonal tone. For example: 'The figures indicate that sales staff need to cut the cost of expenses by x per cent. Consequently all journeys over x miles should be agreed by the Sales Manager.'

By emphasizing points, by appealing to the recipient's emotions, repeating selling points, using reassuring terms and asking questions that lead the recipient to a series of benefits, you can create a persuasive message. For example, the following statement has a persuasive tone: 'How can Home Care help you? With Home Care you can be assured of quality care in the comfort of your own home. No more struggling with the cooking and cleaning . . .'

Activity 4.2

Rewrite the sentences below, avoiding the use of jargon and clichés, and correct any unnecessary wordiness.

1 The practicability of planning to meet possible future service requirements should be explored.
2 The supplies manager has been at pains to explain that the availability of the product is diminishing rapidly.
3 Inflationary land prices have rendered it an uneconomic proposition to relocate the production operation.

(**See** Activity debrief at the end of the unit.)

The mode of communication

The communication format (whether that is a written report or an oral presentation at a meeting) or the media (whether that is the telephone or electronic means or some form of advertising media) that you use to transmit your message will influence its structure and style.

In addition, when communicating internally, you will need to consider the purpose of the communication and the audience you wish to communicate with, to help you decide the correct communication format. For example, there will be some occasions when it is suitable to put a notice on the notice-board to communicate with colleagues and at other times it will be more appropriate to send a memo or organize a face to face meeting.

For external communications there will be occasions when it is suitable to send a fax message and at other times it will be easier and more confidential to send an e-mail.

Where you need to raise awareness about an issue or a new product, your choice of media will influence the style you will adopt.

For example, if you were trying to raise awareness about the dangers of driving without seatbelts you could either use a press campaign or a radio campaign to communicate your message. However, the treatment of the message would be different in each case. For radio, you could use sound to communicate an emotional message of a family talking about the death of a loved one. For the print advertisement, you could go into more detail as you would not have the same time constraints as a short radio commercial. So you could include more facts and figures about the number of car accidents caused by not wearing a seatbelt. Such a detailed message would be totally inappropriate if it was read out loud in a radio commercial but could be absorbed by people reading it in their own time and at their own pace.

Activity 4.3

Suggest an appropriate communication style and mode of communication for each of the following situations:

1 You work for the city council and wish to use an advertising campaign to inform motorists that tolls will be introduced on routes into the town centre.
2 You work in the research and development department of a factory that makes cleaning materials. You wish to demonstrate the prototype of a new window-cleaning product and the main findings of a financial viability study to senior management as you need their approval to proceed to the next stage of product development.
3 You are the distribution manager at a chemical company. There have been problems with deliveries from the warehouse to a number of distributors. You have collated your findings about the problems and now need to communicate them to the Sales and Marketing Director.

(**See** Activity debrief at the end of the unit.)

Relating customer behaviour to external communications

Understanding how customers behave and what influences their purchase behaviour helps determine effective and relevant communication and promotional activity. When designing and implementing communication plans it is important to consider who your customers are, what their lifestyles are, their educational background, the type of jobs they do, their income levels and their attitudes.

Influences on consumer behaviour

One approach is to consider a customer as a 'black box' with a variety of inputs that influence purchase behaviour. Some of these inputs or stimuli are SLEPT (social, legal, economic, political and technological) factors over which you have no control. However, consideration of these factors can help you to communicate with your customers. For example, at a time when the cost of borrowing money is low because of low interest rates, a financial services company might want to invite current mortgage customers to extend their mortgage. In drafting a mailshot to communicate this message to customers, you would probably want to make reference to the economic situation as part of your selling message.

Other influences that affect purchase behaviour are controllable factors, such as your organization's marketing mix offering. So, for example, the knowledge that in the washing powder market on-pack price promotions and money off influence customers to change brand (at least in the short term) may be a vital piece of information when manufacturers are planning customer communications.

There are a number of other buying influences that affect consumer behaviour.

Social influences

Through research into your organization's customer base you should be able to identify a profile of your target audience which enables you to develop the right messages and tone of voice in communications that will appeal to them.

The following are powerful social influences on consumers:

- *Social class* in terms of a person's job, income, educational background and social status, which may influence the newspapers people read, where they spend time socializing with friends and the type of holidays they go on.
- *Stage in the life cycle* in terms of whether a person is single and has high disposable income or is married with young children and therefore spends large amounts on household products.
- *Culture* in terms of religion or ethnic grouping, which can affect people's food choices, the clothes they wear and the magazines they read.

Individual differences

The following are some of the influences that shape people's individual tastes/needs:

- *Motivation* affects people in different ways. Some people are highly motivated by status and therefore tend to buy expensive brand-named goods that are a 'status symbol'. Others are more interested in self-fulfilment and prefer to spend their disposable income improving themselves, for example, learning how to play a musical instrument or learn a foreign language.
- *Personality* can affect a person's consumer behaviour. Although everyone has their own distinct personality, there are specific traits that are identifiable in some groups of consumers. For example, if you ran a travel agency that specialized in adventure holidays, then your advertising would be designed to appeal to people who could be described as having an 'independent' personality.
- *Beliefs/attitudes* relate to a person's opinions about things. So, for example, The Body Shop appeals to consumers who have strong beliefs that testing products on animals is wrong. The Body Shop communicates this message in all its advertising, packaging and in-store promotions.

Lifestyle

Lifestyle refers to how consumers spend their free time and what they spend their disposable income on. For example, if you were marketing a magazine that focused on health and fitness for men, then you would want to target men whose lifestyle was oriented around keeping fit, playing sport, being a member of a gym and going on activity holidays. This customer profile or visual image of your target audience would enable you to develop communication messages and strategies that would appeal to them.

Consumers are generally recognized as going through a number of stages as they proceed from initially identifying that they have a need for something to the point of purchase (see Figure 4.2). Sometimes consumers can proceed through the various stages in a matter of seconds, when they buy on impulse. Typically, consumers are unaware that they are going through a process, it just happens subconsciously.

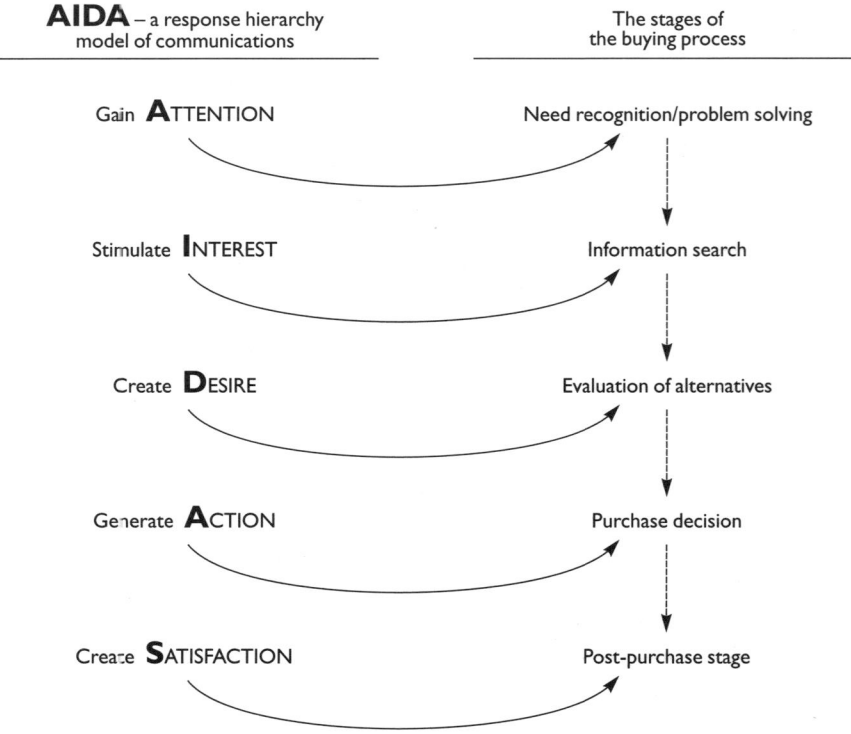

AIDA – a response hierarchy model of communications

The stages of the buying process

Gain **A**TTENTION	Need recognition/problem solving
Stimulate **I**NTEREST	Information search
Create **D**ESIRE	Evaluation of alternatives
Generate **A**CTION	Purchase decision
Create **S**ATISFACTION	Post-purchase stage

Figure 4.2
Relating communication objectives and messages to the stages of the buying process

Using the AIDA model (see Figure 4.2) you can see that customer communication strategies and messages can be tailored to fit in with the buying process that a consumer might go through.

For example, when consumers purchase a car, they will go through various 'problem-solving' stages. Communication messages to prospective car buyers therefore need to be staged to match their progression through the decision making-process.

The buying process

Need recognition/problem solving

Consider the case of a young woman who decides she needs to buy a car as she has moved to a new job that is not convenient for public transport. She may also consider that she would like a car because all her friends have one. At this stage she has recognized she has a need.

As far as customer communications are concerned, car manufacturers may tailor their messages to young people to trigger their need/desire to own a car. They may appeal to a young person's desire to have freedom and a good time. Knowing the attitudes and lifestyle of the target audience is key to developing communications that have appeal. This corresponds to the *attention* stage of the AIDA model. Therefore communications should be designed to grab the target market's attention at this stage.

Information search

The next stage after recognizing a need/problem would be for the young woman to search for information relating to the prospective purchase. At first she may be in a state of heightened attention, where she is more receptive than ever before to information about this product category. She will look at poster sites and magazine advertisements for cars with a new interest. She may listen to friends' conversations about their cars.

Next she is likely to undertake an active information search about different types of cars. Her sources of information may be friends/family and memories she has about various cars she has driven. She will also look at advertising, read consumer magazines and car programmes, talk to salespeople and even perhaps have a test drive.

The implications are that car manufacturers need to take advantage of every opportunity to communicate with prospective customers and have product information widely available in the media and in car showrooms. In addition, they need to have cultivated a strong brand image and other satisfied customers in the target market. This corresponds to the *interest* stage of the AIDA model, indicating that communications should be designed to create interest.

Evaluation of alternatives

After searching for information, she is likely to evaluate the various car models and makes that are on the market. The communications task for the car manufacturer at this point is to get the brand into the customer's 'choice set' and to desire the product. This corresponds to the creating *desire* stage of the AIDA model. However, research should have identified what exactly the target market desires in terms of the product's main attributes. Having identified the most important attribute, it is essential that this *unique selling point* is communicated clearly to the target audience.

The purchase decision

Having got to the intention to buy stage, the consumer's personal circumstances, attitudes and beliefs will affect the purchase decision. But it is at this stage that customer communications, whether they are through advertising or the face to face approach from a salesperson, should move the consumer to the purchase decision. This corresponds to the *action* stage of the AIDA model.

Post-purchase evaluation

Having bought the product, consumers will either be satisfied or dissatisfied, depending on their expectation of the product and the product's actual performance. Even at this stage, communications with the consumer are important in order to foster a favourable opinion of the product. This is mainly because customers tend to discuss purchases with friends/family, and so word-of-mouth advertising becomes a powerful communications tool. In addition, a favourable memory of the product may influence a repeat purchase decision in future years. At this point it is possible to add a final communications stage to the AIDA model, creating *satisfaction*.

Activity 4.4

Using the AIDA model and the model that illustrates the buying process, complete the table below to indicate which promotional tool a car manufacturer might use at each stage.

The buying process	AIDA model of communication	Promotional tool
Need recognition	Gain attention	
Information search	Stimulate interest	
Evaluation of alternatives	Create desire	
Purchase decision	Generate action	
Post-purchase decision	Create satisfaction	

(**See** Activity debrief at the end of the unit.)

Summary

In this unit you have looked at the communication process in some detail. You have also examined a number of barriers to the communication process and the problems they can cause in the workplace.

You have acquainted yourself with the PASS mnemonic. This provides you with a framework to help you plan what you want to communicate and how it should be communicated.

You have also seen how an understanding of customer behaviour can help you devise more relevant and appealing communication messages. In addition you have looked at how communications can be staged to fit in with the stages that consumers pass through when making purchase decisions.

Activity debrief

Activity 4.1

Barrier	Problems caused
Technical noise caused by crackly telephone line.	Mistake by the agency in arranging the duration of the placement.
Social noise caused by Sally's prejudice about Peter's age, gender and appearance. He lacked credibility in her eyes.	This irritated Peter but also stopped Sally working effectively with him.
Psychological noise caused by Peter's anger.	Peter misinterpreted what Sally said to him and this caused conflict.
Contradictory non-verbal communication caused by Peter smiling and saying one thing but really thinking something else.	Sally received the wrong message.

Activity 4.2
Here are some ways of rewriting the sentences:

1 We should attempt to plan ahead to meet future service requirements.
2 The supplies manager has pointed out that the product is difficult to obtain.
3 It is difficult to move as the price of land has gone up.

Activity 4.3

1 You could use a poster campaign along the roads where the tolls will be introduced. As with all poster campaigns, you would need to keep the message simple because people need to be able to take in the message as they go past at speed.

2 You could do a demonstration and a short presentation. Your communication style would be persuasive in order to show the benefits of the new product. To communicate the financial data you might use visual communication, such as graphs and tables. Any slides or acetates that you produce may just feature key words that you will explain as part of your presentation.

3 You may write a lengthy, formal report to the Director which deals with the problems and suggests solutions. You may adopt an impersonal tone, using a 'third person' style. For example, 'It appears that the road works on the local motorway network have caused significant delays when our vans depart for the mid-morning delivery run.' As you are writing to your line manager you would not use an authoritative 'tell' style of communication. In your report you would not necessarily avoid longer, more complex sentences or technical terms.

Activity 4.4

The buying process	AIDA model of communication	Promotional tool
Need recognition	Gain attention	PR
Information search	Stimulate interest	Advertising and point of sale material in car showroom
Evaluation of alternatives	Create desire	Test drives, sales brochure
Purchase decision	Generate action	Sales force
Post-purchase decision	Create satisfaction	Direct marketing material, follow-up calls to check customer satisfaction, warranty material

Past examination question (June 1996)

Question 2(a) Draw a diagram to represent the communications process and illustrate where 'noise' can occur. (4 marks)

Question 2(b) Explain how each of the following can create a barrier to communication and use an example for each to indicate how the impact of noise could be reduced.

(i) Lack of credibility (4 marks)

(ii) Perceptual bias (4 marks)

(iii) Information overload (4 marks)

(iv) Contradictory non-verbal signals (4 marks)

(a)

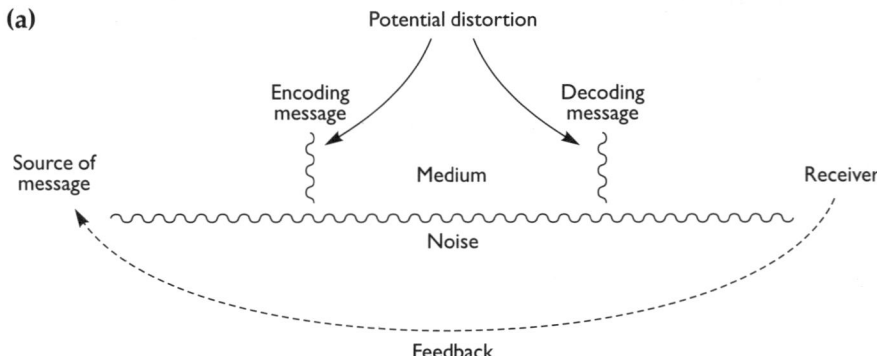

Figure 4.3
The communication process

(b)

(i)

Lack of credibility can be a barrier to communication if, for example, a young, inexperienced salesperson lacking in product/market knowledge tries to sell a high-value, specialist, technical product. This barrier to communication could only be overcome if the salesperson had thorough training in both sales technique and the product/market.

The noise could be reduced if the salesperson had a professional appearance in terms of dress and used a professional demonstration kit to illustrate the product to potential customers. It would also be useful if the salesperson worked for a well-known company and had testimonials from previously satisfied clients. In this way customers would concentrate less on the weak traits of the salesperson and be more aware of the credibility of the product and the manufacturer.

(ii)

Perceptual bias refers to people hearing what they want to hear. By filling in the gaps and making assumptions a significant barrier to the real message can be created. For example, if staff had heard rumours about potential job losses prior to a staff meeting they might 'tune out' from the information being delivered during the meeting and may only select the negative aspects of what was being said.

The noise could only be effectively reduced if the manager addressed the rumours and allowed staff to ask questions so that he could allay fears and ensure that staff heard the whole message.

(iii)

Information overload is a barrier to communication because if a person is given too much information then the key message is not digested. For example, if a person delivered a talk to their local CIM branch on the effectiveness of an advertising campaign and the speaker provided too many facts and figures, the overall message might be lost in the detail.

To avoid information overload, the speaker could reduce the amount of detail and emphasize the main points using visual aids, illustration, demonstration and anecdotal examples. In-depth background detail to the campaign could be provided in the form of notes or a handout for those who wanted to read this information in their own time.

(iv)

Contradictory non-verbal signals might be conveyed by a person whose words say one thing whilst their body language says something else. For example, when a customer is complaining about the service in a bank, the cashier dealing with the complaint could be apologizing for the mistake made but at the same time avoiding eye contact and sounding disinterested and bored by speaking in a monotone voice.

To reduce the noise, the cashier would need to support the words being used by adopting a sympathetic tone, eye contact and positive body language such as nodding to show empathy with the customer's viewpoint.

Unit 5 Effective communication skills

Objectives

In this unit you will:

❑ Appreciate how non-verbal cues can add to or detract from communications.

❑ Understand how to be a better listener.

❑ Build on your telephone communications knowledge.

By the end of this unit you will be able to:

❑ Use non-verbal communication effectively in a variety of situations.

❑ Be a better listener in all face to face interactions and when using the telephone.

❑ Make and receive telephone calls in a professional manner.

❑ Deliver effective presentations.

Study Guide

This unit covers indicative content areas 2.3.3 and 2.3.7 of the syllabus. It provides you with a basic understanding of the role of non-verbal communication and active listening and extends your knowledge in the areas of telephone use and the delivery of presentations.

It will take you a minimum of three hours to work through this unit.

Study Tips

Choose two countries that friends, family or colleagues have visited on business. Find out if there are any differences between the two countries in relation to how non-verbal communication is interpreted.

Communication skills in marketing

Effective non-verbal, verbal and listening skills are essential in marketing as there are so many face to face and telephone interactions when you need to use good oral skills and be able to listen to verbal and watch for non-verbal cues.

Non-verbal communication consists of:

- The body language you use, such as eye contact, facial expression, posture, gesture and physical space.
- The impression/atmosphere you create by your punctuality, hospitality, manners and personal appearance.
- The voice characteristics you adopt – tone, pitch and volume.

Non-verbal communication can convey messages without words or add meaning to whatever words are being used.

Eye contact

The look in someone's eyes can have a variety of meanings. In a romantic scene, the way an actor looks into the leading lady's eyes conveys a very different meaning to the way a person can stare in defiance or in a challenging way. In a business context, avoiding eye contact can convey disinterest or shiftiness but making positive eye contact while you are delivering a presentation shows that you are relating to and connecting with your audience.

Facial expression

Your facial expression and coloration can convey various meanings. A flushed face can indicate embarrassment, while the colour draining out of your face can indicate shock. Pursed lips can reveal your irritation at something, a frown can show disapproval and a smile can indicate happiness, approval or a welcome.

Posture

If you adopt an upright posture, it can show you are attentive and the opposite can show you are disinterested. If you were lounging in your seat when your Managing Director walks past, it could indicate that you do not respect the individual.

If you sit hunched up in your seat in a group, it could either indicate a lack of confidence or hostility.

Gesture

Your gestures might include a clenched fist to indicate anger, or a shrug of your shoulders to convey that you do not really care, or you may tap your fingers and, without knowing it, indicate that you are impatient with the person or the situation you are in.

Physical space

Sitting on a big chair behind a big desk so that people who enter your office have to sit on a lower chair opposite you, with the desk as a barrier, can communicate your authority and the level of formality you expect from others. Alternatively, you can achieve informality in meetings by using a horseshoe shape layout.

Physical space also refers to the invisible line that surrounds people and is referred to as *personal space*. By breaching someone's personal space you can intimidate them and be perceived as overbearing and insensitive.

An accepted move into someone's physical space in Britain is the friendly handshake. In Europe and other countries, kissing on the cheek may be acceptable. Different countries and cultures have different norms.

The impression/atmosphere

You can create a favourable impression in a business situation with a smart appearance in terms of your clothes and personal grooming. If you are punctual and use the appropriate greeting, for example a formal handshake, particularly when meeting new business contacts, this can influence whether you are seen to be acceptable by conforming to the norms of business behaviour.

Similarly, your hospitality can be judged not just by the words you express but if you are seen to be helpful and considerate to visitors. This can include taking their coats, checking that they are warm/cool enough, whether they need a drink and ensuring that your body language is positive, for example, smiling rather than looking at your watch as if you are in a hurry to get rid of them.

You can create a different impression with different types of body language. Consider the difference between a nervous cough, a bored sigh and a snigger. You can also use your body language to indicate that a meeting has finished by edging out of the door, getting up from your chair or gathering up your paperwork.

Voice characteristics

Consider the expression 'Oh, that's just great'. A different message can be conveyed depending on how the voice is used to express the words. For example, said in a friendly tone of voice when someone has received something they are pleased with, it conveys a friendly, grateful message.

If the same expression is shouted at someone, it could be a sarcastic message that in fact they are not pleased with something and things are not in fact 'great'.

The same words said quietly in a deep and husky voice in an intimate situation would convey a completely different message.

So the tone of voice, volume and pitch that are used can affect the message being conveyed.

Using and interpreting non-verbal communication

You can use non-verbal communication to your advantage in meetings, interviews, negotiations and presentations to do the following:

- To create a positive impression.
- To show that you fit in with the culture of an organization.
- To convey enthusiasm and confidence.

By recognizing the messages intrinsic in the non-verbal communication displayed by others you can do the following:

- Recognize other people's true feelings.
- See potential problems.
- Read situations better and modify your message accordingly.

Activity 5.1

You are responsible for internal communications within an import/export company with offices around the world. The firm has recently moved to team working within departments, which means that managers hold regular briefings with their teams. Write a memo to managers giving guidance on the importance of appropriate body language when briefing teams.

(Adapted from a past examination question from June 1999 – 10 marks possible.)

(**See** Activity debrief at the end of the unit.)

Listening skills

Good listening skills are important in marketing, simply because you will use them during meetings, interviews, negotiations, other people's presentations and when you are in a selling or briefing situation.

You need to work at your listening skills so that you possess all the necessary and relevant information, avoid wasting time and maintain good relations with both internal and external customers. Listening skills are particularly important if you are dealing with a customer who is trying to air grievances.

Many people imagine that listening is something that just happens. However, it is important that you distinguish between hearing and listening. *Hearing* is what might happen when you have the radio playing in the background whilst you do something else. *Listening* means engaging your mind and your memory, and you are active in selecting information, organizing, interpreting and storing it.

Barriers to listening

Your thought processes operate four times faster than most people speak, and as a listener you may become bored and allow your mind to wander. You may regard what is being said as dull or irrelevant and close your mind, thus missing vital pieces of information.

You may have prejudices or fixed ideas about things and, if you are listening to something with which you disagree, you may react by pretending to listen but may 'tune out' to the message or become angry and distracted from the message that is being communicated.

You may be listening to someone who is talking about something technical that you do not understand, with the result that you stop following the conversation and may become too embarrassed to ask questions.

You may be listening to a great number of facts and figures and lose track of what is being said because of information overload.

How can we be better listeners?

1 Through active listening you can actively concentrate on what the person is saying and make a conscious attempt to understand. You could even make selective notes of the key points that have been made.
2 By being a patient listener and letting the person speak without interruption.
3 By being open-minded and guarding against prejudice and stereotyping so that you do not 'tune out' from the message.
4 By seeking clarification you can check with the person what they have said, paraphrasing in your own words.
5 By being sympathetic and showing empathy, particularly if you are listening to a complaint. You can demonstrate this with appropriate body language, such as making eye contact, nodding your head in agreement or making encouraging sounds/statements, such as, 'mm-hmm', 'that's interesting' and 'I understand'.
6 By being helpful, particularly in a complaint situation, you need to resist the temptation to argue and look for solutions to the problem instead.

Activity 5.2

A colleague has been promoted and will have to interview staff in future. He lacks interview experience and asks for guidance on listening in interviews. Suggest four ways in which he can be an effective listener in interviews.

(Taken from the June 1997 examination paper – 4 marks possible.)

(**See** Activity debrief at the end of the unit.)

Using the telephone

Advantages of using the telephone

With all the various methods of communication available to people, the telephone remains a popular tool for the following reasons:

- It provides quick, easy access over long distances (even if the recipient of the communication is not available it is usually possible to leave a message either with a colleague or on an answer machine/voice-mail system).

- It is a relatively cheap means of communication.
- It is interactive (it provides a two-way form of communication).
- It is possible to protect the time of others by deciding whether or not to put the caller through.
- It is easier to hide your emotion on the telephone if you wish, because people cannot see your facial expression and body language.
- It is much easier to terminate a conversation with someone on the telephone than if you are in a face to face situation with them.

Disadvantages of using the telephone

- There is no permanent record of the communication and it is therefore difficult to verify the contents of a telephone call unless you record it.
- There is no opportunity to judge body language, which can make negotiation situations difficult. Equally, some customers may not feel confident doing business this way, particularly with important or complex financial decisions, such as buying mortgages or pensions.
- You can become involved in a 'telephone tennis' situation, where messages go back and forth and the caller never actually gets to speak to the person they want to communicate with.
- The truth of a situation, whether someone is actually in a meeting or not, is difficult to gauge.

Planning telephone calls

The most effective approach in using the telephone in terms of saving time and money is to adapt the PASS planning framework, to ensure you make effective and efficient telephone calls.

Purpose
Plan your call and be sure of the purpose of your call. This will guide you in deciding what you have to say. Have all the relevant information to hand, such as the correct telephone number. And, for example, if you were trying to arrange a meeting, you would need your diary. If you were ringing to query an invoice, you would need the original letter with the quote and the invoice that you received.

Audience
Consider who you are contacting, as this will influence what you say and how you say it.

Structure
In planning your message it may be helpful to make a checklist of points you wish to make as a reminder for use during the telephone conversation.

Style
When making a business call you may adopt a different style to the one you use for personal calls. The style you adopt is made up of the words you use, the way you order sentences, your pronunciation and your tone.

You may indeed adopt a telephone voice that close friends and family do not recognize. You do not need to do this but you should communicate in a clear, organized and succinct way. You may need to spell out words, using other words to indicate the letter you mean where there may be confusion. For example, you may say 'F' for foxtrot, not 'S' for sierra to distinguish like-sounding letters. You may also group numbers together, if you are communicating a telephone number or reference number of some sort. For example, you may read out a telephone number as zero, one, six, one, and then pause before reading out the rest of the number.

In business calls you should avoid slang or words that are over-familiar, such as 'OK', 'yeah', 'ta ra then'.

You should be confident when making a business telephone call, or at least sound confident. One of the advantages of telephones (at least those that are not videophones) is that the recipient of the call cannot see you. When someone is slightly nervous on the telephone, they sound hurried and use careless speech. Consequently you should speak slightly more slowly than your usual pace. This is also important because the recipient of the call cannot lip read, so it is important that you pronounce words clearly.

The tone of voice you use in telephone conversations is very important, as your body language cannot be seen. (See Figure 5.1.) You can overcome the barrier of not being seen by adopting the tone of voice that is relevant to the message being communicated. (See Voice characteristics in the section on Non-verbal communication skills in this unit.)

You should also vary the tone of voice you use, as a relentless monotone can give the impression either that you are boring or are bored with the conversation.

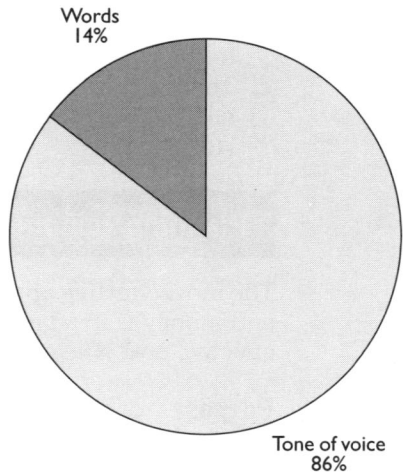

Words
14%

Tone of voice
86%

Figure 5.1
How we receive messages by telephone

Guidelines for making effective telephone calls

Once you get through, greet the person who answers, identify yourself, your company and ask for the person you wish to speak to. At this point you may have to give a brief outline of the purpose of your call.

Having made sure that you are speaking to the right person, make your call in a courteous, clear and concise way. You should be prepared for the person you need to speak to not being available and be able to give a shortened version of the message you wish to communicate. Alternatively, if it is not appropriate to précis your message, you should politely ask for the recipient of the call to ring you back.

Guidelines for receiving calls

Organizations have their own procedures for answering the telephone, so you will find that this section provides some guidelines which may have to be amended to fit in with your own organization's system.

Whatever procedures are set down for staff to follow, it is essential that a friendly and efficient image be conveyed to anyone who contacts the organization.

Callers should not be left waiting while the telephone rings. Some organizations stipulate how quickly the telephone should be answered. It is inappropriate for a caller to be left waiting for several minutes while information is being retrieved. It is equally unacceptable for a caller to be passed around several departments or to be made to feel as if they are an unwelcome interruption. Good telephone technique is vital for the maintenance of good public relations.

Putting a customer on hold

Ideally, customers should not be left hanging on the line. If you consider it is going to take some time to get the right person on the line, it is better to take down the relevant details so that the right person can contact the caller later. If, however, you do need to put the customer on hold, then you should ask for their permission first and briefly tell them why you need to do this. If you have been finding out information while the caller was put on hold and you go back to them, it is only good manners to thank them for holding.

Callers are rarely asked if they mind being put on hold. What usually happens is that when callers draw breath at the end of a sentence, they are summarily sent to telephone limbo and forced to listen to music, while the person on the other end of the line tries to transfer them or consults their files.

Transferring a call

Customers become intolerant when they are transferred over and over again, and particularly when they have to explain their situation several times.

The best approach, if it is possible to do so, is to explain why the call needs to be transferred and to whom. You should also ask if the customer minds being transferred. Before you hang up, make sure there is someone to pick up the call. Before the customer talks to the person they have been transferred to, you should briefly outline the nature of the call, so that the caller does not have to repeat details again.

Taking messages

It is very important to get the details of a message right first time. This is where your listening skills will be very useful. It will mean taking the time to clarify the caller's name, company, telephone number, the nature of the call and the action required.

You need, therefore, the right equipment, such as a pen and message notepad, to hand. Most organizations have pre-printed pads where you complete the relevant boxes with a tick to indicate the action required. Always print your name on the message pad so that the recipient of the message can come back to you if they need to clarify any details.

Answering calls

The circumstances may vary:

- *Answering your telephone extension where calls come in through a switchboard operator.* The caller knows the company they have reached and you only need identify yourself by giving your name. For example: 'Good morning Andrew Kelly speaking, how can I help?'
- *Answering the telephone on behalf of a department.* You could give your name and the name of the department. For example: 'Good morning, Technical Support, Andrew speaking, how can I help you?'
- *Answering the telephone on behalf of the company.* The caller needs to be given the company name and perhaps your name. For example: 'Good morning, Pine Box Productions, how may I help you?'

The greeting should be used to demonstrate friendliness. The telephone should be answered within a certain number of rings; three to five is normal.

You need to be prepared with the right equipment so that you can deal with the enquiry or instructions given to you during the telephone conversation. This will vary depending on your circumstances but usually comprises at the very least: pen, message pad, company extension list, notepad and diary.

Conference calls

The technology exists to have several different people in different locations talking to each other at the same time. While these conversations lack the impact of a face to face meeting, they can be a convenient and relatively inexpensive method of getting people together for instant feedback.

However, it can be difficult to avoid situations where everyone speaks at once and the conversation flow is often inhibited by the lack of non-verbal cues.

Activity 5.3

You are the Marketing Manager for a chain of hotels. Write a memo for circulation to all reception staff about the effective use of telephones. In particular, you should focus on the appropriate way to deal with incoming calls, the transfer of calls and message taking.

(Taken from Question 6 on the December 1997 examination paper – 8 marks possible.)

(**See** Activity debrief at the end of the unit.)

Presentation skills

Types of presentations

For most marketers it is an inevitable part of their professional career to give speeches or presentations. In the early part of your career you could be asked to give an informal briefing to colleagues on a recent training course or a demonstration on how a piece of equipment works. As you become more established you may find yourself going through the results of a campaign to a group of managers, giving colleagues a progress update on a project, putting forward your proposals to a client or even delivering a sales pitch.

Planning an effective speech or presentation

As with all communications, the PASS framework is a relevant planning framework and will help you plan the content and delivery of your presentation.

Purpose

The planning of the presentation begins with objectives. Consider the purpose of the presentation, why you are delivering it and what you hope to achieve. At the end of the presentation you should be able to determine if you have achieved your objectives.

Audience

To help you decide on the message you want to deliver and how you should deliver it, you should consider who is your intended audience. Consider what their needs are in terms of what they need to know, how long you have with them, the size of the group and the type of room they will be in.

Structure

Knowing what your purpose is and what your audience's requirements are will help you decide on the structure of your presentation. You should decide on the key points, the order that they should go in and how you will link the material together.

Style

To determine the style of the presentation you will have to decide the level of formality and involvement that is appropriate. For a small group you could deliver a presentation on a complex matter in a fairly informal way with a high level of participation from the audience. You also need to decide if you are going to use visual aids.

Composing the message

Decide what you are going to say, having first, if necessary, researched your topic. List the points you *could* include and select those that you *must* include. Allocate time to each point and develop a sequence.

You should try to make your presentation conversational rather than trying to learn hundreds of words off by heart. One way could be to write out your talk in longhand, reduce it to shorthand notes and reduce that to crib cards. Your delivery should then be based on the crib cards.

Another approach is to imagine that your audience will get your message from a picture. Once you have an outline picture, then you can take people into the detail by creating a series of smaller pictures by breaking down the argument more simply.

To develop this approach you could use a mind map. The idea is that you draw a circle with your topic heading in it and from that draw branches that are labelled with four or five key areas. Then draw a branch off each of these branches to indicate other detailed points. For example, if you were giving a presentation about the opening of a DIY store your mind map might look like the diagram in Figure 5.2. You could then use prompt cards to remind you of the key areas and sub-points from your mind map.

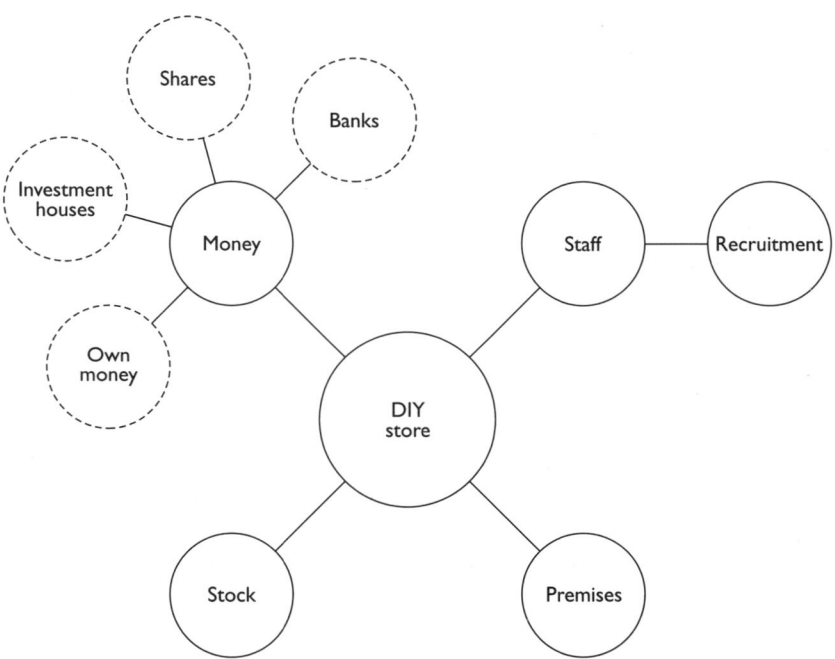

Figure 5.2
Example of a mind map

Whatever method you use to compose the content of your message, you should plan your talk so that it has a beginning, a middle and an end. A well-known quote that describes this approach is as follows: 'Tell them what you are going to tell them, then tell them, then tell them what you told them.'

Preparing for the talk

You should ensure that you have prepared the stage management aspect of the presentation. If it is a large, organized conference that you are speaking at, then this will be done for you. If not, then you need to check the following:

- The layout of the chairs and tables (for a small group a horseshoe shape is often better than lining people in rows).
- That there are enough chairs and tables for the audience.
- That you will be visible from where you are going to stand.
- That there is a lectern or table for your paperwork.

- That the equipment for visual aids works.
- That the lighting is adequate.
- That the room is tidy and has adequate heating/ventilation.

Delivering the talk

A good presentation can be broken down into message, body language and voice. A common assumption is that the message is the most important element but, according to Gray and Wnek in an article in *Marketing Business* (1996), it accounts for only 6 per cent of the total package that people listen to and observe. Body language contributes a massive 82 per cent and voice the remaining 12 per cent.

Body language

The nerves that some people feel before delivering a presentation are usually connected with having to stand up in front of an audience that is totally focused on you. You should try not to be seen to be nervous by having control of your body language. You should aim to do the following:

- Don't look tense – relax your jaw muscles and smile (be careful if you are delivering bad news, though).
- Stand upright with your shoulders relaxed.
- Do not fold your arms across your chest.
- Don't hunch up/bend your head down to read from your notes – just refer to them occasionally.
- Maintain eye contact with the entire group – don't stare at one individual or one section of the group. This can be difficult if you arrange the group in a horseshoe shape.
- Avoid gesticulating wildly or other distracting mannerisms, such as jangling change in your pocket or scratching.

Voice

Except in specific circumstances where you might need to use an authoritative tone, you would normally use a friendly tone to deliver a presentation.

You should consider practising your talk to calculate how long it takes you to get through it. One problem to avoid is an attack of nerves that tempts you into the 'racehorse' syndrome of getting your head down and charging through to the end of the presentation. Take care to consciously slow yourself down.

You can use pauses not only to slow down the pace but also to place emphasis on important points. You also need to give people time to absorb the information in any visual aids you use.

Try to vary the pitch of your voice. Another technique for slowing yourself down is to modulate your voice. If you make your voice rise and fall, as you do when you tell a joke or a story to others, you are less likely to end up with a fast monotone that sends the audience to sleep. This will enable you to put emphasis on certain words or parts of your speech. You also need to sound energetic and enthusiastic to convince people that you are worth listening to.

Use of visual aids and technology

Visual aids, such as overhead projector slides or acetates, pictures, slides of still photography or flip charts, can be used to give variety and impact to a presentation, particularly when you are presenting lists or numerical information. However, they should be produced to a high standard or they can give rise to a negative reaction.

If you are using visual aids, you should be careful how you use them. Check that you have pens to use on the flip chart or that the stand works. Check that you can focus the overhead projector. Always check that all the audience can see visual aids.

When you use visual aids, do not stand in front of them and obstruct the audience's view. Do not read from them verbatim – it is better to talk around the issues that the visual aid encapsulates. When you have finished with the topic, remove the visual aid so that it does not distract the audience.

We work in an age of specialized software such as Powerpoint, video walls and a plethora of acoustic equipment that can enhance a presentation. Used sensibly, these tools can bring clarity and add impact to a presentation. But it is essential to remember that technology is an aid, not a crutch. Unlike a brief television commercial, a successful speech is rarely a triumph of style over content. If you do not get the words right, your audience will quickly lose interest.

The use of video walls at conferences is growing as companies want their brands and the people speaking on their behalf to appear larger than life. Unfortunately for presenters, it means that every nervous lick of the lips and gravy stain can be seen in close-up. They can also have an unfortunate effect on people's clothing. Clothing with big patterns, very bright colours and glittering jewellery can blur and produce a strobe effect. The presenter can also blend into the background if the colour of their clothing is the same as the background.

Always assume that the technology you plan to use for your presentation is going to fail. If your speech does not stand up on its own without the technology, you should question whether the script is good enough.

Verbal skills

To help you decide on how you should deliver your talk, you should consider how people listen and take in information. People tend to take in information at the beginning and at the end and only snippets throughout.

So it is a good idea to pepper a presentation with devices that bring the audience back to you. You can do this with metaphors or analogies (comparing something to something else that everyone is familiar with; for example, the business was an acorn but has now grown into an oak tree) and anecdotes or examples (stories from real life). These can be very effective tools, but do not over-use them or you might confuse your audience.

As a general rule, use punchy sentences and avoid unnecessary jargon. Beware of jokes. They can be hard to carry off as they require excellent timing. Also, you risk offending your audience.

You need to connect with your audience, so use vocabulary that fits in with them. You can add emphasis by using the following devices:

- Repetition, for example, 'This campaign has increased our turnover by £500,000 – that's right, half a million pounds!'.
- Rhetorical questions, for example, 'You may ask me what are we going to do about it but I am asking you "What are you going to do about it . . .?"'.
- Quotations, for example, 'As Martin Luther King said: "I have a dream . . ."'.
- Statistical evidence, 'A dissatisfied customer tells nine other people about their dissatisfaction . . .'.

Questions and feedback

The great advantage of presentations is that they are interactive. You can sense how your message is going down with your audience and even get instant feedback. However, you may find it very disruptive to handle questions during your presentation. If this is the case, you should say that you would be happy to answer questions at the end. You should then leave time at the end for questions and comments from the audience.

Techniques for handling questions/feedback

- Repeat any questions so that the audience can hear and be involved in this part of the session.
- If the question or comment is relevant, then either answer the question directly or thank the person for their contribution.

- If the question is rambling or unclear, try to clarify and retrieve one simple question from the narrative.
- If the question is irrelevant, you could say that it is outside the scope of the presentation.
- If the question is hostile or you don't agree with the points made, accept as much as you can of the points made but do not get drawn into a long argument.
- If you cannot answer the question, admit that you cannot but enlist the help of the audience, or you could say that you will get back to the person once you have had a chance to look into the matter.

Evaluating objectives

At the end of the presentation, consider whether you persuaded people to do something or make a decision about something, or did you sell something, clarify something, change people's minds about something, inspire people to think about something in a different way – in other words, did you achieve your objectives?

Exam/Revision Hints	Do not rote learn the body language section but be prepared to apply your understanding of it in questions that are set in a variety of contexts, such as managing staff, in interviews, dealing with customers and delivering presentations.
	Be prepared to answer questions on the use of listening, telephone use and presentations in much the same way as they have appeared in past papers under the Business Communications syllabus.
	In addition, refer to Questions 1(c) and 5(b) on the specimen paper in Unit 11 for examples of the kind of questions you could be asked.

Summary	In this unit you have seen that reading non-verbal cues and displaying appropriate non-verbal communication are a vital skill in face to face interactions. You have also seen that active listening is a skill that can be used in a variety of situations. You have read about effective telephone usage and hopefully can implement the guidelines in your working lives. You have also been provided with some general guidelines about the delivery of presentations whatever their purpose or context.

Activity debrief

Activity 5.1

MEMORANDUM

To: All Managers

From: Maggie Yorke, Communications Manager

Date: 30 July 20XX

Subject: Weekly team briefings

A number of managers have asked for some guidance on the best way to present themselves in the regular team briefings that have recently been introduced in all departments.

I have observed a number of the meetings and body language is one important area where some simple tips could improve the way messages are put across to teams.

It is important to communicate your verbal message and keep in the back of your mind how the following can either add to or detract from the message you are trying to put across:

Facial expressions

Staff will react more favourably to you if you have a warm, friendly smile instead of looking rather tense or aggressive, which is the message that can be communicated if you have a furrowed brow or pursed lips.

Posture

You may feel more comfortable sitting down with your team round a table rather than standing up in front of them, which creates a more formal atmosphere. If you do sit down, avoid folding your arms as that can appear as if you are creating a barrier. Make sure that you sit upright rather than slouched in the chair as that could communicate that you are too tired or bored to be bothered with the briefing.

Gesture

Many people like to use their hands to express themselves but too much hand waving can be distracting for those listening. Even if you are displeased with the team's performance or recent events, it is better to avoid emotional displays such as banging one's fists on the table.

Eye contact

It is very easy to find yourself making eye contact with just one person in the team. However, this may make the person feel uncomfortable as they will feel they are being stared at. Another problem could be that you are tempted to read from your notes and may end up not making eye contact with your team. You should avoid this as it can result in the team not being involved in what you are saying.

I am sure that most of you are happy with your departmental team briefings. However, I do hope that you find these tips helpful so that we can continue to improve our internal communications which are so important in helping to motivate and inform the workforce.

Activity 5.2
There are a number of ways in which you can ensure that you are listening effectively in interviews:

- Be patient and let the person express themselves – do not interrupt or complete sentences for the interviewee.
- Use appropriate body language, such as eye contact and nodding, to show interest in what is being said – this will encourage the interviewee to answer your questions fully.
- Ask questions to clarify your understanding of what has been said.
- At intervals sum up what the interviewee has said, to show that you have listened and understood.

Activity 5.3

BLUEBIRD HOTELS
MEMORANDUM

To: All reception staff
From: George Stakis, Marketing Manager
Date: 9 August 20XX
Subject: Effective telephone use

A recent research survey into the service provided by Bluebird Hotels has revealed a number of areas where we can improve our service. One of these areas is the way customers' telephone calls are dealt with. The following recommendations need to be adopted by reception staff when dealing with calls.

Incoming calls

All calls should be answered by the fifth ring. Too many callers are left waiting for several minutes before their call is picked up.

When calls are answered, it is important that they are dealt with correctly. Staff should clearly state their name and that of the hotel, followed by the question, 'How can I help you?'

Transfer of calls

It is important that reception staff are familiar with the extension numbers for the hotel's various departments and the numbers in guests' rooms, so that calls can be transferred quickly and efficiently.

It is apparent that many calls are being cut off whilst they are being transferred. Therefore it is vital that reception staff ensure that they press the gate # button before dialling the extension number they require.

Many suppliers have complained that they are transferred to various departments in the hotel when they are in the middle of speaking to the person on reception. Before transferring calls, please briefly explain to the caller why you need to transfer them and ask for their permission to do so.

Message taking

If the extension number is engaged or not answered, then it is important that an accurate message is taken. Messages should be noted on hotel message pads only. They should state the date and time of the call, name of the caller (company name if it is appropriate) and the telephone number of the caller. Messages for staff should state the purpose of the call. All messages should be put in guest or staff pigeonholes immediately after they have been taken.

Thank you for your co-operation with this matter.

Past examination question (December 1996)

You have been asked to contribute to your company's training programme. Your topic is 'Guidelines on how to prepare for and deliver presentations'. Draft out your plan for this presentation. Use clear headings and bullet points to show the structure and content of the training session.

Specimen answer

Presentation plan

How to prepare for and deliver presentations.

Introduction

- Introduce yourself.
- Explain why good presentation delivery is both important and relevant in your job.
- The presentation will cover the following areas: preparation and delivery of presentations.

Main body of presentation

Preparation – stage 1

- Identify the purpose of the presentation (key message and information needed).
- Identify sources of information.
- Identify amount of time available for presentation.

- Identify specific needs of the audience:
  - Size of audience;
  - Their experience/prior knowledge;
  - Specific interest in relation to this topic.

Preparation – stage 2

- Organization of information/logical sequence/links.
- Three parts – beginning, middle and end.
- Avoiding information overload.
- Timing.
- Practice.
- Use of cue cards.
- Preparation of visual aids.
- Arrangement of room.

Delivery

- Style needs to suit audience needs and type of room (formal/informal, participative/lecture style).
- Use of language.
- Use of tone, pitch and pace.
- Use of body language (eye contact, dress, gestures, etc.).
- Use of visual aids.
- Using participation effectively to maintain interest.
- Using cases/anecdotes to establish common ground.

Summary

- Sum up the main points only – don't introduce new ones.
- Allow time for questions.

Communicating in meetings and interviews

In this unit you will:

❏ Learn about planning and arranging meetings.

❏ Acquire the skills necessary to prepare and conduct meetings.

❏ Recognize the appropriate terminology and documents needed for meetings.

In this unit you will achieve the following:

❏ Recognize the purpose of interviews.

❏ Learn how to plan an interview.

❏ Appreciate the different types of interviews used by business organizations.

❏ Consider the different types of questions that can be asked in interview situations.

By the end of this unit you will be able to:

❏ Prepare yourself for meetings.

❏ Understand all the terminology and documentation needed to conduct successful meetings in business.

Study Guide

Meetings fulfil the need of individuals in organizations to exchange views and information on a range of matters that affect decisions and plans and provide an opportunity to solve problems.

Meetings may be required because of statutory legislation or the constitution of the company, or may be held for a number of other reasons, formal and informal. In the marketing and sales functions the need for a meeting may arise for a number of reasons, to discuss tactical issues relating to one or more of the marketing mix variables in the context of a plan that is currently being actioned, or may be significant in respect of discussing strategic initiatives and so on.

Generally speaking, meetings should be constructive and productive, which means that they have to be carefully planned and should focus attention on one subject at a time or have a structured and logical agenda that provides a reasonable sequence for discussion.

In business organizations a considerable amount of time is spent in meetings, therefore group interactions which are unproductive lead to frustration, wasted time and effort and are not cost-effective.

Interviews are a distinct type of face to face interaction because they are primarily designed to solicit specific information from the interviewee. In marketing or sales, interviews may take place in a survey situation with respondents addressing a number of issues related to your marketing research – these are left to the marketing texts to discuss as we are concerned with *your* skills and needs in an internal interview situation.

One important field of discussion that usually takes place in an interview-style situation (i.e. relatively formal, usually with a pro forma that is completed prior to the interaction, additional notes made during the communication and follow-up sanctions thereafter) is the appraisal, which leads to recommendations by the interviewer (usually a line manager or superior in the department/organization) for promotion or suitable training to help in your personal, professional or career development.

Obviously, your first face to face interaction with the organization will be when you attend for a job interview, and the impressions created will last for some time.

Interviews can also take place due to organizational problems, conflict, need for negotiation with certain parties or because of change factors – all these will be discussed in this unit, which requires about three hours of study time and a further two hours to complete the activities and address the questions.

This unit covers indicative content area 2.3.6 and will take about three hours, as well as another two to three hours to complete the activities.

Study Tips

The route to understanding how to be effective in personal communication within the context of meetings, discussions and interviews is first to observe, second to listen and third to interact.

You should approach colleagues and superiors to participate in meetings, discussions and possibly interviews and also to ask them to give feedback on your performance in handling the above.

In terms of observation, you should look out for the way in which group norms develop, the roles played by members of the group and personal objectives that may constrain the ability of the group to reach a decision, or one that is in the best interests of the department or organization.

Listening skills should be used to understand the content and level of discussion taking place.

If you have the opportunity to interact, do so in a constructive manner, using non-verbal skills.

My main recommendation to you is observe the rules established in this unit and then aim to follow them in all internal and external interview situations, whether you are the interviewer or interviewee.

Another useful way of acquiring effective skills as an interviewer is to be present in interview situations and observe the verbal, non-verbal and written communication that takes place. If you are not allowed to be physically present, ask if a video- or tape-recording of different interview types and levels at which they take place can be made. You can then carry out an evaluation of the processes involved.

Question 6.1

What is the purpose of meetings?

Question 6.2

Do you think that *personal goals* can affect the success of meetings?

The main factors that all business meetings have in common are the following:

1   An objective. There should be a clear purpose of holding the meeting, whether it is to inform, persuade, collaborate, provide counselling or solve problems.
2   An outcome. Some action should have arisen as the result of the meeting which can be resolved in time.

Types of meeting

There are numerous situations that may call for a meeting and I have narrowed them down to the following:

1   Making decisions on strategic and tactical issues. This requires that information relevant to the decision is on hand and that sufficient time is allowed for discussion that will enable a decision to be reached.
2   Solving problems on internal and external issues. The discussion needs to be relevant to the problem under consideration and opportunity needs to be given to all participants so that different perspectives and interpretation can be identified, which may throw significant light on the issue. This, however, must be controlled.
3   Informing and collaborating on a range of organizational issues. This may be achieved formally with a structured presentation or informally through a casual discussion.
4   Negotiating to resolve conflict. The discussion will invariably take place with a minimum of two parties who need to achieve an outcome to satisfy their objectives. The skills needed in handling negotiations are more sophisticated than in most personal communication and cannot be detailed here.

Meetings are usually face to face interactions and therefore have the following advantages:

1   Group discussion can take place.
2   Immediate feedback can be received and further information exchanged.
3   It is an opportunity for fast and efficient dissemination of information.

Meetings do not generally work well if the following factors prevail:

1   The purpose of the meeting is unclear or no background information to the meeting has been provided for the participants.
2   The meeting does not provide relevant facts and information to facilitate valid discussion and decision making.
3   The leader/chair does not control the meeting effectively or is biased in some respect.
4   The participants do not wish to contribute or communicate ineffectively at the meeting.

Preparation for the meeting

In general, the following rules should be observed:

1 Be clear on the need for the meeting – what is its purpose and aim? The success of a meeting will depend on whether a clear aim has been established and the approach that will be taken in its conduct. Meetings will usually arise because of the need for information exchange, decision making, problem-solving, brainstorming or training personnel.

2 Identify the main subjects or topics and subtopics for discussion, by having analysed the situation leading to the call for a meeting and any (superficial) observations you have made.

3 Select the participants, namely key personnel who can make a positive contribution to the subject under discussion, limiting the size to reflect the level and aim of the meeting, with a chairperson who is objective, tactful and patient and to whom the speeches should be directed.

4 Set and distribute the agenda. This is the prepared list of matters to be discussed at the meeting, which should be agreed in advance with the chairperson and secretary of the committee. A list of the participants, time, location of meeting and order of business are also included and the agenda should be distributed several days in advance, to allow preparation by the participants and a strategy by the leader. Preparation of the agenda is discussed below.

5 Prepare the location. The room chosen should reflect the number of participants that will be present and non-tangible factors such as acoustics, room temperature, lighting, timing and availability of refreshments, handouts and accessibility of visual aids (you may even use tele- or video-conferencing) to yourself and the participants.

6 If you are the leader, follow the agenda as set. Do not dominate or monopolize the meeting, but keep control, interest and a pace that will cover all the issues that need to be discussed, to ensure successful completion of the meeting.

7 A record of the proceedings needs to be made and someone will have to be designated for this task, from which the minutes (a record of what took place, discussed below) will be produced and distributed (within 24 hours, if possible).

8 Finally, summarize or conclude the essence or main points of the meeting which the participants are likely to agree (or at least to agree deferment of the point/discussion) and close with a review of action that is to be taken, by whom and dates, as appropriate.

Terminology of meetings

There are a number of vocabulary items that are often exclusive to meetings, such as the following:

1 Proposer – speaks about the statement/argument that they have proposed.

2 Seconder – supports the proposal.

3 Quorum – the minimum number of members that must be present at a meeting, according to the rules.

4 Motion – a proposal to be considered at the meeting.

5 Amendment – to the proposal which will have to be voted for and, if carried, accepted.

6 Collective responsibility – a rule by which all participants agree to be bound by a decision.

7 Casting vote – by the chairperson if there are an equal number of votes on either side of an argument.

8 Adjourn – this means that a meeting will be held over to another time or date.

9 Constitution – a set of rules by which the members of a group are expected to abide.

10 Ex officio – an individual given rights and powers by reason of the position he or she holds.

11 Mover – an individual who speaks on behalf of a motion.
12 Opposer – an individual who speaks against a motion.
13 Point of order – drawing attention to the breach of rules or procedures.
14 Proxy – this means on behalf of another person, e.g. proxy vote.
15 Resolution – a motion that has been carried.

Constituting a meeting

A meeting is only properly constituted if it is convened (called) according to a set of regulations (statutory or otherwise). The main issues are as follows:

1 A meeting must have a *chairperson* who oversees the conduct and progression of the meeting.
2 A meeting must have a *quorum*, i.e. a minimum number of persons who are physically present, as stated in the regulations.

Informal meetings which are called from time to time by a colleague or superior in the department or organization may follow simple procedures and be tantamount to a group discussion. In this situation some notes may be taken and possibly documented. After the meeting has concluded, a summary of the main issues raised and decisions made may be circulated to the participants.

Formal meetings are completely different in their organization and procedure. A set of strict rules and conventions is followed and formal documents are required before the meeting takes place. The main documents are described below.

Motions and resolutions

Definition 6.1

Proposals put to a meeting and which require a decision, usually through a vote, are called *motions*.

Each motion must have a proposer and usually a seconder, i.e. a person who supports the proposal. Motions always begin with the word 'that', for example, 'it is proposed that we initiate a new sales campaign based only on below-the-line initiatives for the next financial year'.

The motion is then discussed at the meeting and if participants approve and agree to take this forward, it is known as being 'carried' and becomes a *resolution*.

Sometimes the motion is changed because of issues that have emerged during the debate, and if this is the case it is known as an 'amended' proposal, which must also be agreed before it can be carried.

The chairperson to a meeting can reject a motion if they feel that it will not slow down the progress of the meeting, it is against the regulations laid down for the meeting or that it will prevent a full and equal discussion from taking place, particularly if it represents the view of only a minority of people.

Adjournment

Sometimes it is necessary to 'put off' discussion of an agenda item and leave it until the next meeting. This is known as an *adjournment*. On rare occasions the whole meeting may also be adjourned.

There are many reasons why a meeting may be adjourned. One reason is that not enough data or information is available for consideration by the participants and therefore they are not in a position to make reasonable decisions.

(a) Can you think of a motion that would be a suitable proposal for a meeting in which you may be a participant in the near future?
(b) For what possible reasons could the meeting be adjourned?

You have been asked to chair a meeting on the past experience and future expectations of undergraduate students of marketing and management who have had work placements in your organization. The informal feedback received to date identifies that some departments are keen to continue with this activity, whilst others wish it to end. The decision will determine whether work placements will be made available next year.

Your task is to consider what type of meeting this should be, how it is to be conducted and suitable items for the agenda.

Meeting documents

The notice

The notice will be prepared and circulated before the date of the meeting, according to the constitution of the company and any other regulations with which the organization may have to comply.

If a large number of participants are to attend, it may be impractical to communicate with them all individually, therefore notices of the meeting may be placed on notice boards as a main channel of communication, especially if these are regularly accessed by potential participants.

Where individuals can be contacted directly, the following channels of written communication may be used:

1 An invitation printed on a card or note.
2 An internal memorandum.
3 A personal letter.

If the agenda (described below) is already drawn up and available for circulation, it is usually included with the notice to enable the participants to study its content before the meeting.

The minutes of the last meeting (also described below) may be attached to the notice so that any issues in respect to the points made can be stated in advance of the meeting, especially if the minutes of the previous meeting have to be approved as a matter of procedure. Figure 6.1 gives an example of a notice.

Figure 6.1
A notice

Friedman & Sons Ltd **Memorandum**

To: Jenny Hamson (Sales Director)
            Andrew Stevens (Marketing Research)
            Alison Perkins (Advertising and Promotions)

From: Clare Simpkins (Marketing Director)
Subject: Notice of Marketing and Sales Group Meeting
Date: October 1st 20XX
The next meeting of the Group will be held in the 'Oak Room' on the first floor of 'General Building' on Tuesday October 10th 20XX at 11am.
I enclose a copy of the minutes from the last meeting and an agenda. Please bring any relevant documents with you or circulate beforehand.

The agenda

This is the schedule of 'things to be done', i.e. the subjects to be discussed, which is prepared by the secretary after having enabled all participants to propose items for the agenda. Although an agenda is not an obligation for the conduct of a meeting, it is a useful tool for guiding the discussion and ensuring that the full scope of the meeting is covered.

Once the agenda has been set, it is then discussed with the chairperson in terms of suitability of subject matter and order of items which the meeting will follow.

The agenda will then be distributed to all the participants so that they are aware of the subject matter of the forthcoming meeting and the order of proceedings, together with any supplementary material that needs to be considered and the minutes of the last meeting. This communication process enables the participants to prepare themselves in advance and also to decide whether their presence is necessary for the full duration of the meeting.

Copies of the agenda are either sent out with the notice of the meeting or distributed to participants as they arrive at the designated location.

A special agenda is prepared for the chairperson, which contains more details than the document circulated to the participants and the names of any particular participants that will be making a special contribution (e.g. presenting a report), with space for the chairperson to make notes on the meeting for personal reference.

Agendas normally contain the following items:

1　Apologies for absence – announced by the chairperson once the meeting has been officially opened and the time and date recorded by the secretary.
2　Minutes of the previous meeting – the chairperson will ask members whether the minutes represent an accurate record of the previous meeting and if so, he/she will sign them as such.
3　Matters arising is an opportunity for participants to declare views or report back on developments since the last meeting.
4　Correspondence from parties outside the meeting may be read and considered.
5　The main agenda items are then opened and discussed in turn, with the chair trying to keep the meeting moving ahead (particularly if a time constraint was imposed at the start) and aiming to reach a consensus on the main points. The types of items discussed will reflect the nature of the meeting, which may be to produce plans, solve organizational problems, deliver reports or feedback, debate proposals or to reach decisions.
6　Any other business (AOB) is stated and discussed. If an item is of relevance to the general discussion or appropriate for the meeting, it may be raised under this section. If the issue is considered unimportant or unsuitable for the present meeting, it may be carried over to another or a separate meeting called.
7　Date of the next meeting is discussed and agreed and the chairperson closes the meeting by thanking the participants for attending the meeting.

Finally, agendas will vary from meeting to meeting and may be a reflection of the following:

1　Degree of formality required for the meeting, which will determine the style of layout in the agenda and state the procedures to be followed.
2　Length of the meeting, which will be determined by:

   (a)　The number of subjects to be discussed.
   (b)　The complexity of the subject matter.
   (c)　The number of important items relative to routine – both may be postponed or made the subject of a further meeting if the time allocated for the present is insufficient to cover all the ground. Figure 6.2 gives an example of an agenda.

```
┌─────────────────────────────────────────────────────────┐
│                  Brown & Co. Squash Club                   │
│                  Annual General Meeting                     │
│                Wednesday October 31st 20XX                  │
│                       at 7pm sharp                         │
│           Venue: 'The Chinese Room', Building Annexe        │
│                                                             │
│                         AGENDA                             │
│                                                             │
│   1   Apologies for absence.                                │
│   2   Minutes of the AGM held on Oct. 30th 20XX.            │
│   3   Matters arising.                                      │
│   4   Report of the club committee for last year.           │
│   5   Annual accounts and Report of the Treasurer.          │
│   6   Election of officers.                                 │
│   7   AOB.                                                  │
│   8   Date of next meeting.                                 │
└─────────────────────────────────────────────────────────┘
```

Figure 6.2
An agenda

The *chairperson's agenda* is different to the one described above in two respects:

1   Each item on the agenda has additional notes which are pertinent to the discussion that will take place in the meeting and for which the chairperson should be suitably prepared with background information or sensitivity in handling material presented and discussed or points raised.
2   A right-hand margin, which is wide enough for the chairperson to make notes during the meeting, is incorporated into the layout of his/her personal agenda.

The *duties of the chairperson* are as follows:

1   Keep the meeting to the agenda and in good order so that the business can proceed smoothly.
2   Be unbiased and fair in allowing the members and participants to make their contribution without taking too much of the meeting's time.
3   Allow only one person at a time to address the meeting and take a decision on the sequence of speakers if more than one wishes to make a contribution.
4   Ensure that all issues and points of debate are addressed to the chairperson, thereby avoiding the deterioration of the meeting into fragmented groups or arguments.
5   Conduct the system of voting if this is deemed necessary during the meeting or at its conclusion.
6   Keep an overall sense of the meeting according to the original agenda and the logic of the discussion.

The minutes

These are a written record of the transactions that took place and should be as accurate as possible, reflecting the duration and general tone of the meeting.

The minutes are usually taken by the secretary, who should have them typed and distributed as quickly as possible after the meeting as they are an important channel of communication and source of reference.

The style or format used to present them, i.e. narrative or structured in some way, should reflect the type of meeting and needs of the participants.

There are three types of minutes:

1   Narrative minutes – these are a brief summary of the meeting which led up to the resolution (decisions) and include the comments made by the participants which have gone on record as their judgement of the arguments preceding the resolution.

2   Resolution minutes – these are minutes where only the resolutions are recorded and therefore do not reflect the tone of the meeting or specific points made leading to the resolution.

3   Action minutes – these minutes indicate the specific courses of action that need to be taken as a result of the resolutions made in the course of the meeting and the individuals responsible for the action items. Figure 6.3 gives an example of a minutes document.

**Research and Development Group
Minutes**

Minutes of the Meeting held in the 'Panelled Room' at 'Building Headquarters', Bromley, Kent on October 15th 20XX at 4 pm.

Present: T. Stones (Chair), A. Peters (Secretary), L. Simons, K. Andrews, J. Clarke

1   Apologies for absence.
    Apologies for absence were received from J. Thyme, L. Young and P. Ankers.

2   Minutes of the last meeting.
    The minutes of the last meeting were taken as read and signed as a true record.

3   Matters arising.
    Further to item 2, the Chairman has received a report of the new innovation currently in prototype stage and will circulate a copy to all members before the next meeting.

4   Proposal to cut the budget by £1 million to be phased in over a period of three years.
    All members present argued for a strong statement to be issued to the M.D. on the consequences for new and existing projects as a result of this budget cut and seek clarification if jobs are also to be lost in this process.

5   New Product Development.
    Len Simons and Ken Andrews presented a visual report on the new products to be commercialized by the end of the financial year.

6   AOB.
    Jane Clarke raised the need for a new laser printer. Angela Peters will receive literature and circulate this to members of the group before the next meeting.

7   Date of next meeting.
    The next meeting of the R&D group was scheduled for January 10th 20XX at Building H.Q.

    Signed X   T. Stones (Chair) Director R&D. Date Nov. 10th 20XX

Figure 6.3
Minutes

Summary

In this unit I have introduced you to the following:

1   The notion of meetings in business organizations, which are designed as an opportunity for a group of individuals to discuss issues that are significant to the organization in a face to face interaction that give immediate feedback and a convenient method for decision making, solving problems, hearing presentations and debating facts. Clearly, the marketing and sales functions will hold meetings for all these reasons but as they cost both time and money they should be justified and the most appropriate participants invited to attend at a convenient and suitable location.

2   Good preparation for meetings requires the following:
    (a) Being clear on the purpose for the meeting.
    (b) Clearly identifying the main subjects and topics to be discussed.
    (c) Selecting suitable participants who will make a valid contribution.

    (d)   Keeping the size of the meeting to a manageable level.

    (e)   Preparing the location suitable for the number of participants and their needs during the meeting and ensuring that the venue is convenient.

3   A complete range of vocabulary that may be used in a variety of meetings.

4   The constitution of meetings is made valid by having the following:

    (a)   A chairperson who carries out their duties according to the rules and regulations.

    (b)   A quorum of people, as stated in the regulations.

5   The documents that are required at meetings, in particular:

    (a)   The notice.

    (b)   The agenda.

    (c)   The chairperson's agenda.

    (d)   The minutes, whether they are narrative, resolution or action.

In this unit I have described that interviews are an opportunity for face to face interaction where information exchange, motivation and professional judgements of people can take place.

Interviews are conducted for a number of different reasons, such as to make policy decisions, recruit staff and judge performance levels.

The key to success in interviews is careful planning beforehand, professional conduct, which includes using the correct vocabulary, terminology and documentation, and appropriate follow-up, as soon as possible after the event has taken place.

In interview situations it is important to ask the right type of questions that reflect the relationship of the parties, purpose of the interview and nature of the discussion.

Interviews

Question 6.4

What is the purpose of interviews in business organizations?

Definition 6.2

Interviews in business organizations tend to be planned formal face to face interactions which are used for a variety of purposes.

1   Information-gathering and dissemination for the purposes of giving instruction, planning or co-ordinating effort.

2   Changing attitudes or behaviour, particularly in the case of conflict.

3   Negotiating on policy matters or personal issues, either with the internal market or with customers and suppliers who are part of the external market.

4   Motivating personnel to achieve greater levels of performance or to maintain interest in their role.

5   To persuade people to behave in a particular way.

6   Selecting potential employees or those suitable for promotional opportunities.

Face to face interactions have a number of advantages:

1   Immediate exchange of information and feedback is possible. In this context questions can be raised and responses given.

2   The quality and understanding of the verbal communication are enhanced through the observation of non-verbal cues, such as body language and reactions to the issues discussed.
3   The parties to the communication can develop a better relationship through exploring their sensitivity, degree of trust, sharing cooperation, empathy and sympathy to the issues under review.
4   The opportunity to exercise good listening skills will better facilitate the interview process and aid the interviewer's understanding of the information being received than is the case in more distant verbal communication, such as through telephone calls.

Planning the interview

The key to success in conducting interviews that are efficient and constructive comes from being in control throughout the event and this is largely a function of careful planning.

1   Before the interview, spend a suitable amount of time thinking about the purpose and aims of the interview, whether this is to select an applicant, solve a problem or negotiate for a contract or pay claim and so on.

    You should reflect on the nature of the discussion to be facilitated in the interview process and draw up a list of tentative points which will help to guide the interview proceedings and ensure continuity and completeness.

    The discussion should largely go backwards and forwards from the interviewer to the interviewee so that the interviewer maintains the position of controlling the proceedings.

    The interviewer also has the responsibility for setting the general tone of the interview, which will reflect the relationship of the parties and the nature of the discussion.
2   The interviewee will also have a general purpose for attending the interview, i.e. to obtain or pass information. However, they may also have a personal agenda in attending the interview which is not explicit and, whilst it may be wasted effort to speculate on this issue, it is useful to consider the possible reaction of the interviewee to the discussion that will take place during the interview and to plan further points of action, if appropriate.
3   Choose an appropriate location and time and collect all necessary background data that will set the structure for the interview.
4   During the interview, listen carefully for facts and feelings expressed by the interviewee. This will help you to make an assessment of the real issues under discussion and the personal qualities and judgement of the interviewee, which may be significant in appreciating the overall value of the interview.

    You should also make notes on critical issues during the course of the interview and close with a summary of the main points raised, highlighting any further action to be taken. If possible and suitable, finish on a positive note.
5   After the interview, spend a few minutes making additional notes that may be useful for reference later, whilst the meeting is still fresh in your mind. This may also be the best time to draft a short response in the form of a memo or letter to the interviewee, to thank them for attending the interview and enclose a summary of the discussion and outcome, if applicable.

Your final task is to put into action any items that needed to be resolved as a result of the interview.

Interview questions

The aim of the interview and the relationship of the parties will determine the type of questions that are set before the interview and asked when it takes place.

Questions are asked for a number of different reasons:

1 To obtain information on the general or specific issues to be discussed.
2 To enable and stimulate the interviewee to answer honestly and suitably for the purposes of the interview.
3 To establish a rapport with the inteviewee, particularly in the early stages of the interview which helps them to relax and feel comfortable in the interview situation and therefore to express themselves fully and openly.

Types of questions

1 Open-ended questions allow interviewees to express themselves in detail, as they are able to form opinions and explain these, for example asking a panel survey of customers: 'What do you think about our new products that were launched last week and you have tested in the home?'
2 Closed-ended questions require short answers or simple 'yes', 'no' or 'don't know' type responses. For example: 'Have you acquired our latest catalogue and price list?'
3 Restatement questions enable the interviewer to check that they have:

   (a) Not misunderstood a piece of factual information given in response to a question.
   (b) Informed the interviewee correctly.

For example, 'You stated that you do not use our executive lounge because it is always overcrowded. Is that correct?'

Types of interviews

Interviews are usually controlled by a person or panel (interviewers), who will ask questions and expect responses from the interviewees on a range of issues.

If both parties achieve their goals through the interview process, then it will have been a success.

Each interview will have a specific purpose and require a particular type of approach:

1 Employment interviews are used by an interviewer/employer to learn about the skills, qualifications and experiences of a prospective employee. The interviewee/applicant must use the opportunity to obtain information about the organization as a whole, the functional area for which they have applied and the related conditions of service; they will also want to make a good impression, therefore appropriate choice of vocabulary, clear speech characteristics, listening skills and body language are all important to express what you wish to say.
2 Appraisal interviews or joint performance reviews are used by superiors/managers to the employee as an opportunity to provide feedback in terms of an evaluation of the role and tasks achieved and to identify future expectations and needs of the subordinate, both specific to the job and any general issues that they may wish to raise.
3 Counselling interviews are used for a variety of purposes, in particular to resolve personal or professional problems that constrain the ability of the employee, or to motivate individuals and groups to improve their performance at work.
4 Disciplinary interviews are used by superiors/managers to try to change the behaviour of an individual or group, because company policy or rules/procedures have not been followed. The exchange is likely to be hostile, which therefore requires a great deal of tact and diplomacy by the interviewer, whilst objectively explaining the context and stand to be taken.

5 Exit interviews are used as an information exchange opportunity, before the employee leaves the organization, voluntarily or by dismissal; they are also used for employees transferring to another department. The focus of the interview should be away from personal issues and on positive aspects of the employee's time at work.

Activity 6.2

In the situations below, think about the interview from the perspective of both parties and address the following:

1 For each party, what is the purpose of the interview?
2 How should the interview be staged so that the process is effective and an outcome achieved?
3 What is the type of information that needs to be presented and received?

   (a) You approach a senior in the organization to discuss an increase in the budget for the marketing department to achieve the targets that have been set for this year, though you are only at the end of the first quarter.
   (b) You have produced a job description of your current role and the evaluation indicates that you are carrying out a number of additional tasks, some of which are appropriate to the next grade. An interview has been arranged with your line manager/superior.

Revision Tips

You must be able to address the following:

1 What is a meeting in business? Give examples of business situations in which only a meeting will be suitable as a channel of communication.
2 What points should be considered when preparing for a meeting?
3 Identify some of the terminology that is used in meetings.
4 (a) What is meant by the term constitution in the context of meetings?
   (b) What are the two main requirements for a valid meeting?
5 Identify and briefly explain the main documents needed for a meeting.

You must also be able to address the following:

1 Explain the purpose of interviews in business organizations.
2 Identify the benefits of face to face interaction during the interview process.
3 Describe the steps in planning an interview.
4 Identify the different types of question that can be asked in an interview situation and give an example of each.
5 State and briefly describe the different types of interviews used in business organizations.

Exam Hints

Clearly you will need to learn whether a meeting or informal discussion is required in a given situation. If it is the former, you may be asked to explain the steps that need to be taken to plan and hold the meeting. It is therefore important that you are conversant with all aspects of meetings, notably the issuing of a notice, setting the agenda and producing minutes.

You may be given a fictitious scenario and out of this asked to set an agenda and/or issue a suitable notice – all settings will have a marketing context and you may need to rely on your knowledge from other parts of the Certificate course to place suitable details in these documents.

You will be expected to know the general rules and guidelines in the planning of interviews and to explain these in the examination. You may also be given situations in which it is important to identify whether a meeting, discussion or interview needs to take place, the preparation involved and the approach to be taken. Clearly you need to be aware of the different types of interview that can take place in business and how the use of different questions can help you to solicit the required information. You should also expect to comment on any body language, speech and listening skills as important tools in interviews for successful communication.

Past examination question (December 1995)

A new Social Committee has been established at Datasend, the company you work for. You have been appointed Social Secretary and will be acting as Chair for the first meeting. Other members of staff have been elected to the committee, and in reply to a memo you circulated you have found out that they are keen to discuss the following topics: the setting up of corporate membership at a local sports club; the forthcoming office party; and a fund-raising event for a colleague who has developed a chronic illness.

(a) Draw up the agenda for the first meeting. Include one item of business in the form of a motion which is proposed and seconded.

(8 marks)

(b) Draw up a guide to meetings procedure for new staff and explain what the following terms mean. Give one example for each.
  (i) a quorum
  (ii) a procedural motion
  (iii) a point of order.

(12 marks)

Specimen answer

(a)
                  Social Group Committee Meeting
                  4 December 1995 at 5.30 p.m.
              Venue: Trinidad Conference Room, Datasend

                            AGENDA

1 Apologies for absence
2 Corporate membership at the Tobago Sports Club
3 Christmas Office Party
4 To propose a fund-raising event for John Ralphs, seconded by Helena May
5 AOB
6 DONM

(b)   *GUIDE FOR SUCCESSFUL MEETINGS*

The procedure for meetings is as follows, and should be observed for effective and successful mettings. It begins with a series of questions that you must address.

1 Decide on the nature of the meeting, i.e. is it solely to give or receive information or both? Is a facilitation of a discussion important?
2 Who should be invited to the meeting and what is to be each individual's relative contribution?
3 A notice of the meeting must be issued.
4 An agenda must be prepared.
5 Minutes should be taken and produced and circulated after the meeting has taken place.
6 A chair for the meeting must be appointed and their agenda drawn up.

7 Finally, a suitable room/location must be prepared and ready to receive the participants.

   (i)   A quorum is the minimum number of members that must be present at a meeting, according to the rules of the firm.
   (ii)   A procedural motion is a proposal to be considered at the meeting.
   (iii) A point of order is when participants have their attention drawn to a breach of the rules or procedures.

Specimen examination question

1 Define the purpose of interviews.   (6 marks)
2 You have been asked by the training manager to write a set of guidelines when planning interviews for all new junior employees joining the company from next month.   (14 marks)

Specimen answer

1 Interviews in business organizations tend to be planned, formal face to face interactions which are used for a variety of purposes:

   (a) Information-gathering and dissemination for the purposes of giving instruction, planning or coordinating effort.
   (b) Changing attitudes or behaviour, particularly in the case of conflict.
   (c) Negotiating on policy matters or personal issues, either with the internal market or with customers and suppliers who are part of the external market.
   (d) Motivating personnel to achieve greater levels of performance or to maintain interest in their role.
   (e) To persuade people to behave in a particular way.
   (f) Selecting potential employees or those suitable for promotional opportunities.

2 The key to success in planning interviews that are efficient and constructive comes from being in control.

   (a) Before the interview, spend a suitable amount of time thinking about the purpose and aims of the interview, whether this is to select an applicant, solve a problem or negotiate for a contract or pay claim, and so on.
        You should reflect on the nature of the discussion to be facilitated in the interview process and draw up a list of tentative points which will help to guide the interview proceedings and ensure continuity and completeness.
        The discussion should largely go backwards and forwards from the interviewer to the interviewee so that the interviewer maintains the position of controlling the proceedings.
        The interviewer also has the responsibility for setting the general tone of the interview, which will reflect the relationship of the parties and the nature of the discussion.
   (b) The interviewee will also have a general purpose for attending the interview – to obtain or pass information. However, they may also have a personal agenda in attending the interview which is not explicit and, whilst it may be wasted effort to speculate on this issue, it is useful to consider the possible reaction of the interviewee to the discussion that will take place during the interview and to plan further points of action, if appropriate.
   (c) Choose an appropriate location and time and collect all necessary background data that will set the structure for the interview.
   (d) During the interview, listen carefully for facts and feelings expressed by the interviewee. This will help you to make an assessment of the real issues under discussion and the personal

qualities and judgement of the interviewee, which may be significant in appreciating the overall value of the interview.

(e) You should also make notes on critical issues during the course of the interview and close with a summary of the main points raised, highlighting any further action to be taken. If possible and suitable, finish on a positive note.

(f) After the interview, spend a few minutes making additional notes that may be useful for reference later, whilst the meeting is still fresh in your mind. This may also be the best time to draft a short response in the form of a memo or letter to the interviewee, to thank them for attending the interview and enclose a summary of the discussion and outcome.

Extending Knowledge

If you have access to minutes from meetings held at different levels in the organization, make an attempt to retrieve these and analyse them. You are trying to determine how the meeting was conducted, the number and position of participants and the type and level of decision reached.

Meetings are relatively formal settings for group interactions as they require both planning and following a set of rules. Many departments in organizations hold discussions, both formal and informal, and you may like to analyse which of these are the most suitable in different situations and whether they save time and are considered valuable by the participants. A systematic analysis over a period of time may reveal some interesting results for your department or organization.

For a humorous look at face to face interaction in the process of conducting meetings, refer to the text *The Secrets of Successful Business Meetings* by Gordon Bell, published by Butterworth-Heinemann.

Interview skills are not difficult to acquire, especially if you have the opportunity to practise them, which I recommend forms part of your training in management. Although good basic communication skills are general to all interview situations, your sensitivity, personality, preparation and conduct of the interaction may play a significant part in the eventual outcome and you should plan for these aspects as well as the formal research needed before the event takes place.

Unit 7 Using statistical data

Introduction

In Unit 10 we will look at the value of information technology in enhancing the process of business communication to make it faster and more accurate for managers to take decisions on a range of business issues.

Clearly, *factual* information is the key to the whole process of making decisions and solving problems and essentially there are two types of facts that can be gathered: primary and secondary.

Definition 7.1

Primary data is collected specifically for the investigation or survey being carried out by using observation, experimental techniques, depth interviews and panel surveys or questionnaires. These are frequently used in marketing as the basis for planning a complete range of initiatives.

In collecting information through primary techniques, it is unlikely that the entire universe or population can be surveyed, therefore a representative sample will have to be selected and tested. A number of sampling techniques are available and will be chosen to reflect the purposes of the research brief and time available to carry out the survey. These are discussed more fully in *The Marketing Customer Interface* workbook.

Definition 7.2

Secondary data is information that has already been collected and published elsewhere, such as internal customer records, sales reports or external HMSO publications, periodicals and newspapers, which can be used for the research.

Primary data has the advantage of being up-to-date and tailored specifically to the research in hand, but is expensive and time-consuming to collect. Secondary data is usually relatively cheap to obtain, but may be out-of-date or unreliable.

Most data, particularly primary data, is usually collected in the *raw form* and then transformed into *statistics* to make the numbers more meaningful.

Definition 7.3

Statistics are a group of figures which relate to some important attribute or variable, e.g. market share or sales turnover, which are presented through a statistical method, e.g. tables, charts, diagrams, etc., allowing interpretation of the information more easily than would be the case if a mass of numbers were shown.

However, statistics prove nothing in themselves – they are merely indicators of what is likely to happen, based on past experience, and also used as forecasting models for the future.

The type of statistical data used and its visual presentation must reflect the business situation, the needs of the audience and the level of understanding and time available. Different types of graphical presentation lend themselves to different types of data and the needs of an audience will depend on their familiarity with the data and/or ability to interpret the information; some graphs are more complex than others in their presentation of data and interpretation.

Once data has been collected, it is usually divided into groups and recorded in a frequency table (frequency is the number of times a value occurs). The system of recording the data is called a tally.

Example

The number of brands managed by each of the 15 brand managers in a confectionery company are as follows:

Brand manager	A	B	C	D	E	F	G	H	I	J	K	L	M	N	O
No. of brands	4,	6,	3,	6,	7,	2,	4,	6,	7,	3,	6,	6,	6,	7,	6

The raw data which has been tallied and identified in terms of its *frequency* of occurrence can now be presented as a table (Table 7.1). The table makes it much easier to 'visualize' the raw data.

Table 7.1

No. of brands	1	2	3	4	5	6	7
No. of managers and managing brands	0	1	2	3	0	6	3

The table can now be used to produce a range of graphs. A couple of the most commonly used ones have been presented below; these are also the quickest to produce and present.

Figure 7.1 is a line graph/chart and Figure 7.2 is a stacked bar chart. You will be shown how to prepare and present these later in the unit.

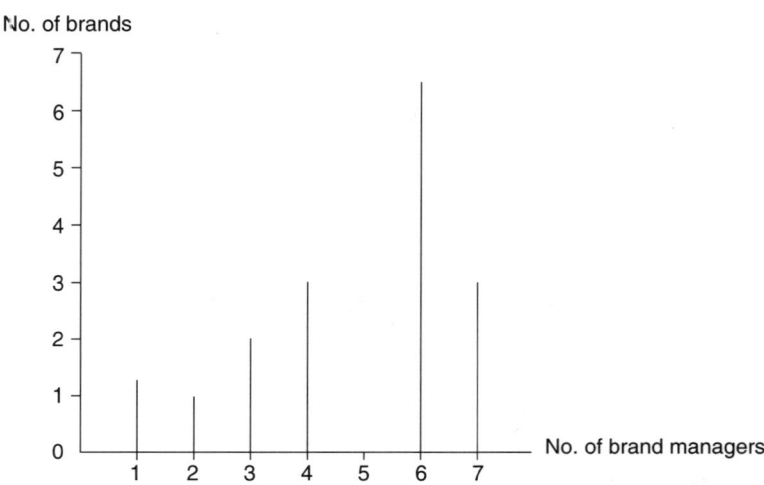

Figure 7.1

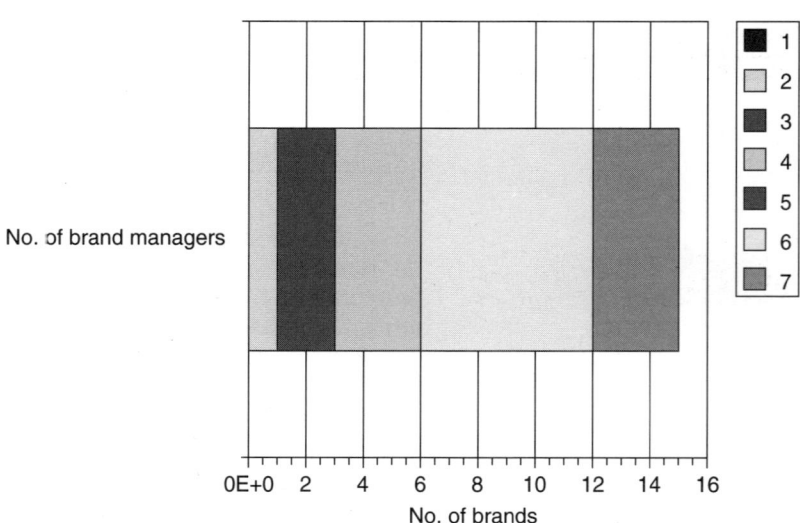

Figure 7.2

86

We can begin to see that the presentation of raw data can be made more effective when it is used visually through a table or graph/chart.

Other attributes of graphical presentation are detailed below.

Graphical presentation

Graphical presentation can cut the time needed to present long and complex sets of statistics and data on all aspects of marketing (e.g. costs, value and number of sales, profits, market shares), but will only be appropriate if the audience is able to follow the trends identified and understand the logic of the message, which will enable them to make sound business decisions. However, statistics prove nothing in themselves – they are merely indicators of what is likely to happen, based on past experience.

Definition 7.4

Graphs show the relationships between two variables – discrete (where only certain values are possible) or continuous (where any value over a certain range is possible) – by means of either a straight line or curve; they particularly demonstrate how the magnitude value of one variable changes, given a change in the other.

There are two axes on each graph, a horizontal axis (the x axis) and a vertical axis (the y axis). The horizontal axis is used to represent the independent variable (e.g. month or years) and the vertical axis to show the dependent variable (e.g. changes in sales figures), whose value depends on the independent variable (e.g. when demonstrating figures of promotional expenditure relative to sales turnover, promotional spend would be the independent variable and any changes shown in the sales figure would be dependent on the spend that had taken place).

Analysing data

Once the research process has been completed and the raw data made available, it must be analysed to provide significant meaning. You are looking for any patterns in the relationships between attributes or variables in order to form initial conclusions, on which you, or the recipient of the information, will base recommendations or decisions at a later stage.

The first step is to manipulate the data so that its significance can be determined. There are several ways to do this:

Definition 7.5

1 Averages are measures of *central tendency* and, through the use of mean (most frequently used), median or mode, are used to find the number which is representative of a group of numbers, i.e. the middle value.

Definition 7.6

(a) The arithmetic mean is found by totalling the sum of all the numbers in the group and then dividing by the number, in that group. This gives the average and the other numbers in the group can then be established relative to this average, i.e. either above or below.

$$\text{The arithmetic mean} = \frac{\text{sum of the observations}}{\text{number of observations}}$$

(b) The median is the value of the middle number and is particularly useful when analysing extreme values in a distribution of numbers. The median is found by arranging the items in ascending or descending order of value and then selecting the number in the middle of the list.

$$\text{The position of the median} = \frac{n + 1}{2}$$

(c) The mode is the most frequently occurring item in a list of numbers. For example, if the following organizations had market shares of 20%, 13%, 15%, 8%, 13%, the mode would be 13%. If a list has two lots of items with the same frequency, the mode would be the average of those two values. The mode is useful when a frequency from a list can be commonly and easily identified.

Figure 7.3 calculates the averages of mean, median and mode.

SKINCARE UNLIMITED PLC

Location of branch retailer	Annual turnover
Appleby	£ 125 000
Barchester	£ 230 000
Collingwood	£ 216 000
Dedworth	£ 129 500
Eastling	£ 230 000
Fordingham	£ 215 500
Grange Town	£ 230 000
Harlington	£ 130 000
Jankley	£ 250 000
Total	£1 756 000

(i) The mean is £195 111.
(ii) The median is £216 000.
(iii) The mode is £230 000.

Figure 7.3
Calculates the averages of mean, median and mode

Finally, consider the *range* of numbers that are being analysed in the list of data and use the opportunity to look closely at the relative values to identify any significant variations, which could be the basis for further research or investigation.

2 Trends are patterns and relationships that can be identified using data over a period of time (including the use of past information). However, be prepared for the fact that this analysis may raise more questions than provide answers.

3 Causal relationships can often be established based on trend analysis, i.e. if we manipulated x variable, what would be the effect on y variable? Correlations are often used in business and are particularly useful in planning for the effect on variables; when another is changed, what would be the effect on quantity demanded as a result of an increase in price?

Based on the following information, calculate the mean, median and mode and briefly conclude from the observations made from the data.

Competitor	Brand X Market share (£000s)
Competitor A	30 000
Competitor B	12 000
Competitor C	15 000
Competitor D	14 000
Competitor E	12 000
Competitor F	14 000
Competitor G	19 000
Competitor H	7 000

From your knowledge of marketing, think of the effect on some variables, if another is changed. Make a list below, using the marketing mix as a guide to your thinking.

We have just studied averages which help us to understand data better. The information which follows is a detailed account of how to produce tables, charts and graphs, some of which have been used and described briefly above.

Tables

A table is a matrix structure where data is placed in titled rows and columns.

Tables are particularly useful for the presentation of detailed, specific information and, although only two variables can be demonstrated simultaneously, they do permit the reader to compare and contrast this information, particularly at points of intersection, from which similarities and differences can be observed. Tables can be used within the text to present the facts being considered and are introduced with a preceding sentence, or set apart as an independent piece of information, possibly in the appendices of a report, to which reference is made in the main text. Tables can be complex, such as reference tables, or relatively simple, such as spot tables, where only a few items are presented. Both figures and words can work equally well in tabular form.

Guidelines for producing tables

1. Analyse the audience to whom this information will be presented and reflect their needs in terms of the amount and level of data used.
2. Keep the table simple, uncrowded and easy to handle, not tedious or difficult.
3. Label the table clearly, with a suitable brief introduction as appropriate.
4. Provide a key for complex headings or clearly label the columns and rows.
5. Use comfortable figures, such as decimals and percentages, rounded up, not fractions.

6 Label and number reference tables so that they can be easily identified and found.
7 Briefly explain any significant differences in the data by using a footnote to the table.
8 If appropriate, present a total column on the right-hand side and a total figure at the bottom of each column.
9 Use shading to highlight titles or significant features – this enhances the appearance of the table whilst drawing attention to important aspects of the information being presented.
10 In figure tables, clearly identify the units that will be used, e.g. percentages, £s, thousands, etc.

Example

Salesperson name	Product line sales turnover (£000s) 1996–97					Total (£)
	A	B	C	D	E	
Helen Jenkins	13	15	8	12	10	58
Jane Atkinson	8	10	9	6	5	38
Andrew Salter	16	12	10	12	14	64
Luigi Romero	23	26	13	28	22	112
Karen Mann	33	34	24	22	30	143
Sunil Singh	12	16	11	17	15	71
George Vassiliades	4	7	3	8	11	33
Alan Bennett	11	12	12	12	11	58
Tony Taylor	15	7	7	9	8	46
Christine James	22	13	21	10	15	81
Total (£)	157	152	118	136	141	704

Activity 7.3

Observe the raw data below and manipulate it such that you can produce an effective table. In order to turn the data into information for decision-making, identify what further data or information might be required.

The brands listed below achieved a decrease or increase in sales during and up to 1996, compared with previous years:

Brand X: 1990: £120,000; 1991: £130,000; 1992: £120,000; 1993: £50,000; 1994: £145,000; 1995: £113,000; 1996: £189,000

Brand X1: 1990: £115,000; 1991: £131,000; 1992: £200,000; 1993: £500,000; 1994: £150,000; 1995: £131,000; 1996: £180,000

Brand Y: 1990: £11,000; 1991: £13,000; 1992: £12,000; 1993: £30,000; 1994: £14,000; 1995: £13,000; 1996: £18,000

Brand Y1: 1990: £200,000; 1991: £100,000; 1992: £100,000; 1993: £100,000; 1994: £140,000; 1995: £100,000; 1996: £100,000

Charts

Charts are usually used to convey a few main points (and possibly relationships between them) clearly, rather than the more detailed information which is used in tables. There are many different types of chart that can be used in the graphical presentation of data:

1 Column/bar charts.
2 Pie charts.
3 Line and surface charts.
4 Flow and organization charts and maps.
5 Diagrams, photographs, pictograms and drawings.

We will consider each in turn.

Column/bar charts

Column/bar charts demonstrate relationships and differences in variables by the respective heights of the columns/bars, which can be displayed vertically or horizontally, with the data on or near the bars. They are particularly useful when you want to:

1 Compare the size of several variables in one presentation.
2 Demonstrate important differences between the variables.
3 Demonstrate changes over a period of time.
4 Demonstrate the composition of variables.

Therefore, there are three types of column/bar chart that can be presented:

1 Simple column/bar charts.
2 Multiple column/bar charts.
3 Component (stacked) column/bar charts.

Guidelines for producing simple column/bar charts

Simple column/bar charts demonstrate the value of one piece of data by the respective length of the column/bar(s) on the chart. They are particularly useful for demonstrating the changes in the variable and for making comparisons based on the lengths of the columns/bars.

1 The chart must be titled and each axis of the graph must be labelled.
2 There must be a scale to indicate values on the corresponding axis (as on the y axis, where market share percentages are shown, below).
3 The vertical axis must always start at 0, so that the relative values can be accurately demonstrated, or indicate with a staggered line that the data does not begin at 0.
4 If possible, the data should be presented in some order of value, i.e. lowest to highest or vice versa; this is usually not possible if time comparisons are made.
5 Use spaces between columns/bars for ease of interpretation.
6 Use shading to highlight the columns/bars, making them easier to view.

Figure 7.4 demonstrates how to draw a simple column/bar chart based on the data below.

The following data can be shown as a simple column/bar chart:

Year	Market share of Brand A
1988	0.4%
1989	0.7%
1990	1.9%
1991	2.6%
1992	3.0%
1993	3.0%
1994	2.8%
1995	1.4%
1996	1.0%
1997	0.2%

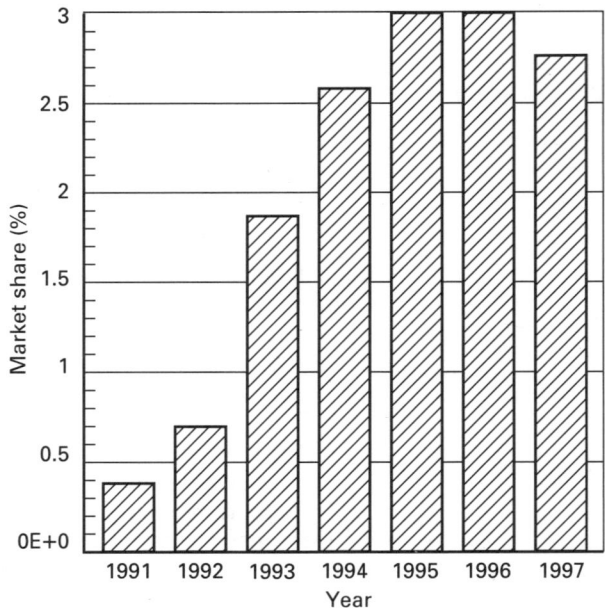

Figure 7.4
Market share of Brand A for the
years 1991–97 inclusive

Based on the following data, draw up your own simple column/bar chart and briefly conclude from the observations made.

Month	Turnover of Brand A (£m)
January 20XX	4.4
March	5.7
May	5.3
July	5.8
September	6.6
November	7.5
December	9.0

Multiple column/bar charts

Multiple column/bar charts use several columns/bars for each variable, each column/bar demonstrating a particular aspect of the overall data.

Guidelines for producing multiple column/bar charts

1 Two or more columns/bars are used to present aspects/divisions of the data.
2 Shading must be used to distinguish the columns/bars representing different data.
3 Use spaces appropriately to draw attention to similarities, differences or trends, either in the columns/bars separately or groups of data.
4 Columns/bars can be drawn horizontally or vertically.

	Market competition for Brand A		
	1995 Sales (000s units)	1996 Sales (000s units)	1997 Sales (000s units)
Competitor B1	150	170	220
Competitor B2	230	240	210
Competitor B3	340	560	480

Figure 7.5 demonstrates how to draw a multiple column/bar chart based on the data below.

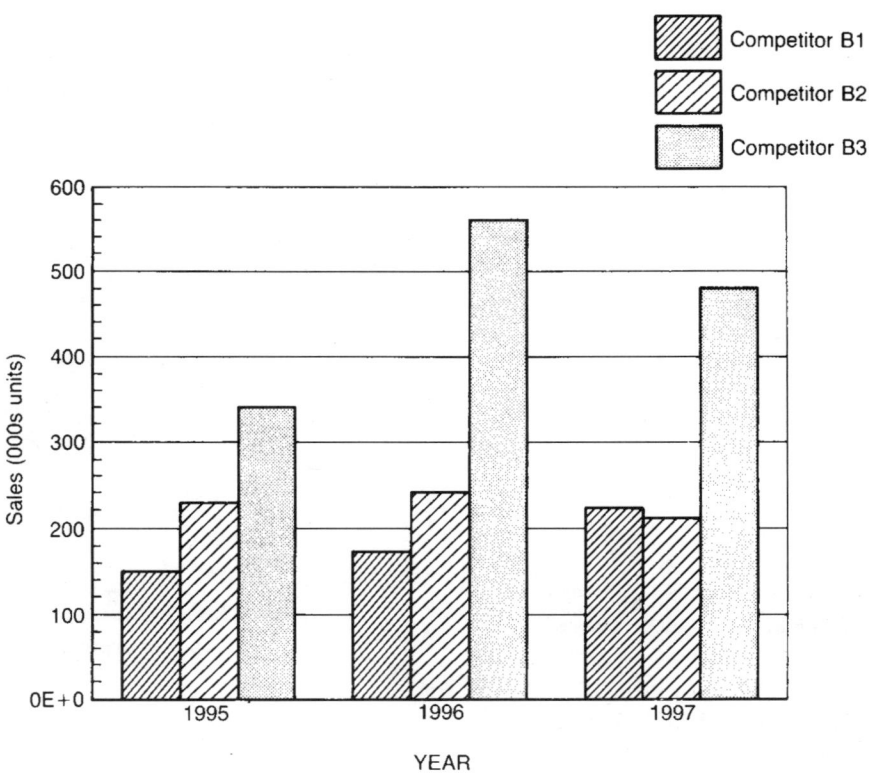

Figure 7.5
A multiple column/bar chart of market competition for Brand A

Based on the following data, draw up your own multiple column/bar chart and conclude from the observations you have made.

	1995 Sales (000s units)	1996 Sales (000s units)	1997 Sales (000s units)
Brand X	120	140	110
Brand X1	125	185	199
Brand Y	85	100	90
Brand Y1	230	270	290
Brand Z	55	140	230

Component (stacked) column/bar charts

Component (stacked) column/bar charts can be segmented or broken lengthwise to show the relative size of components of an overall total. An example is presented in Figure 7.6 using the following data:

The launch of Brand X in 1997 was made up of the following promotional expenditure:

Media advertising 40%, public relations 10%, sales/promotional incentives 20%, demonstrations/exhibitions 10%, sales force training and special conference 15%, press releases 5%.

Guidelines for producing component column/bar charts

1 The components can be ordered in any way on the column/bar, but must remain consistent if more than one column/bar is demonstrated.
2 The relative values should be kept in order, with either the highest or lowest at the top, and then presented in ascending or descending order.
3 Use shading and/or a key if the components cannot be labelled directly.

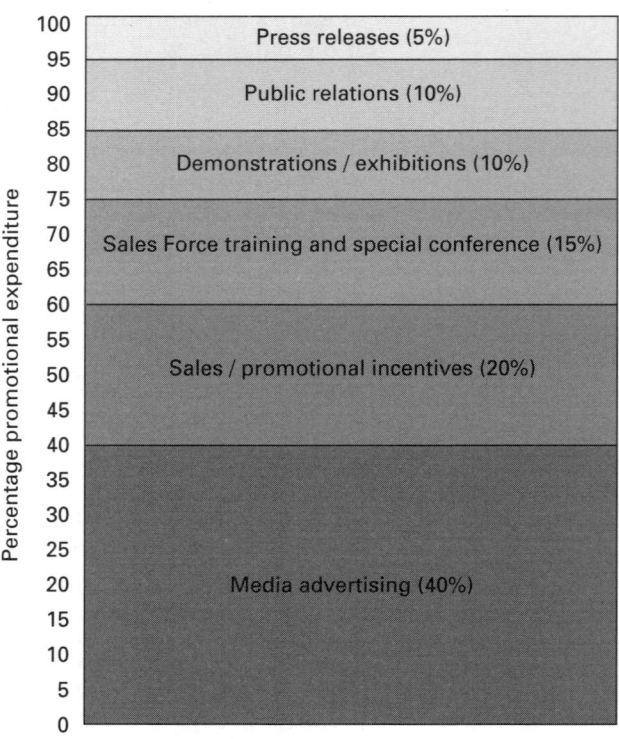

100 — Press releases (5%)
95
90 — Public relations (10%)
85
80 — Demonstrations / exhibitions (10%)
75
70 — Sales Force training and special conference (15%)
65
60
55
50 — Sales / promotional incentives (20%)
45
40
35
30
25
20 — Media advertising (40%)
15
10
5
0

Percentage promotional expenditure (vertical axis)

Figure 7.6
A component column/bar chart

Types of expenditure on Brand X in 1997

Histograms

Guidelines for producing histograms

1 The horizontal axis must show the intervals of the distribution.
2 The vertical axis must show the frequency of the intervals (if the intervals have different widths, it will show the frequency density).
3 The height of each rectangle (bar) must be proportionate to the frequency (or frequency density) of the base interval.
4 The mode must be calculated.
5 The class interval, class boundaries, lower and upper class limits must be established.

Figure 7.7 demonstrates how to draw up a histogram based on the information below.

The size of 15 rejects in a chocolate-bar manufacturing plant were measured in centimetres and are as follows:

3.98, 2.45, 1.33, 5.66, 4.75, 8.78, 8.76, 4.61, 3.43, 3.56,
2.45, 6.30, 7.45, 7.23, 8.10

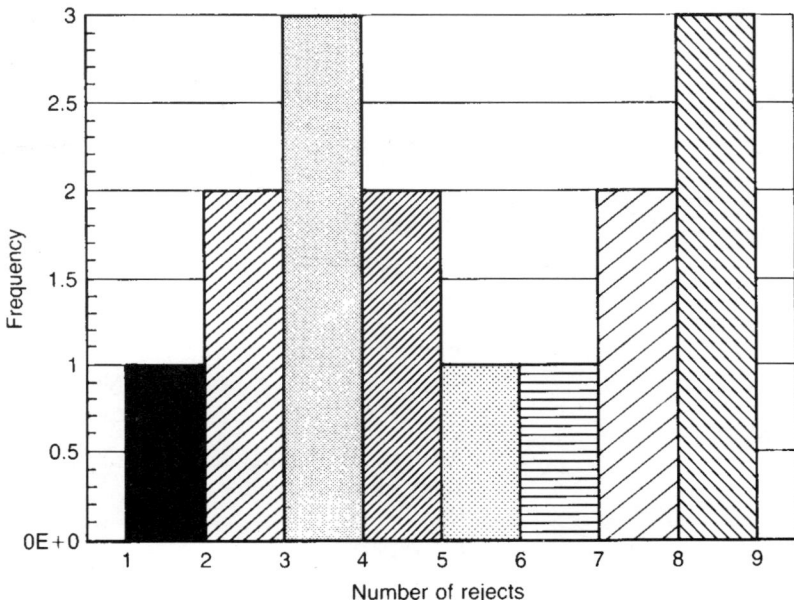

Figure 7.7
A histogram of chocolate bar
rejects based on the data below

Grouping the data into classes we can see that the smallest value is 1.33 cm and the largest value is 8.78 cm.

A class width of 0.99 cm gives the following (eight) classes:

Class (cm)	Tally	Frequency
1.0–1.99	1	1
2.0–2.99	11	2
3.0–3.99	111	3
4.0–4.99	11	2
5.0–5.99	1	1
6.0–6.99	1	1
7.0–7.99	11	2
8.0–8.99	111	3

In the above table, 1.0–1.99 cm is the class interval, with 1.0 cm the lower class limit and 1.99 cm the upper class limit.

The class boundaries are 1.0, 2.0, 3.0, 4.0 cm, etc.

The class width is the difference between the upper class boundary and the lower class boundary, i.e. 1.99 – 1.0 = 0.99 cm.

Pie charts
Pie charts are circular diagrams that are particularly useful for showing the composition of all the data, with the segments demonstrating the relative values of the data.

Guidelines for producing pie charts

1 Pie charts should be drawn accurately with a compass to represent the 360° of a circle and divided up equally into segments.
2 The component parts must represent 100%.
3 To draw the segment sizes accurately, use a protractor by putting the base line across the middle of the circle and mark off degrees to represent percentages (which must be worked out, based on numerical values). For example, 180° represents 50%, 90° 25%, etc.
4 Keep the maximum number of segments to seven, otherwise the chart will look too congested and be more difficult to interpret.

5   Place the most important (largest) segment at the 12 o'clock position and the others relative to it in some logical order.
6   Use shading to draw attention to salient features, usually largest and/or smallest segments.
7   Label all the segments and show their relative values either on the segments or beside the graph. A key will be necessary for this.

Figure 7.8 demonstrates a pie chart based on the data below.

In 1997, these graduates in media studies found jobs in the following sectors:

Sector	Number of graduates	Percentage
Advertising agencies	3 400	28
Television	1 300	11
Radio	2 100	18
Newspapers	1 900	16
Magazines/journals	2 500	21
Public relations	600	4
Other media	350	2
Total	12 150	100

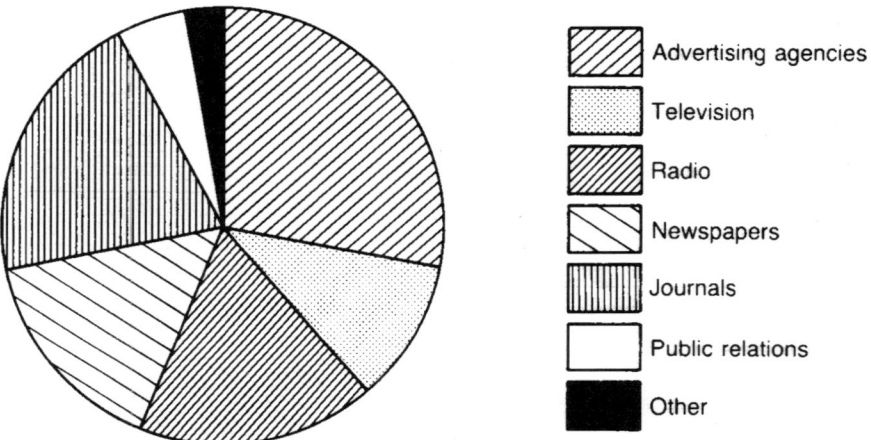

Figure 7.8
A pie chart

Based on the following data, draw up your own pie chart and briefly conclude from the observations made. Can you identify the limitations of using pie charts?

The following are statistics on the socioeconomic profiles of daily consumers of wine in the UK:

Socioeconomic group	Relative amount of wine consumed (%)
A	76
B	67
C1	33
C2	21
D	13
E	4

Line charts

Line charts are a series of points joined together to form a straight or curved line and are usually used to reflect a trend over a period of time, or the interaction of two variables. They are similar to column/bar charts, but with lines instead of columns/bars, to represent the value of the variables, and in many cases several lines will be used to show comparisons between the data.

Guidelines for producing line charts

1 The horizontal axis should show the time period (years, months, hours, etc.).
2 The vertical axis should show the amount or value being measured.
3 Both scales should begin at 0 and increase in equal amounts, or indicate with a staggered line that the data does not begin at 0.
4 Both negative and positive values can be shown on line charts.
5 Use different colours for more than one line on the same graph, to distinguish between them.
6 Use solid lines or broken lines to distinguish between different data or to draw attention to significant features of the data.
7 In order to avoid clutter and to make observation of the chart easier, a maximum of three lines on any graph should be used, especially if they are likely to cross over.

Figure 7.9 demonstrates a simple line chart, based on the data below.

Product line (XYZ)	Turnover 1997 (£)
Brand X	150 000
Brand X1	225 000
Brand Y	130 000
Brand Y1	195 000
Brand Z	85 000

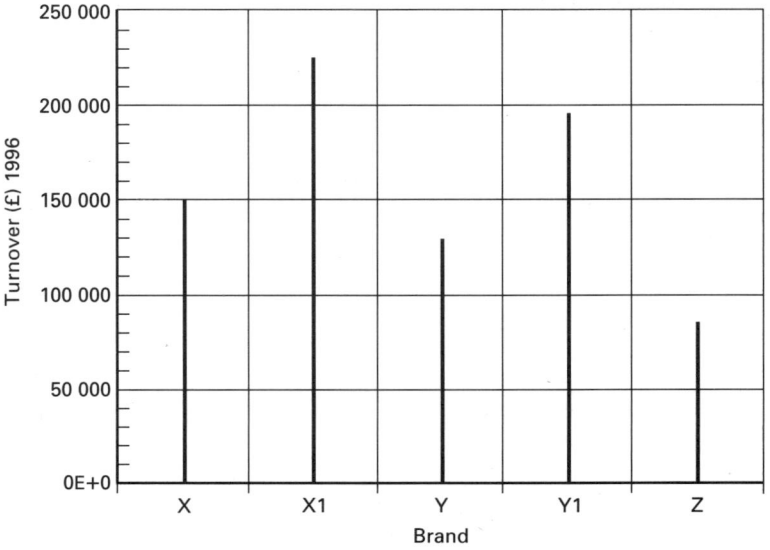

Figure 7.9
A simple line chart

97

Figure 7.10 demonstrates a multiple line chart, based on the following data:

Year	Product lines (XYZ)	Advertising spend (£m)
1993	Brand X	0.5
	Brand Y	0.7
	Brand Z	2.4
1994	Brand X	0.7
	Brand Y	1.0
	Brand Z	1.9
1995	Brand X	0.9
	Brand Y	2.3
	Brand Z	2.5
1996	Brand X	0.9
	Brand Y	2.3
	Brand Z	2.5
1997	Brand X	1.4
	Brand Y	2.7
	Brand Z	2.5

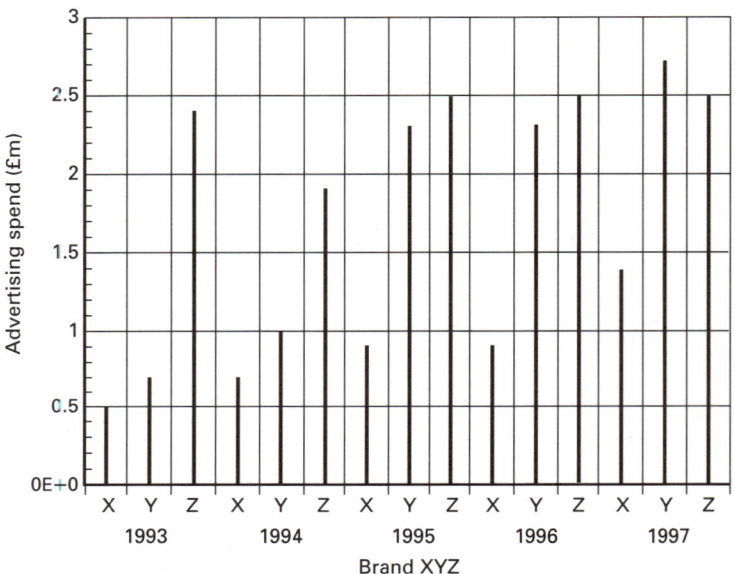

Figure 7.10
A multiple line chart

Activity 7.8

Based on the following data, draw up your own simple line chart and briefly conclude from the observations made.

Year	Total advertising spend (£m) of Company Z
1991	5
1992	7
1993	7.5
1994	7.5
1995	8.3
1996	8.5

Based on the following data, produce your own multiple line chart and draw brief conclusions from the observations made.

Year	Total advertising spend for product line (XYZ) (£)	Medium
1992	450 000	Newspapers/magazines
	200 000	Radio
	500 000	Direct mail
	2 450 000	Television
1993	550 000	Newspapers/magazines
	400 000	Radio
	300 000	Direct mail
	2 350 000	Television
1994	750 000	Newspapers/magazines
	650 000	Radio
	600 000	Direct mail
	3 700 000	Television
1995	500 000	Newspapers/magazines
	650 000	Radio
	800 000	Direct mail
	3 750 000	Television
1996	700 000	Newspapers/magazines
	900 000	Radio
	500 000	Direct mail
	4 500 000	Television

Gantt charts

Gantt charts are a type of column/bar chart which show dimensions of a variable over a period of time and can be used to measure a number of different aspects of business activity in terms of actual, planned and cumulative. They are often found in marketing plans to show how the plan will be 'phased in' over a period of time.

Figure 7.11 demonstrates a simple Gantt chart.

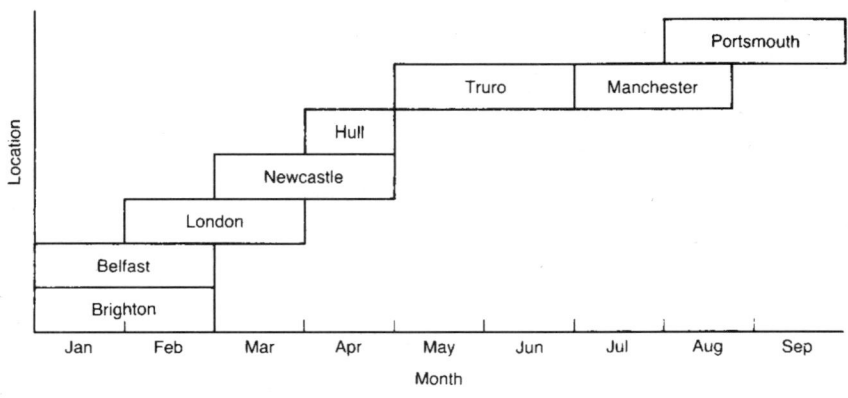

Figure 7.11
Gantt chart. Rolling national launch of Brand Q in different regional cities in the UK from January to September 20XX

Pictograms

Pictograms are charts in which the data is represented by a line of symbols or pictures. They are usually used for presenting information in a novel format and are often used in the transmission of simple messages, such as in some types of advertising. They can enhance the presentation of data by making it easy to view.

Guidelines for producing pictograms

1 Use a symbol which will be clearly representative of the subject matter, eye-catching and appealing.
2 The number of pictures or symbols must reflect the values they represent.
3 Use a key to indicate the value of one picture or symbol.
4 Keep the size of the pictures and graph consistent with the overall presentation.

Activity 7.11

Based on the following data, draw up your own pictogram and briefly conclude from the observations made.

Volume sales of Widgets by Company A1.

Year	Volume sales (000s)
1993	5
1994	6.5
1995	7
1996	9.5
1997	10

Figure 7.12 demonstrates some pictograms.

= 10 000, = 5 000

Number of people in the UK who regularly eat (three bars a week) chocolate

1993
1994
1995
1996

Advertising spend of the 'top five' chocolate manufacturers in the UK in 1996. £ = £10 000

Company A £ £ £ £ £ £ £ £ £ £ £ £ £ £ £ £ £ £

Company B £ £ £ £ £ £ £ £ £ £ £ £ £

Company C £ £ £ £ £ £ £ £ £

Company D £ £ £ £ £ £

Company E £ £ £

Figure 7.12
Some examples of pictograms

Map charts

Map charts (cartograms) also use symbols to represent values, usually of geographical data, such as the difference in market share of products and brands (or the whole organization) in regional areas of the UK, EC and international markets. The maps can be produced in a number of different ways – shading using lines, dots and complete colouring are some of the techniques used.

Figure 7.13 illustrates a map chart.

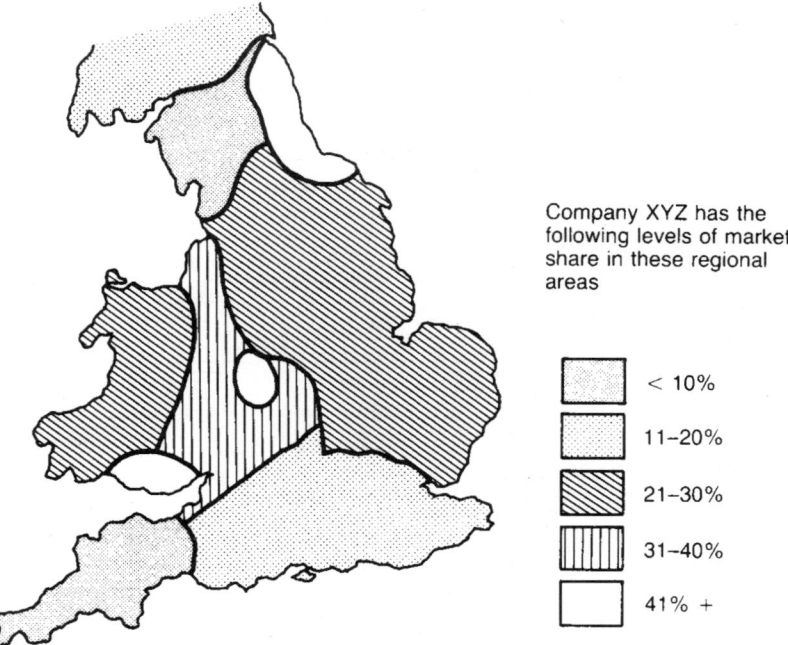

Company XYZ has the following levels of market share in these regional areas

	< 10%
	11–20%
	21–30%
	31–40%
	41% +

Figure 7.13
Map chart

Activity 7.12

Use information from your organization to produce map charts of the UK and an international market (if applicable) indicating market share, volume sales and turnover of the whole organization and a selection of its products or brands or services.

Photographs

Photographs are often found in annual reports of organizations and other brochures and flyers as they are visually appealing and of interest to readers, especially if it is important for them to put a name to a face.

They are commonly used in surveys of large geographical areas and selective locations to show a number of important characteristics, such as suitable land sites and their proximity to towns, cities and natural resources, for the purposes of building processing and manufacturing plants, distribution centres and so on. They can also be used to highlight dangerous physical situations and in evidence to settle disputes.

Drawings and diagrams

Drawings and diagrams can be extremely useful in showing the dimensions and parts of products, equipment and machinery and how they operate; they are extensively used in instruction manuals for a large range of technical products.

Figure 7.14 is a diagram of a typewriter and its components.

Flow charts

Flow charts are useful for demonstrating conceptual relationships, processes and procedures and business activities, where numerical values are not important. The relationships between various parts of the activity being demonstrated are shown in sequence from beginning to end and use geometric shapes to distinguish between various aspects.

Figure 7.15 demonstrates a flow chart.

Organization charts

Organization charts are frequently used in business organizations to show the hierarchical positions and relationships of employees, which also represent the main formal channels of communication.

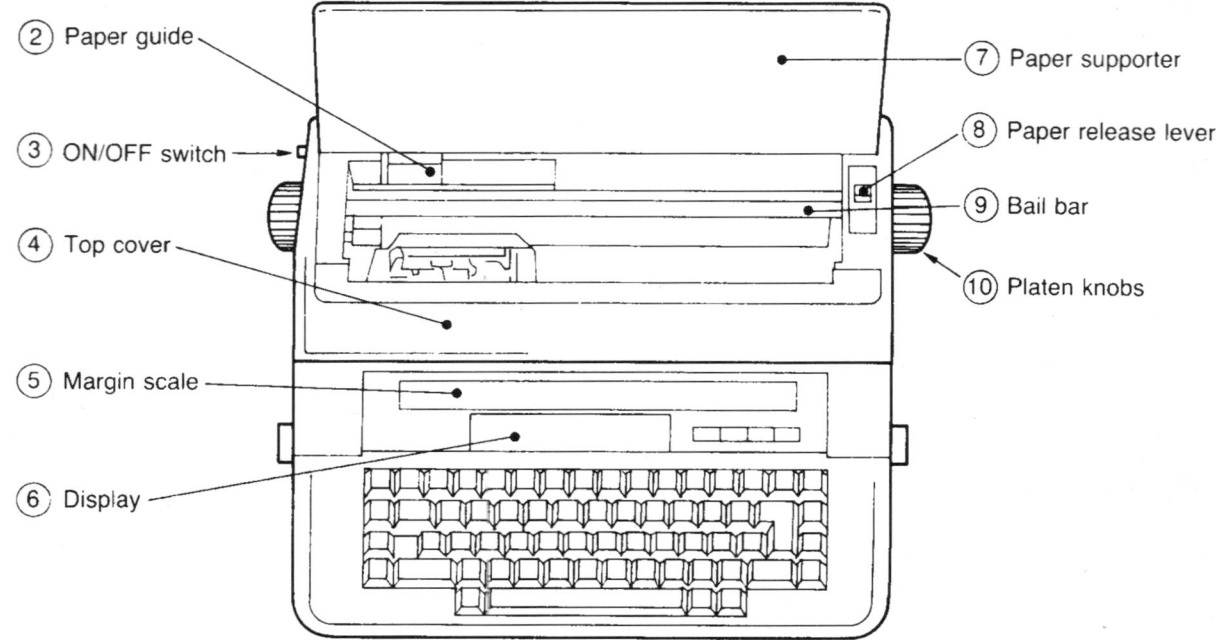

Figure 7.14 Diagram of a typewriter

- (2) Paper guide
- (3) ON/OFF switch
- (4) Top cover
- (5) Margin scale
- (6) Display
- (7) Paper supporter
- (8) Paper release lever
- (9) Bail bar
- (10) Platen knobs

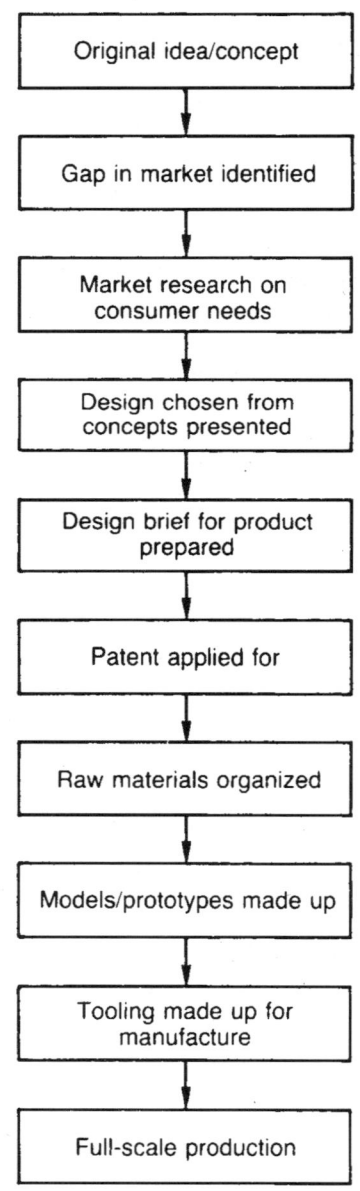

Original idea/concept

↓

Gap in market identified

↓

Market research on consumer needs

↓

Design chosen from concepts presented

↓

Design brief for product prepared

↓

Patent applied for

↓

Raw materials organized

↓

Models/prototypes made up

↓

Tooling made up for manufacture

↓

Full-scale production

Figure 7.15
A flow chart for the stages involved in the introduction of a new product

Summary

Graphical presentation of statistical data through the use of tables, charts, maps, diagrams and pictograms demonstrates the significance of important variables and the relationships between them. They are used extensively in business to enhance and complement the information to be communicated and frequently by the sales and marketing functions.

Graphs must be kept as simple as possible and be attractive to the reader. They must also reflect the needs of the audience in terms of type, level and format for presentation of the information. Using colour, contrast and shading can make the visual easier to follow; greater appreciation of differences can take place and its appeal will be enhanced.

Revision Tips

You must be able to do the following:

1 Explain why graphical presentation of data is important in business communication, especially in a marketing or sales environment.
2 Briefly, distinguish between primary and secondary data and determine that statistical information is derived from primary sources.
3 Present data based on raw information using:

  (a) Tables.
  (b) Charts.
  (c) Histograms.
  (d) Pictograms.
  (e) Cartograms.
  (f) Drawings and diagrams.

Exam Hints

This unit has taken you through a selected range of statistical techniques that can act as important visuals in business communication, either as part of a verbal presentation such as a speech or meeting or a written document, for example a report.

It is vital for the purposes of the exam that you learn the rules that govern each of the statistical techniques described and use one or more that are *most suitable* in a given context where the raw data will be provided.

The compulsory question is the one most likely to ask you to present raw data in a statistical format, and other questions are likely to ask for your *written* interpretation based on a chart or graph which is presented.

You have recently joined Robinsons's, a grocery chain with 96 outlets in the north of England. Following a survey which was carried out by the magazine, 'Food Retailer', you are required to analyse the information given below and to deliver a presentation to senior management. For use with an overhead projector, draft out the visual information you would include on 3 acetates/slides. Draw out *any graphs or charts in a way which gives a clear indication of how* you consider the material should appear.

Survey Details

A total of 1750 shoppers were interviewed in the north of England. Most of those interviewed were women. The area was divided into convenient sections and electoral registers were used to make random selections of houses. The refusal rate was under 0.7 per cent. The average age of women interviewed was 40, and 78 per cent of those interviewed had children.

Table 1 How often do you shop for groceries not including the times when you have forgotten something?

	%
More than twice a week	7
Twice a week	17
Once a week	60
Every two weeks	11
Every three weeks	1
Less often	2
Miscellaneous	1
No response	1

Table 2 On what day or days of the week do you usually do most of your grocery shopping?*

	%
Monday	12
Tuesday	4
Wednesday	8
Thursday	24
Friday	40
Saturday	31
Sunday	6

* results add up to more than 100% because respondents could choose more than one day.

Table 3 What is the main reason you do most of your grocery shopping on that day?

	%
Most convenient time	45
Fits in with pay-day	30
Good day for special offers	26
Habit	19
Not crowded	8
Stock up for the weekend	7
Leaves weekend free	6
Run out of food on that day	6
Better selection of groceries	3
Miscellaneous	13

Table 4 At which one store do you shop for groceries most often?

Top UK Retailers	%
Sainsbury	11.2
Tesco	10.4
Co-op	6.9
Asda	5.7
Safeway	4.7
Robinsons	4.5
Fine Fare	4.5
Gateway	4.4
Spar	4.2
Kwiksave	3.2
Others	40.3

Table 5 What are your reasons for shopping at (name of shop) most often?

	%
Convenient location	42
Special offers/low prices	38
Good meat	25
Carry all brands	22
Friendly assistants	20
Quality of fresh produce	17
Good display	14
Adequate parking	12
From habit/miscellaneous	47

Table 6 What are your reasons for not shopping at the other stores?

	%
Prices too high	45
Too far to travel	27
Slow check-out	22
Prefer the shop I go to	17
Very few special offers	17
Poor selection	15
Unattractive store	7
Too small	7
Too overcrowded	5
No particular reason	3
Miscellaneous	28

Table 7 On your major grocery shopping trips, how often do you buy advertised special offers?

	%
Frequently	35
Occasionally	15
Seldom	10
Never	38
No response	2

Table 8 Which of the following are your best source of special offers? Which second and which third?

	Source		
	First	*Second*	*Third*
Newspapers	40%	10%	21%
Store leaflets	25%	24%	15%
Leaflet drops	15%	31%	19%

Table 9 Please look at all these advertisements and tell me the reference number of the one you like best.

	%
Safeway	20
Fine Fare	16
Asda	14
Gateway	13
Kwiksave	10
Tesco	9
Sainsbury	8
Co-op	6
Robinsons	2
Aldi	1
No response	1

Table 10 Why do you like the advertisement you picked?

	%
Special offers are easy to find	42
Eye catching	38
Easy to read/large print	27
Easy to find specific brands	19
More bargains	17
Good variety of items	15
Other replies none more than 8%	45
No response	3

Specimen answer

The first point to note is that 15 marks are allocated to this part of the question, and therefore we can safely conclude that 5 marks per drawing of a chart or graph will be awarded. The tables are all reproduced below (by kind permission of the CIM) and it is a question of personal choice as to which are to be used in answer to the question. You must make sure that each graph or chart is clearly labelled, both on each axis and also given a title.

I have presented below a different graph for each set of data corresponding to the first five tables.

Table 1. I have chosen a column/bar chart to represent the data in this table.

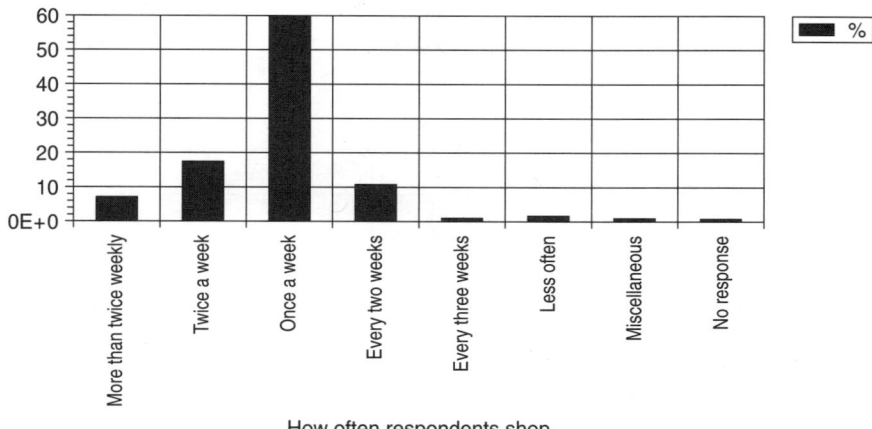

Figure 1
Shopping for groceries

Table 2. I have chosen a pie chart to represent this data.

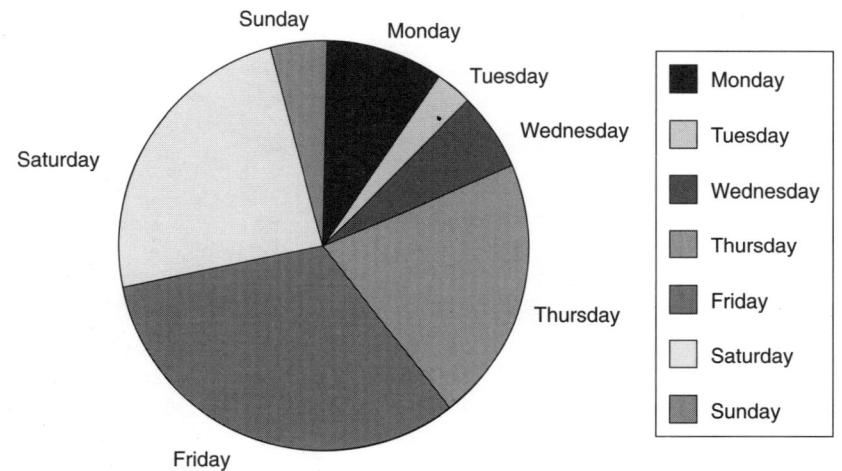

Figure 2
Shopping days

Table 3. I have chosen an area graph to represent this data.

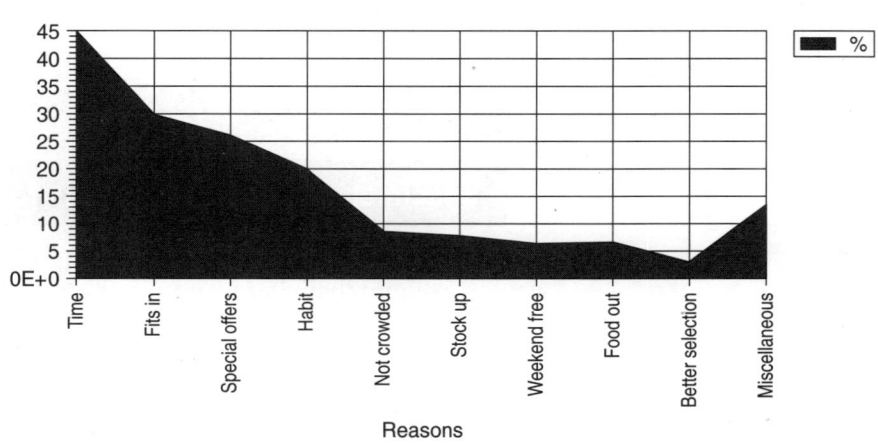

Figure 3
Reasons for choice of day

Table 4. I have chosen a standard line graph for the data in this table.

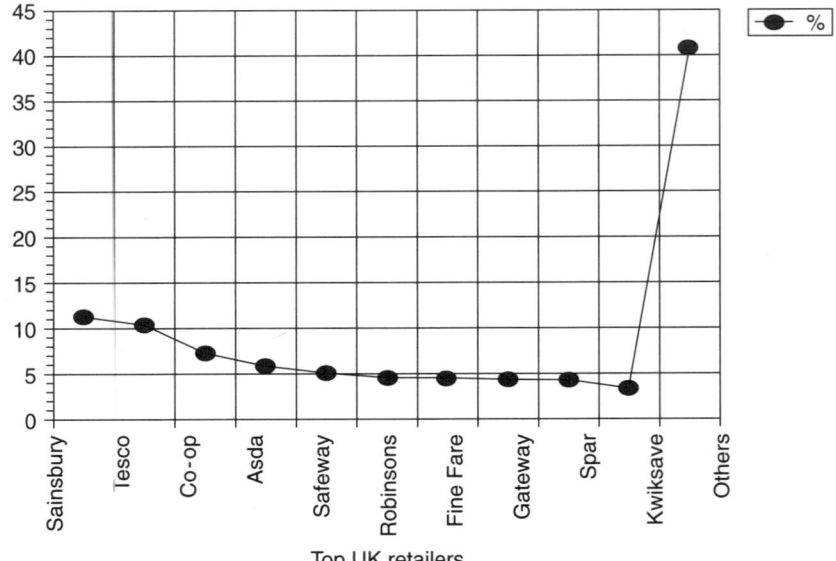

Figure 4
Store shopped at for groceries most often

Table 5. I have chosen a 3-dimensional column/bar chart for this data.

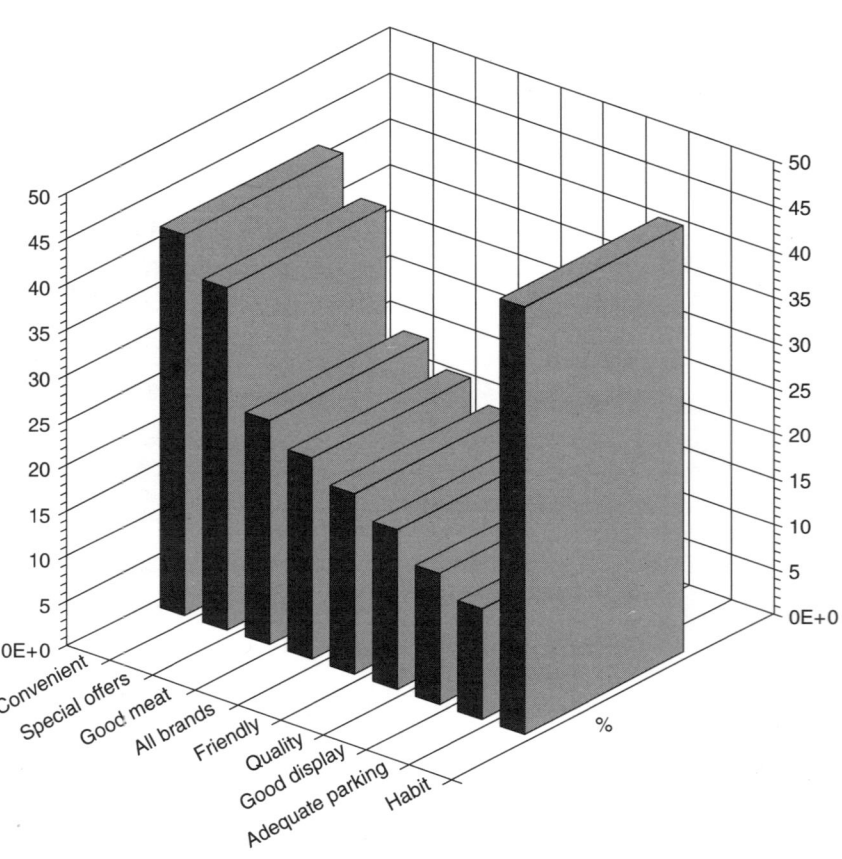

Figure 5
Reasons for shopping at a certain shop

Specimen examination question

(a) The sales manager has asked you to write a brief note on the value of column/bar charts and pie charts in the presentation of sales data.
(10 marks)

(b) Study the undernoted information on the American cigarette market and choose a suitable method for graphical presentation of the data.
(10 marks)

The American Cigarette Market, 1993
Courtesy: Merrill Lynch. Source: *The Sunday Times*, March 1994

Brand name sales	(billions of cigarettes)	Percentage share of the market
Marlboro	108.5	24%
Basic	24.4	5%
Benson and Hedges	11.5	2%
Merit	10.6	2%
Virginia Slims	10.4	2%
Winston	31	7%
Salem	18.1	4%
Camel	17.9	4%
Carlton	6.9	1%
Pall Mall	5.8	1%
Kool	12	3%
Newport	23	5%
Other	181.3	39%

Specimen answer

(a) Pie charts are represented by a circle, divided by radial lines into sections, so that each one is proportional to the size of the figure represented. It therefore shows the sizes of component figures in proportion to each other and to the overall total. There are many uses for pie charts in presenting sales data, as whole numbers or percentages can be depicted, but the main value is that by using shading or contrast the segments can be easily distinguished and, if this is compared to past data, it serves a useful basis for planning.

Column/bar charts represent data by a series of columns/bars and are a valuable visual as the differences between the data are easy to distinguish, enhanced by the use of contrast or shading.

Column/bar charts can be used to show the relative values of data or brand performance in terms of turnover, percentages, perhaps relative to other brands, internal or external (if the data is available).

(b)

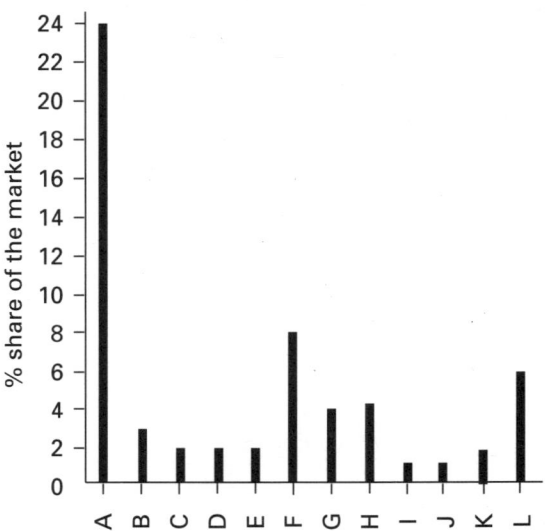

Figure 1

109

Clearly the number of statistical techniques or other visuals to present sales or marketing data are enormous and you need to learn how each can be used to best advantage in the presentation of information. In meetings and discussions or when written communication is received, analyse whether any visuals have been used and, if not, could they have contributed to a better appreciation of the information presented?

Experiment with the range of techniques developed in this unit and ask for feedback on their effectiveness and value to the recipients in your own business communications. Monitor and evaluate this activity over a period of time until you feel confident that the most suitable visual is used in a given situation.

Unit 8 Written communication formats

In this unit you will learn that:

❑ There are a number of different vehicles used for transmitting written communications. The most commonly used are the business letter, the memorandum, briefs and reports; each will be dealt with separately in the unit.

❑ Each of these written communications is used in different business contexts, and you will appreciate the reasons why one may be used relative to another.

❑ Finally, each of these may be communicated through traditional methods such as the postal system (internal and external to the business organization), but increasingly are transmitted via electronic equipment such as facsimile machines, etc. These enable a number of advantages, which are discussed.

By the end of this unit you will:

❑ Know the difference between the main vehicles used for transmitting information either internally or externally.

❑ Appreciate the different situations, in which each would be appropriate.

❑ Be able to write a business letter, memo, brief or report with some confidence.

❑ Understand that transmission through electronic aids enables communications to be more efficient and can also save money in the long run.

Study Guide

In this unit I have combined the three main ways in which written material is communicated, i.e. business letters, memoranda and reports, together with a short emphasis on briefs, and information on planning and composing business messages.

The aim of the unit is therefore to give you a thorough grounding in the principles that underpin the successful preparation of letters, memos and reports in a business context. However, despite the many examples contained in this unit, you do need to supplement your experience of this area by looking at good and bad practice exhibited by professionals in the business environment.

Collectively, this unit represents about ten hours of private study together with another eight hours required for the various tasks, activities and questions.

This unit covers indicative content area 2.4.1 of the syllabus.

In order to become proficient in verbal and written communication you should do the following:

- Collect records of written communication sent by others. Analyse them against the rules established in this unit. You will be able to determine the skill of the sender and how the communication could have been improved; this is an effective way for you to learn.
- Keep records of written communication that you send and ask for a response from the recipient; this will help you to determine the effectiveness of your communication and will put you on the learning curve to improvement.
- Attempt to make recordings of verbal communication by tape or video so that they also can be analysed and used to improve your skill in planning and composing verbal messages.

Question 8.1

Give examples of the different types of message that might be used by business organizations in written communication for both the internal and external markets.

Types of written message

Business organizations have to send a variety of communications both internally and externally. Some of these will be routine, others non-routine and will generally convey either positive or negative messages.

1 Routine messages are used in business for a range of positive activities such as announcements to regular clients of changes in merchandise or prices, information on personnel changes to the internal market, etc.
2 Non-routine messages are specific to the purpose in hand. For example, you may wish to make an enquiry regarding the merchandise of a supplier or place a one-off order on behalf of a customer; these types of correspondence messages usually require a reply to the communication.

Positive messages are frequent occurrences in written communication, whether to the internal market through a memo or to the external market through a letter. Written communication which is designed to be positive should follow these guidelines:

1 The opening paragraph should be clear and concise, with a supportive tone that is positive and pleasing.
2 Subsequent paragraphs should contain increasing levels of detail that identify the reasons for the communication and any information that will be of significance to the recipient.
3 The closing paragraph should be polite and courteous, finally stating any action that may be required of the recipient.

Messages that are designed to convey bad news or negative messages require a great deal of tact and diplomacy in their composition and delivery. These types of written communication are usually used when refusing requests, for example for credit or information, or turning down applicants for positions in the organization. The following guidelines in planning a negative communication may be observed:

1 The opening paragraph should recognize the situation leading to the communication and explaining the nature of the negative message.
2 Subsequent paragraphs should give increasing levels of detail but remain clear and concise, firm, fair and positive.
3 The closing paragraph should have a polite and courteous tone. Avoid using clichés and make a suitable suggestion, if appropriate.

The communication messages described above may be used for the internal or external market but in respect of the latter, there are further initiatives that can be taken.

Definition 8.1

The AIDA (attention, interest, desire and action) is a useful principle when planning written communication and, although it is usually used in communicating with a large, impersonal audience, its basic constructs can be used to guide the preparation of correspondence.

Attention arises from a bold headline or statement. In the case of a letterhead this is likely to be positioned in the logo or style of lettering used and therefore must be both immediately visible and stimulating. *Interest* will emerge from the content of the message which, as a general principle, should give an appropriate level of detail whilst remaining clear and concise. Good use of language and written communication skills (which varies for memos, letters, advertising copy, job descriptions, etc.) are needed to successfully communicate the message. *Desire* will make the recipient 'read/listen' and want to know more. If you have requested specific *action*, the quality of the message should be such that it makes the recipient respond.

Activity 8.1

Consider the type of message (routine, non-routine, positive, negative, personal or impersonal) that would be most appropriate for the audiences in the following situations:

1 Internal audiences:

(a) Employees who need to be motivated on issues of change in the organization.
(b) Colleagues from other departments who need to support you on a new proposal for product development.
(c) Colleagues in the department who seek your support for proposing a budget increase in advertising expenditure.

2 External audiences:

(a) Retailers whom you wish to stock your brand of merchandise.
(b) Suppliers who need to be more flexible in responding to your business needs.
(c) Voluntary organizations that seek your support in the community.

The business letter

Undoubtedly you will have been already involved in writing business letters as millions are composed, produced and delivered daily. Every organization has its own style (which is important in reflecting image and efficiency) but there are a set of basic rules of layout that all will follow:

1   A blocked layout with all entries starting from the left-hand margin or an indented style where the main body of the letter is set to the left-hand margin and all other parts are centred; either method may be used but should be consistent throughout the organization or department (Figure 8.1).

(a) Blocked layout

(b) Semi-blocked layout

Figure 8.1
Layouts for business letters:
(a) blocked; (b) semi-blocked

2   Business letters are made up of the following parts:

   (a)   Letterhead and/or logo – communicates the corporate image through its graphic style and usually also contains the address, telephone, telex and fax numbers of the organization.
   (b)   Letter references – initials of the typist and author.
   (c)   Date – usually the month is placed first, fully written – not numerals, followed by the day.

(d) Recipient's title, name and address.
(e) Salutation – for example, Dear Sir, Dear Madam or Dear Mrs Jones.
(f) Subject heading – this is usually indented and underlined, for example, Conference on Marketing Communication, September 25th 20XX, Queen Elizabeth's Hall, London.
(g) Body of the letter – short paragraphs centred on the page.
(h) Complimentary close – 'Yours sincerely' for named recipients, i.e. Dear Mr Brown; 'Yours faithfully' for formally addressed recipients, i.e. Dear Sir(s), Dear Madam; and 'Sincerely' or 'With kind regards' when the recipient is addressed by first name only, i.e. Dear Angela.
(i) Signature – usually in the sender's own handwriting.
(j) Position title of sender.
(k) References to enclosure and copies.

Figure 8.2 shows a model business letter.

LETTERHEAD

Letter references

Date

Inside address of recipient

Attention leader

Salutation

Subject heading

      Body

Complimentary close

Signature
Name
Position

Enclosure reference

Figure 8.2
A model business letter

Structuring business letters

1 The opening paragraph sums up the reason for the communication, and acknowledges any correspondence received and any other information which will provide a context for the rest of the letter.
2 The middle paragraphs set down the detail of the message and the sequence will either follow a direct approach (deductive), where the main idea comes first, followed by the supporting evidence or, where this is first, followed by the main idea, an indirect approach (inductive) is used. The method chosen will be determined by the likely reaction of the recipient: *deductive* for receptive audiences and *inductive* with those who may be displeased or harder to persuade.
3 The closing paragraph will summarize the main points of a complex communication and state any action that is needed from the recipient, and finally end on a courteous note with the suitable complimentary close.

Writing order letters

Definition 8.2

Letters for placing orders are used infrequently because preprinted order forms are usually more convenient and efficient. However, if an order letter is written, state your needs clearly by presenting the information in column form, with double-spacing and totalling the balance of prices at the end, explaining to which account the balance should be charged. State the delivery address (it may be different from the address on the letterhead) and the mode of transport which should be used.

Figure 8.3 gives an example of an order letter.

MAKE-IT BUILDING SUPPLIERS
Churchyard Grove
Pickwick
Lancashire LUI 5TF
Tel: 0123 668791

Our ref: HBJ/abc

October 1st 20XX

The Timber Merchants Ltd
Station Road
Ripon
Yorkshire YU8 TR3

For the attention of Deborah Jones

Dear Ms Jones,

Account Number: 5690   Special order under invoice 123

Further to our last order, would you supply the following additional items:

1	20 metres of extra hard-wearing timber for fencing.	£5.95 per metre excl. VAT	=	£119
2	5 litres of creosote liquid in natural colour.	£2.75 per litres excl. VAT	=	£ 13.75
3	24 litres of indoor wood varnish in antique pine.	£1.44 per litre excl. VAT	=	£ 34.56
		Balance		£167.31
		VAT on items		£ 29.28
		Total balance		**£196.59**

The balance should be stated on the above invoice and charged to our existing account. I would appreciate delivery by November 15th, latest.

Yours sincerely,

Harold Jenkins
Purchasing Manager

Figure 8.3
An order letter

Activity 8.2

Draw up an order letter based on the following information:

To: ABC Printers Ltd, Queen Street, Wolverhampton, Staffs, WV5 EL8
For the attention of Jonathan James. Account no. PC 123.

You wish to receive the following:

1 300 copies of the sales promotion literature for Brand Y, cost per copy: 20p.
2 2000 leaflets for the mail-drop campaign, cost per leaflet: 7p.
3 500 of your latest catalogues and price list, cost per catalogue: £1.50, cost per price list: 15p.

Answering order letters

If an order letter is received from a new customer, you should send a personal reply, which can also be used to state or clarify the terms of payment and other administrative procedures.

From time to time, you may also have to deal with non-routine order letters from customers, which will usually mean conveying some bad news about back orders, unfillable orders or having to make substitutions.

Your overall aim should be to keep instructions clear, remaining positive and confident in the tone of the letter so that the customer is pleased to respond, and attempting to ensure that the sale, as close to the original, is made and goodwill is maintained.

If a letter based on an unclear order is received, your first task is to get the information necessary to complete the order, which may be in writing if the order is long or complex and the customer needs time to restate the information, or by phone, if time is short and it is relatively easy for the customer to deal with the data required.

If the letter is written, begin by confirming the original order and emphasize again the positive features of your goods. In the next paragraph, state the nature of the problem and in the close, tell the customer how to solve the problem and how soon you expect to hear from them.

When dealing with back orders, you will either be able to fulfil some of the order, or none if the organization no longer makes the product and you are not able to offer a substitute. If some of the order can be fulfilled, this will convey some good news (see above), but if you cannot meet the customer's needs, then tact is necessary for conveying the negative message (see above).

Writing letters of enquiry or request

Definition 8.3

Letters of enquiry or request can deal with a variety of questions, such as asking the reader to supply certain information, make a presentation or inviting them to attend a function. They almost always require a reply and some action to be taken, therefore they should be sent out in advance of the action date and be well-written and tactful.

The opening paragraph should state the nature of the enquiry or request clearly and simply with a personal tone that will make the reader want to respond.

If further explanation or justification is needed, explain the importance of the information required and the situation which prompted the inquiry or request and, if appropriate, the benefits to the reader. Next, specify the desired action in a positive manner and present the questions logically.

Close the letter with a courteous statement and explain the type of action needed, the deadline by which a reply should be made and assurance that the information will be treated as confidential (if appropriate).

Figure 8.4 gives an example of a letter of request.

ULTIMATE COMPUTER COMPANY Ltd
3 The Gateway
Hounslow
Middlesex TW15 6TU
Tel: 0181 967 6345

TRJ/abc

October 1st 20XX

Mr Andrew Collins
Marketing Communications Consultants
'The Nook'
Twinkle Lane
Beaconsfield
BUCKS DU18 74R

Dear Mr Collins

Ref: 'Computers of the World' Exhibition, London, 20XX

I had the pleasure of using your professional services in helping us to prepare and present at the above last year.

We are now in the process of planning to exhibit our new product range again this year and would like to know whether you would offer us your services. I am pleased to enclose our latest catalogue.

Please contact me at the end of next week to arrange for a meeting at our offices.

I look forward to hearing from you.

Yours sincerely,

Timothy R. Jones
Marketing Manager

Enc. Catalogue of product range X.

Figure 8.4
A letter of request

Activity 8.3

Write a letter of request and inquiry based on the following information:

To: Jennifer Stevens, Sales Manager, Graphics Galore, The Hyde, Palmers Green, London N3 6TV, asking for the latest catalogue and price list of software packages for producing graphical visual aids. You are also interested to know whether they will have any packages available in 3-D in the near future.

Answering letters of inquiry and request

The *perception* of your organization is partly based on how efficiently, courteously and thoroughly enquiries and requests are handled, whether written or verbal, and the style in which they are expressed.

The majority of enquiries and requests are routine, so it helps to have prepreparedinformation that can be sent out quickly (this may simply mean a brief covering letter, together with a catalogue, brochure or price list).

Non-routine enquiries and requests, especially those that may involve a potential sale, which require a specific letter should contain the following:

1 An opening statement acknowledging the enquiry or request.
2 A favourable response of key information regarding the enquiry or request, making references to enclosures (if appropriate).
3 A personal close leading towards a sale (if appropriate), but encouraging goodwill and appreciation.

Writing claim or adjustment letters

Definition 8.4

In marketing, claim and adjustment letters are likely to deal with faulty, mishandled or lost merchandise and other types of customer complaint.

BEAUTY POTIONS LTD
2–6 Staines Road
Windsor
Berkshire BK7 9LE
Tel: 01753 576423

JK/abc

October 1st 20XX

Variety Fragrances
10 Harrow Road
Wembley
Middlesex 8TU 65R

For the attention of Mr Gardiner

Dear Mr Gardiner,

On September 5th 20XX, we received your order 1112, together with the invoice, 2224.

You will note that the first item on the invoice is listed as 50 × Fragrance 'Irresistible', but unfortunately we received 50 × Fragrance 'Uncontrollable'. A copy of the invoice is attached.

Please be kind enough to collect the wrong items and have them replaced by 50 × Fragrance 'Irresistible' at the same time.

I look forward to receiving the correct order by November 1st 20XX.

Sincerely,

Joanna Kemp
Sales and Purchasing Manager

Enc. Copy of invoice 2224

Figure 8.5
A letter making a claim for adjustment

Your motive for communicating is to have the claim sorted out and therefore written documentation is better than verbal communication as there is evidence of action you have taken.

In writing a claim letter, you should contain the following:

1 Opening paragraph with a clear statement of the problem.
2 Further information that will verify the claim or adjustment needed.
3 Closing statement with a polite, non-threatening request for action, emphasizing that the business relationship need not be affected if the matter is resolved satisfactorily.

Figure 8.5 gives an example of a letter making a claim for adjustment.

Activity 8.4

Write a letter making a claim for adjustment based on the following information:

To: The Sales Manager of Ladies Fashion Shoes Ltd, Northampton Business Park, Billings Road, Northampton NNE 5XT.

You are the manager of a retail shoe shop and ordered eight pairs of shoes in style 'Italian', but were sent size 5 instead of size 6. They were ordered on pro forma no. 876 and are urgently needed for a wedding in 2 weeks' time.

Answering letters for claims or adjustments

This type of letter will usually be most significant when a claim or adjustment is refused. In this situation, the following rules should be observed:

1 An opening statement with reference to the claim or adjustment but with a notable point on which both parties might be agreed.
2 An explanation which is tactful and maintains the goodwill of the organization, whilst ensuring that the claimant accepts (some) responsibility for the nature of the claim.
3 The refusal, possibly with the suggestion of an alternative course of action.
4 A pleasant close.

Writing letters of credit

In most organizations today, the process of buying and selling goods and services is facilitated by credit. The credit manager has responsibility for accepting or rejecting an application for credit, which is based on an assessment regarding the person or organization's financial viability and outstanding debts, in relation to the type and value of credit required.

Approving credit

1 A pleasant opening paragraph which grants the credit request.
2 Details of the terms and conditions under which credit is granted, addressing any specific points which may not be in line with company policy, but have been raised.
3 A courteous close.

Refusing credit

1 An opening statement appreciating the request for credit. Make the refusal, but with a notable point that both parties may agree.
2 Details for the refusal in positive terms which are specific to the reader, whilst maintaining a tactful tone to ensure goodwill.
3 A courteous close, with a sales pitch in relation to the correspondence, if appropriate.

Figure 8.6 gives an example of a letter approving credit.

```
                    CATERING WHOLESALERS LTD
                         35 Redruth Avenue
                            Tunbridge
                          Kent TN15 UCI
                         Tel: 01932 57311

HB/abc

October 1st 20XX

Mr R. Anderson
The Manager
'The Restaurant'
76 Sevenoaks Road
Sevenoaks
KENT


Dear Mr Anderson,

Thank you very much for your recent application for credit. I am pleased to
inform you that this has been approved.

Our terms and conditions are as follows:

1   A credit limit of £2000 is available for your establishment.
2   Invoices must be settled within 15 days of the date of issue, after which an
    interest charge of 5% will be levied on outstanding balances.

Yours sincerely,



Harry Bains
Credit Manager
```

Figure 8.6
A letter approving credit

Activity 8.5

Write a letter refusing credit to: Sonia Grant, Sales Manager of The Jewellery Store, Cirencester, stating that her establishment can continue to purchase on a 'cash-with-order' or 'cash-on-delivery' basis. You are a jewellery wholesaler with whom Sonia Grant has been a customer for 1 year and it is company policy to trade with customers for a minimum of 18 months before credit is made available.

Writing sales letters

Definition 8.5

Sales letters are designed to motivate people in a variety of different ways – in making purchases, endorsing the activities of an organization, participating in campaigns and so on.

Before a sales letter can be written, the sender must be clear on the main idea and message they wish to express, the target market or audience to whom the communication is directed and the appropriate format for the letter.

The main idea or message will usually be about a product or service: new, repackaged, relaunched, changes in price, distribution or marketing communication, i.e. new advertising campaign or different channel of communication, and so on.

The target market will be determined by identifying potential buyers of the product or service, based on traditional market segmentation variables such as age, sex, position in family life-cycle, socioeconomic group, etc. or psychographics and behavioural aspects of consumer behaviour. Clearly the size of the target market will determine the number of letters that need to be prepared and sent and the costs associated with this activity, which may exceed the designated budget; this may in turn lead to the need for sample coverage.

The format may be just a letter, or may include brochures, response cards and other (promotional) material; it may be (colour) printed or photocopied.

Composing the letter
The letter should follow the AIDA principle:

A   Arouse the attention of the reader by having a personalized opening which responds to the reader's emotions, a surprise statement or a free sample.

ID   Keep the interest and desire of the reader by highlighting benefits to the reader and unique selling points (USPs) or talking about the price.

A   Motivate the reader through positive statements and challenges to undertake the desired course of action.

Figure 8.7 gives an example of a sales letter.

WHOLESALE HOLIDAY Co. Ltd
26–28 Kensington High Street
London W14 XA5
Tel: 0171 635 2146

APJ/abc

October 1st 20XX

Sally Kenkins
25 Rosemary Court
Ipswich IP7 14T

Dear Ms Kenkins,

A FREE CRUISE ON THE MEDITERRANEAN!

You are one of our most valued customers. As part of our fifth birthday celebrations we are offering you this unique opportunity to cruise on the Med for free.

We are also pleased to enclose our latest brochure of holidays for the discerning traveller and if a booking is made for yourself and one other person by November 15th 20XX, a free cruise on the Mediterranean is yours.

Call or write for further information, but this special offer can only be made available on booking from our brochure.

I look forward to receiving your reservation in the next few weeks.

Yours sincerely,

Anthony P. Jones
Senior Marketing Executive

Enclosure: Wholesale Holiday Brochure

Figure 8.7
The sales letter

Write a sales letter based on the following information:

To: Dr Makhan Singh, 36 The Grove, Slough, Berks SL3 7TY, informing him about your new range of garden furniture and the special offer of a free bag of compost with the first order received by November 15th 20XX.

You are also enclosing the new specialist catalogue and price list.

Sales letters and direct-mail

Sales letters tend to be sent as part of a direct-mail exercise, which has rapidly grown as an important medium for both communicating and selling directly to a target market. A direct-mail package has four main components:

1 An outer envelope, which may show the organization's logo and name.
2 The (covering) sales letter, following the AIDA principle.
3 A brochure or catalogue, price list and order form as appropriate.
4 A (postage-paid) return envelope or order card.

In marketing activities today, mailing lists are frequently used to identify potential recipients of the communications. These are available through various sources such as ACORN (A classification of Residential Neighbourhood).

Writing letters of recommendation

Letters of recommendation convey information about people, their characteristics and suitability for the position. Therefore they are usually confidential and must contain the following:

1 The name of the person.
2 The position that the candidate is seeking.
3 The nature of the relationship between you and the candidate.
4 Relevant details to the position being sought by the candidate.
5 Evaluation of the candidate by the correspondent.

If you feel unable to provide a letter of recommendation, be brief and factual in your reasons. Figure 8.8 gives an example of a letter of recommendation.

Write a letter of recommendation for a friend who wishes to join a social or professional club of which you are a member.

Memoranda

Memos are widely and routinely used by organizations, mainly for internal correspondence to convey short specific information such as the schedule of meetings, decisions made and the results of research; these can be stored for future reference and follow composition principles similar to that of writing business letters.

```
FINANCE and INSURANCE Co
The Causeway
Newcastle upon Tyne NN4 65T
Tel: 0191 35202


SB/abc

October 1st 20XX



The Membership Secretary
Chartered Institute of Marketing
Moor Hall
Cookham
Berks


Dear Sir/Madam,

**Re: Caroline Taylor**

I am pleased to support Ms Taylor's application for membership of the Chartered
Institute of Marketing.

Ms Taylor has been in our employment for 6 years working in the area of Direct
Marketing.

I understand that she has passed all her CIM examinations and will be pleased to
receive further benefit as a member of the CIM.

Yours faithfully,



Sheila Brown
Marketing Director
```

Figure 8.8
Letter of recommendation

Memo paper is often preprinted on A4 or A5, in the following format:

(Letterhead)

MEMO
To:
From:
Date:
Subject:

The sender and recipient of the memo are usually addressed by job title
(e.g. sales manager), but may also include the full name. There may need
to be circulation of the memo to other interested parties and this should be
indicated here.

The subject title should be clear and concise and tell the recipient exactly
what the memo is about.

The body of the memorandum should be in short paragraphs, with
summary headings if appropriate.

Figure 8.9 gives an example of a memo.

Activity 8.8

Write a memo to your superior asking for training in one of the areas
identified in a personal communication plan.

MEMO
Medical Software Ltd

To: Carole Francis (Sales and Marketing Director)
From: Clare White (Marketing Manager)
Copy to: Hannah Craven (Secretary)
Subject: Software 20XX Exhibition, Amsterdam, December 1st–3rd
Date: October 1st 20XX

We have 8 weeks before the exhibition takes place and need to finalize the details of the follow-up campaign, particularly the role of our sales force.

Further to our meeting last week, we also need to discuss the sales promotion initiatives to push our products following the exhibition.

Please confirm that a meeting on October 5th at 3 pm in my office will be convenient.

Figure 8.9
A memo

Notices

Definition 8.8

Notices can play an important role in disseminating unconfidential information to a large number of employees who share a common interest.

Effective notices should follow these rules:

1   The size of the paper should correspond to the amount of information to be conveyed and its effect when displayed on the noticeboard and possibly viewed from several feet away.
2   The AIDA principle can again be used with a large, bold heading which captures attention, detail which holds the reader's interest and desire, and clear instructions as to the action which should be taken.
3   The message should be simple and concise.

Figure 8.10 gives an example of a notice.

SAFETY FIRST!

A Special First-Aid Course designed to give you basic introduction will be available free to all employees on the following dates:

October 1st 5–6 pm
November 1st 5–6 pm
December 1st 5–6 pm

The number of places is limited to 20 per class so early booking is advisable.

Contact: Jane Slater, ext. 123

Figure 8.10
A notice

Activity 8.9

Write a notice to all employees in your department or organization stating that a special course on body language will be available on two dates and free of charge, though places are limited to 10 per class.

1   Write a letter to Sharon Taylor, Purchasing Manager of Furniture Makers Ltd, 37 Station Road, Barnsley, West Yorkshire from John Perkins, Credit Control Manager of Timber Ltd, The Yard, Harrogate, approving their request for a credit limit up to £6000.

(12 marks)

2   Describe the main features of a letter of recommendation.

(8 marks)

Timber Ltd
The Yard
Harrogate
Tel: 01234 98765

JP/abc

October 1st 20XX

Ms Sharon Taylor
Purchasing Manager
Furniture Makers Ltd,
37 Station Road
Barnsley
West Yorkshire

Dear Ms Taylor

Thank you for your letter dated September 5th 20XX, requesting credit in relation to orders for our timber. We are pleased that your business with us is growing and happy to extend our services to you.

I am pleased to inform you that your credit has been approved up to a limit of £6000 and the terms and conditions are as follows:

1   A minimum order of £1000 must be placed.
2   Invoices are sent out on the 25th of each month.
3   Payment is due 30 days after the date of the statement.
4   Interest charges for outstanding balances will be 5% above the basic bank rate.

I hope that this information conveys all the details you need and we look forward to continuing to work with you.

Yours sincerely

John Perkins
Credit Control Manager

Letters of recommendation have an important goal: to convince readers that the person being recommended has the characteristics required for the job or other benefit. It is therefore important that they contain all the relevant details:

1   The full name of the candidate.
2   The job or benefit that the candidate is seeking.
3   Whether the writer is answering a request or taking the initiative.
4   The nature of the relationship between the writer and the candidate.
5   Facts relevant to the position or benefit sought.
6   The writer's overall evaluation of the candidate's suitability for the job or benefit sought.

Recommendation letters are usually confidential, i.e. they are mailed directly to the person or committee who request them and are not shown to the candidate.

Reports

Introduction

Reports are factual documents, prepared to fulfil the needs of decision-makers in organizations. They are therefore used for a variety of purposes and can be short (such as progress reports) or long (such as investigative reports or the annual report), formal or informal, routine, occasional or specially commissioned. Before any report can be prepared, decisions about the exact nature and purpose of the report, the recipient, distribution and likely reaction all need to be addressed because these factors will determine the structure, length and style (i.e. the degree of formality) of the report.

Report preparation

There are four main steps in the preparation of a report:

1 Define the issue(s) – this helps to identify the information that will be needed to deal with the main points by asking the right questions and clarifying the exact purpose of the report.
2 Identify the main issues – this will break up the problem into specifics that can be easier to analyse and also help to develop a logical structure to the investigation.
3 Produce a plan of action – the steps you need to take and the sources to be used in conducting the research.
4 Draw conclusions and make recommendations based on the facts and findings, which will aid the decision-maker.

Types and structures of reports

Long formal reports

Long reports are designed to achieve a number of goals (discussed below), but mainly to provide information and arguments based on an investigational problem or opportunity.

Structure

1 The title page (which may be preceded by an additional page with just the title of the report) shows the following:

    (a) The title of the report.
    (b) The name, title and address of the person or organization that prepared the report.
    (c) The submission date of the report.
    (d) The name of the person or organization to whom the report is submitted.

2 Letters of authorization and acceptance ('for the record') which directed the report to you or your organization and your subsequent reply may be included.
3 Letter of transmittal which introduces the report in a conversational tone to the reader and indicates the purpose, scope and limitations,

important points or sections, sources used and helpful suggestions for follow-up or further study. The final paragraph should convey thanks and a willingness both to discuss the report and to offer further services in the future.

A synopsis of the major findings, conclusions and recommendations may also be included, in particular if this is a short report.

4   The table of contents lists the text and supplementary parts of the report with page numbers and any other reference details.

5   The executive summary is a synopsis or overview which enables the reader to review and appreciate the contents of the report quickly. A summary of this type is either informative, where the main points of the report are presented in the same order or descriptive, where actual findings are omitted, but the main emphasis of the report is highlighted.

6   The body of most long reports is usually divided up as follows:

(a)   Introduction. This section provides a background to the discussion and findings of the report which have not been cited in detail in the letter of transmittal. Therefore, identifying the report's terms of reference and purpose, procedures and problem(s) which were tackled, scope and limitations, sources and methods, references and the organization of the report might be stated.

(b)   The discussion should be the largest part of the report, where analysis and interpretation of the findings are presented, supported by the conclusions and recommendations. All additional tables, charts and figures are also presented to make the interpretation easier for the reader.

7   Conclusions and recommendations which are substantiated and justified need to be clearly stated. Conclusions are the analysis of what the findings mean and recommendations are opinions about what should be done, in light of the investigation.

8   The addendum is the final part of the report which includes all supplementary material, such as appendices, which have been used to support the arguments presented in the report.

9   Appendices will contain the statistical charts and graphs that have been referred to in the text or research and any other information which has been useful.

Short formal reports

Definition 8.11

These are usually clear, concise statements pertaining to some organizational problem which can be solved, or a decision made relatively quickly, based on the facts which are presented.

Structure

1   The terms of reference deal with the scope and limitations of the report which has been investigated.

2   The procedures involved in carrying out the data-gathering process are identified.

3   Findings are the details that facilitate an understanding of the report's nature.

4   Conclusions present a final analysis of the findings.

5   Recommendations are the logical arguments about the course of action that should now be taken by the reader/organization.

Informal reports

Definition 8.12

Informal reports are used where the information to be presented deals with relatively simple issues. An informal report has three main sections:

1 Opening section – this puts the report into context with an introduction and essential background that leads logically to the next section.
2 Middle section – this part presents the procedures and findings which have been highlighted in the opening section.
3 Final section – the main points are highlighted through a summary or conclusions and recommendations, which clearly stipulate any action required by the reader.

Information reports

Definition 8.13

Information reports are designed primarily to provide information to others, for example, reports on conference activities or on sales training courses. They are mainly a summary of longer/complex material.

Investigation reports

Definition 8.14

Investigation reports are records of the investigation of a problem/situation or a proposal for change, for example a report on the changing working patterns or reorganization of a department layout. These types of report will usually offer recommendations and proposals for future action or consideration in the final sections.

Summary

In this unit we have seen that:

- There are a number of important steps that should be followed in the planning and composing of messages to be used in business communications. However, it is also important to remember that not only should the message reflect the needs of the recipient and therefore contain enough information (not too much and not too little), but it must also be relevant, timely and written in both suitable format (presentation style, such as a letter or report) and with the appropriate use of tone and language.
- Written business communications must serve a direct purpose, whether this is to provide information, receive information or ask for information. In a business context, they cost time and money to produce and send and therefore must be cost-effective. They may be made more efficient and therefore cost-effective if sent through electronic aids such as facsimile machines.
- Written communications can be used in a number of different business contexts. For example, business letters are designed to communicate important and often sensitive information to the recipient(s), memos are often used in internal, mostly relatively informal communications, briefs provide an update on (business) activities that have taken place over a period of time or in response to a particular issue, and reports are usually designed to provide a decision-maker with information that is relatively complex and often long, compared with other forms of written communication.

Unit Activity

Choose your own organization or one of which you have some knowledge and put yourself in the position of a marketing consultant to the business. Your task is to think about a marketing initiative that could be taken for the business, to carry out the appropriate primary and/or secondary research and to present your findings to the marketing director.

You must be able to:

- Explain the steps used in the planning and composition of business messages.
- Understand that the tone, language used and style of presentation will vary with each business situation, but in time common practice can be identified and used routinely, particularly in relation to the various formats available, memos, letters, etc.
- Identify in a given business scenario which format should be used, i.e. business letter, memo, brief or report.
- Structure each of these along the lines given in the study text in order to make them an effective vehicle of communication.
- Appreciate the relative costs associated with using these, particularly in large quantities, and the advantages of using electronic aids such as facsimile machines to make the communication more effective and cost-efficient.

Exam Hints

From the information studied in this longer unit and also the study and revision tips above, you will have begun to appreciate that this is one of the most important areas in the syllabus and therefore likely to be frequently tested in the examination.

In most of the examination papers so far, there have been at least two or three questions relating to this unit, either as whole questions in Section B or as part questions in Section A, the compulsory question.

The examiner will probably expect you to identify the most suitable *format* for a written presentation. The choice will be to prepare a report, brief, memo or letter and will depend on factors such as amount of information, context or situation, sender and recipient relationship, etc. You will then be expected to use all the information given and to present it in this format — some creative thinking may be required if the information is incomplete.

Specimen examination question 1 (December 1995)

As Sales Manager, you are responsible for a sales team of 18 people who operate throughout the UK. They often have to make calls to head office and to their customers.

(a) You are becoming increasingly concerned about the high cost of their mobile phone bills. Write a memo advising your staff on efficiency and effectiveness when using the mobile phone.

(13 marks)

(b) Write a memo to your finance department, explaining how you believe that mobile phone bills should be checked for cost and effective use.

(7 marks)

(a)   MEMO

To: Sales Team
From: Candidate name (Sales Manager)
Date: December 4th 1995
Subject: Using your mobile phone

Recently, I have received a report from our accounts department regarding the cost of telephone calls associated with using the mobile telephone.

Whilst I appreciate that a number of calls have to be made both to customers and also head office, the cost of these is exceeding our budget allocation.

I must therefore ask you to both restrict the number of calls to those that are urgent and not routine and also cut down the time needed on the telephone; the latter can be achieved through careful planning of the call before it is made and also by having on hand any details that may be required.

Other calls should be made either through the 'non-mobile' telephone (you will be reimbursed for expenses) or by use of a facsimile machine.

I hope that we will all be able to cut costs and therefore retain the use of our mobile telephones.

(b)   MEMO

To: Jean Parker (Finance Department)
From: Candidate name (Sales Manager)
Date: December 4th 1995
Re: Cost and efficiency of mobile phones

I have recently communicated with my sales team of 18 people regarding the collective cost of using mobile telephones.

However, the situation does need to be carefully monitored, and although I would anticipate a reduction in the cost by the next monthly statement, please let me have a copy of the account as soon as it is available.

You may consider it appropriate to investigate a change to another provider, for example from Vodaphone (our current system) to Orange – please advise if there are any details that I should note.

Finally, I would be very pleased if my team could be given a short presentation or some training on the effective use of mobile telephones – I can advise on suitable dates and times.

Specimen examination question 2

Your organization is considering diversification into franchising its range of cosmetics and toiletries in the retail sector. Study Figure 8.11 on the development of the Body Shop and write a short informal internal report to the Marketing Director, Ahmed al-Bayt.

PROFILE: Anita Roddick, founder of Body Shop

Anita Roddick was astonished by the ease of her success – which was due, she says, to breaking nearly all the rules. The following insight by Norma Wright, appeared in the magazine *British Business*.

The Body Shop International, named 'Company of the Year' at the 1987 Business Enterprise Awards, has a current annual turnover of more than £17.5m and almost 300 branches in 31 countries around the world. It has created almost 3000 new jobs – and 98 percent of its products are made in Britain. The inspiration for it all has been its livewire founder and managing director.

'Unemployable' is how Anita Roddick describes herself – but as head of the largest British-owned retail chain overseas, she needn't worry. A former student teacher and United Nations employee in Geneva, she is now the supreme entrepreneur – with a highly unorthodox view of what that means.

'I believe people are confusing entrepreneurship with opportunism', she said in a recent lecture at the City University Business School. 'They measure success by the profit and loss sheet.'

'In reality, entrepreneurship consists of three things: first, the idea one wants to get across; second, oneself – the person promoting it; third, the money that's necessary to make it happen. The third is the least important of all; the first is what matters – the integrity of the idea. You just have to believe in what you're doing so strongly that it becomes a reality.'

'Logically anybody who starts a small business with no money (as I did) can't succeed. But sometimes you do. Because you know if you don't succeed, you don't eat.'

Succeed she certainly did – and in an industry once described by Elizabeth Arden as 'the nastiest business in the world'.

Anita Roddick started her first shop in Brighton 11 years ago, with a loan of £4000 and some revolutionary ideas. She wanted to sell simple herbal and plant-based cosmetics, many of which she had seen used to great effect during her travels abroad; she intended to use the minimum amount of packaging and advertising; and she was determined to sell products that were developed with concern for the environment and were not tested on animals.

Inevitably the business had some teething troubles. The very first Body Shop had as neighbours a couple of funeral parlours who, not unnaturally, objected to its name; and her initial products 'looked and smelled peculiar' because the natural ingredients hadn't been prettified in any way. 'We had to explain to customers why our products looked revolting,' said Anita Roddick. And she only had 15 products in her range 'which looked pretty pathetic in the shop, because they only filled one shelf.'

She now has a range of over 300 products. The Body Shop still uses the cheapest bottles. 'The Sunday Times called them urine sample bottles, and perhaps they are' Mrs. Roddick said. There are now five sizes of each product. 'Because we had so few products at first, we originated the idea of five sizes; then we could fill a whole wall of the shop.' Customers have taken to the idea of a wide range of sizes; they can try the small one first, before splashing out on the more expensive sizes. Today's Body Shop is a franchise operation, each individual shop being 'almost a licence to print money' in Mrs. Roddick's words. The franchising came about almost by accident.

'All our "unique" marketing features happened because we had no money. Because it cost £3000–£4000 to open up a shop about a decade ago, my husband Gordon and I dreamed up what we called the "self-financing" idea; we didn't even know the word "franchising". Now we have a network of marvellous franchisees.'

Community project undertaking

She selects her franchisees with extreme care. Not for her is the man who wants to set up his wife in a little business, because it would be fun and should make a bit of money. She looks for franchisees who share her aims and ideals – and insists that each should undertake some kind of community project.

Figure 8.11

'This is not only altruism – it's survival. We have community projects which are riveting.' They range from running drug dependency groups and visiting elderly or handicapped people, to setting up street theatre. Most of our shops are run by women, who are enthusiastic about community work. And it's all done during working hours, not in their own time.

Anita Roddick has an enormous fund of ideas – 'drawers full of them', she said. And she's an expert communicator. The Body Shop publishes a bi-monthly 'Talksheet' for all members of staff, which contains – amongst others – a swop-a-job feature: staff are encouraged to exchange jobs for a few months, so a girl working in Bondi Beach can sample life in Aberdeen, and vice-versa.

Every month a video magazine, 'Talk Shop', is produced by the Body Shop's own video and film production company, and distributed to the franchisees worldwide. It includes reports on the various community projects and on Mrs. Roddick's overseas trips; she travels for two months of every year to find out how people in other cultures take care of their skin and hair; and to visit the various third world projects which produce products – for example cosmetic sponges – for her shops.

There is also a series of leaflets published for individual customers and for schools, containing detailed product information; and newsletters posted up in the shops. Customers' opinions are actively sought. 'Can you imagine', said Anita Roddick, 'that we are the only high street retailer which has suggestion boxes in its shops? Why spend billions of pounds on market research if you can do it yourself?'

She sees customer education as a major role. 'We reckon that about 25 million people must pass our shops at one time or another, so we use our windows to promote environmental community issues. Every one of our shops is like a major poster site.'

She is super-confident about the future, predicting 'we will become a major communications company and within two years we plan to have a magazine.' She also hopes to open a Body Shop in Moscow in three years' time.

'We think following the route of promoting health is vital for the cosmetics industry – it will not succeed by any other route. In the past it has often tried to create needs that don't really exist. We do things differently. It's so easy to break rules.'

Her advice to young potential entrepreneurs is simple: 'Never stop annoying people, and never stop asking questions. It is knowledge that gives you strength.'

Specimen answer

REPORT ON THE PROFILE OF THE BODY SHOP

To: Ahmed al-Bayt
From: (Student name and title)
Date:
Reference: Diversification into franchising of our cosmetics and toiletries.

Introduction

The Body Shop International is in the business of producing and distributing cosmetics and toiletries through its franchisees. In 1987 it had an annual turnover of more than £17.5m achieved through sales in some 300 branches operating in 31 countries.

Anita Roddick is the founder of this empire, having opened her first shop in Brighton in 1976 selling a few simple herbal and plant-based cosmetics. She has maintained a concern for the environment and that products should not be tested on animals, both concepts being used in her marketing strategy.

Findings

The product range has grown from 15 to 300, with five sizes of each, to satisfy the varying needs of customers from sample to bulk purchase.

The ownership of a Body Shop franchise is 'almost a licence to print money', but franchisees are picked only if they share the values of community involvement and are willing to engage in community work.

The Body Shop also publishes a bi-monthly Talksheet for all members of staff and a video magazine every month for the franchisees. A series of leaflets is also published for customers and schools.

Finally, the founder states that 'the route of promoting health is vital for the cosmetics industry'.

Conclusions

Undoubtedly The Body Shop has been highly successful in creating a new market for cosmetics and toiletries which are cruelty-free, and have educated the buying public to want products that promote health whilst caring for the environment.

The establishment of the franchise system allows for flexibility in controlling the distribution of goods and marketing practice, whilst allowing franchisees the freedom to generate their own profits.

I recommend that we penetrate this lucrative market by setting up a system similar to that of The Body Shop.

Unit 9　The communications mix

Study Guide

This unit provides you with a basic understanding of a variety of external communication formats (sometimes referred to as the *promotional* or *communications mix*) as this is fundamental to an understanding of customer communications. It does not purport to equip you with a comprehensive knowledge of marketing communications or enable you to develop an integrated communications strategy, as these are areas that you will study at Diploma level.

This unit will cover indicative content area 2.4.2 of the syllabus. It will take you two hours to read through the unit and a further two hours to work through the activities.

Study Tips

This unit provides an outline of the main advertising media and their main attributes. To provide further examination of this topic you need to spend some time looking at examples of advertising using different media. For each advert you should specify the advertising objectives, identify the target audience and consider why that particular medium has been chosen.

You could undertake a similar activity looking at sales promotions. List how many different types of sales promotion you can see when you next go shopping. Consider what the objectives are of each promotion.

The communications mix or promotions mix

You have already looked at the various ways that individuals inside an organization use to communicate either with colleagues or others outside their organizations. The *communications* or *promotions mix* refers to those forms of communication that are used not on behalf of an individual but on behalf of the entire organization to promote either itself or its goods and services.

See Figure 1.3 in Unit 1 for an example of the communications mix and see Figure 1.1 for the target audiences that organizations may want to communicate with.

Promotional mix decisions

The communications or promotional mix can be categorized as *above-the-line activity* and *below-the-line activity*. (These definitions will be explained as you work through the unit.) Organizations usually use a mix of both above- and below-the-line activity to communicate with their target audience. In deciding which of these activities to use to communicate with customers, an organization needs to consider the following factors:

- What is to be achieved? What are our objectives?
- Who do we want to communicate with? Who is our target audience?
- How big is our target audience? How can we reach them? What are their media habits?
- What is our message? How can we state our message?
- When do we need to communicate our message?
- How much money do we have to spend?

Promotional objectives

Before deciding what kind of promotion or communication with customers is required, an organization has to tie itself down to one or two realistically achievable objectives.

The following are a selection of objectives:

- To create an image.
- To create awareness.
- To inform about a new feature.
- To change attitudes.
- To correct misconceptions.
- To reassure.
- To remind.
- To generate interest.
- To generate response.
- To encourage trial.
- To prompt purchase.
- To support other promotional activity.

The role of the brief

In the early stages of your career you are unlikely to be developing full-scale campaigns using above- and below-the-line activity. However, one way for your organization and its advertising agency or design consultancy to determine how to communicate with customers is to write down its requirements in the form of a *brief*. You should be aware of the components of a brief.

Below is an example of the headings that could be used in an advertising brief. However, you should note that a brief could be used to determine any kind of above- or below-the-line activity. In addition, you should be aware that every brief will be individual to the company, the product and the market concerned.

An example of an advertising brief:

Client details
In this section you would include the name of the client and the name of the product.

Background information
In this section you would include whatever relevant information you had about the following:

- The company.
- The product.
- The market.
- The competition.
- Previous advertising activity that has been undertaken.
- Any relevant research data.

Objectives
In this section you should outline the objectives of the campaign/project.

Target audience
In this section you should identify who the campaign is aimed at.

Message to be conveyed
In this section you should identify what you want to say and how it should be said. This may include the *unique selling proposition* (the one key benefit that distinguishes the product/service) and any substantiation for the claims being made. It should also determine the desired tone of voice and brand image that should be communicated.

Media
In this section you should specify where you want to place the message.

Timescale
Here you need to specify when the campaign is to run, its length and duration.

Budget
Here you should specify how much money is available for the campaign.

Miscellaneous information
In this section you should specify if there are any mandatory inclusions, for instance, you may have to mention membership of ABTA if it is an advertisement for a travel agent. You also need to include contact phone numbers or certain logos.

Above-the-line promotional activity

'Above the line' is a slightly out-of-date expression that refers to advertising on which a commission fee is paid by the media to the agency that placed the advertising. As the rules and methods for booking advertising and the whole area of remuneration has changed, it has come to refer to the main advertising media of television, radio, cinema, outdoor and the press.

Television advertising
This is the most visual medium, as most people spend at least some time watching television for entertainment. Because it can reach large numbers of people, the cost of one spot or commercial break can be very high.

In order that the television commercial does not look out of place with all the other professionally filmed programmes that appear either side of the commercial, television advertising requires production specialists, which adds to the cost of production. The relatively short exposure time (most commercials last for no more than 30 seconds) means that television advertising has to be repeated many times and, as the cost of airtime is very expensive, this means that it tends only to feature in the marketing budgets of the mass-market fmcg (fast moving consumer goods) brands.

Television is a very creative medium that offers:

- Sound, movement, interesting visual effects.
- Entertainment that famous people are happy to appear in.
- Impact – you can see it in action or being demonstrated.
- Credibility to the product or service.

Television is a very transient medium that can easily be missed. This is more so since people with video recorders can fast-forward past commercial breaks (zipping) and people with a remote control can quickly change channels (zapping) to avoid television advertising. There is also no opportunity to sample or smell a product.

In the UK it is possible to buy television advertising that only appears in one or more of the 13 ITV regions and so target a specific area of Britain. It is also possible to buy national advertising airtime covering all the television regions, which makes it ideal for mass-market products or services.

Until recently it was a difficult tool to use for targeting specific groups, except in a fairly crude way. For example, media planners could make generalizations that mothers mostly watch daytime television, the evening news is watched by upmarket business people, and teenagers watch late-night television.

With the introduction of more channels via cable and satellite television, there are more opportunities for specialist programmes, such as programmes about specific sports. With this comes more opportunities to target specific audiences. For example, MUTV is a channel devoted to the interests of Manchester United fans. With greater audience fragmentation comes greater opportunities for niche advertising.

Radio advertising

Radio relies only on sound. It does not therefore have the same creative impact as television and cannot show products. However, it can tap into the listeners' imagination with the use of evocative sound effects and voices (including famous voices) to make it a very effective advertising medium.

It can reach large audiences as in the UK there are several national commercial radio stations. These stations specialize in particular types of music (from jazz to classical). In addition, most regions have local radio geared to the needs of people in their catchment areas. In this way radio advertising campaigns can be targeted geographically and according to lifestyle/tastes.

Cost varies with the size of audiences reached but production costs are not as high as television. However, advertisers usually have to buy a large number of airtime 'spots' because of the transient (and sometimes background listening) nature of the medium.

Cinema advertising

Cinema advertising has the same creative characteristics as television and perhaps even more impact because there are fewer distractions and potential interruptions from zipping and zapping. In addition, media buyers can ensure that advertisements fit the audience profile that applies to particular films. In the UK most cinema advertising is sold on a national basis through various cinema chains and two contractors. There is some opportunity for geographic segmentation, with a small proportion of advertising aimed at purely local audiences.

Outdoor advertising

This type of advertising covers a whole range of different types of media that can be found outdoors and indoors. It includes large roadside billboard hoardings, small poster sites on bus shelters and bus stations, on underground and ground level train stations, the inside and outside of various types of transport, such as buses, trains, tubes and taxis, and even peripheral sites, such as parking meters and street furniture.

Although a poster site can have plenty of impact, it is limited to short messages with bold images. Usually there is a very short exposure time as people are moving past the advertising. (Exceptions here are people waiting at tube or rail stations.) Most outdoor advertising does not incorporate sound or movement in the message. However, there are some moving poster sites where the image changes every few minutes. There are also some well-known three-dimensional sites. For example, an airline has one in the form of an aeroplane at Heathrow and there was a famous one designed to look like a pub that sold Guinness.

Press advertising

Press advertising comprises all printed media. In the UK this covers national newspapers, local newspapers, specialist trade and technical magazines (one for almost every industry sector and job), general interest magazines (the most popular of which are female interest magazines aimed at different age groups) and specialist interest magazines that cover almost every hobby and interest area, from fishing to stamp collecting.

Therefore advertising in print media can be carefully targeted at demographic and geographic segments. Quite complex messages can be conveyed because print media can be retained and seen more than once. Advertisements can also benefit from the credibility of the newspaper or magazine.

However, advertising in the print media has limited impact and there is little flexibility for creative messages in comparison with television advertising. Although magazines can be in full colour and quite glossy, newspapers tend to be in black and white with only spot colour.

Activity 9.1

Look at the following scenarios and evaluate the proposed advertising media decisions.

1　Calvin Klein are considering using local newspapers to promote their expensive new fragrance, 'y', which is aimed at fashionable young men and women.
2　The manager of a small hotel in Wales would like to use television advertising to attract tourists.
3　Harvey Goldsmith Entertainments sell concert tickets nationally. They are considering using radio to advertise a number of outdoor summer concerts featuring the famous Three Tenors.
4　ASH (the anti-smoking lobby group) has identified that there is a massive growth in the number of young female smokers and is considering using cinema and teenage girl magazines like *Jackie* and *19* to target them in a hard-hitting anti-smoking campaign.

Below-the-line promotion

Basically, any promotional activity that does not come under the five main media already mentioned above comes under the category of below-the-line promotion.

Corporate literature

Corporate literature, such as stationery, brochures, leaflets, annual reports, is a visual record of an organization's corporate identity in which branding and logos are often featured extensively. An organization's corporate literature has a vital role to play in communicating information about a company, its products/services and its annual performance to its stakeholders.

Production of literature

Unless it is specific to your job role, it is unlikely that you will need to have extensive knowledge of graphic design and print production techniques. However, you should be able to critically evaluate rough drafts that designers supply to you for corporate literature and provide layout information for items to be published in-house and by printers.

Here are some points you should look for when studying suggested layouts.

Consistency

Overall, there should be some consistency as regards headings, margins, spacing of paragraphs, white space, text justified or ranged left/right, typefaces and typesizes. It is better that a page has unity, which can be created by a dominant headline or illustration or a combination of both, so that the reader is focused and is not confused by too many visual 'tricks' or devices. However, there is often justification for text and images to be arranged in an interesting way to encourage the reader to follow through the text.

Colour

Colour can be used to provide variety, impact, interest and even to communicate a mood. However, too many colours can bombard the reader and convey a cheap and tacky feeling.

Typefaces

Typestyles are a whole area of study on their own. If you look at the various typestyles or typefaces (sometimes known as *fonts*) on your computer, you will have an idea of the choice and variety available. Different typefaces convey different visual images. Some have an old-fashioned/traditional feel, others appear modern, some give an impression of formality and others appear light-hearted and would be appropriate for a party invitation.

Some typefaces are easier to read than others; others provide more emphasis for headings and sub-headings. You should ensure that there is some consistency with regard to the typefaces used in your organization's corporate literature.

Typesize is also an important consideration and you should ensure that all printed material is legible.

Activity 9.2

You work in the Marketing Department of the local chamber of commerce. An international conference is planned on e-commerce (business on the internet). A gala dinner will launch the event. An expert speaker will make a keynote speech on the topic and dignitaries and interested parties will be invited to attend.

Draft an invitation to the gala dinner to be printed on A5-size card. Include layout instructions for the printer.

(Taken from June 1999 examination paper – 8 marks available.)

Corporate image

An organization's image and that of its products/services are a vital way to communicate with target markets.

A corporate identity or image can be communicated by the following:

- An organization's logo.
- The typeface on an organization's letterhead.
- The materials it uses for correspondence (stationery, business cards).

- Corporate literature (brochures, annual reports, internal training material, application forms, internal newsletters, exhibition stand material).
- Its headquarters and offices (including signs inside and outside the building, its reception area).
- The signs on its vehicles.
- The appearance of personnel (uniforms, badges) and the way they deal with people (they are ambassadors for the organization).
- Its public relations image (the way it is reported in the media and public perception in general).

Brand image

Whereas a corporate image refers to the organization as a whole, the organization may be the umbrella for a number of different brands. For example, Virgin is an organization with a corporate image and there are a number of Virgin brands, such as Virgin Vodka, Virgin One (financial services) and Virgin Trains, each with their own brand image.

A brand can be communicated by any of the following:

- A name.
- A term.
- A design.
- A trademark.
- A symbol.
- A logo.

With brands, consumers can be encouraged to associate certain attributes with a product. These attributes can be used to personify the brand and add value to a commodity. For example, it is much easier to promote Andrex toilet paper using the Andrex puppies than if the manufacturers could only talk about the product and show images of toilet rolls. It allows Andrex to distinguish the product from its competitors and allows the manufacturer to charge a premium price.

Logos

Logos can be just as important as a brand name or brand image in that they can do the following:

- Attract attention.
- Create an impression.
- Create recognition.
- Convey information about a product or organization.
- Provide consistent imagery.
- Differentiate the product/organization from its competitors.

Packaging

Aside from the functional role of packaging, which is to actually provide a container for products, packaging has a role to play in communicating with customers. It communicates the product name and the brand image. Following on from advertising and other promotional activity, this can act as a reminder to consumers at the point of sale to purchase the product in favour of a competing product.

Point of sale display and merchandising

Point of sale display and merchandising refers to the in-store display that can influence consumers to purchase products in shops. It involves the layout and design of the shop and the way the goods or merchandise are presented. Manufacturers can have in-store display material produced to remind customers of their products at the point of purchase. For example, manufacturers of chocolates and confectionery might arrange with shops to display special branded stands, mobiles or life-size cardboard cut-outs of characters used to advertise the chocolate brand. Similarly, cosmetics manufacturers might supply shops with hanging signs or revolving display stands. This is another tool for marketers to communicate brand imagery and act as a reminder at the point of purchase.

Powerful manufacturers that spend vast amounts on advertising tend to have more influence on retailers in terms of where their products are displayed. The most effective display areas are at 'eye level', where products are easy to see and reach for.

Sales promotion

Sales promotion is another communication tool that marketers use. It is often described as 'A short-term tactical marketing tool that gives customers additional reasons or incentives to purchase'.

Sales promotions can offer temporary added value to the customer at the point of purchase (often referred to as a sales *pull* strategy). Manufacturers can also direct promotions to the trade (often referred to as a sales *push* strategy).

There are many different versions of sales promotions that are directed at consumers:

- Price reductions.
- Coupons/money-off vouchers.
- Entry to competitions/free prize draws.
- Free goods.
- *x* per cent free.
- 3 for the price of 2.
- Free samples.
- Free gifts.
- Guarantees.
- £*x* goes to *y* charity if you purchase.
- Reward points/tokens against a free gift (for example, Air Miles).
- Refunds or free gifts on a mail-in basis.

Sales promotions aimed at the trade include:

- Discount on bulk orders.
- Free supplies.
- Incentives (for example, shopping vouchers for Marks & Spencer or a free alarm clock).
- Free prize draw competitions.
- Deferred invoicing.
- Merchandising and display material.

The objectives of a promotion could be to achieve one of the following:

- Encourage trial of product.
- Extend existing customer base.
- Prompt customers to change brand.
- Generate bulk buying.
- Overcome seasonal dips in sales.
- Encourage trade to stock product.

Exhibitions

In many business-to-business marketing situations, organizations have a sales force that visits the customer. With exhibitions, road shows, seminars and conferences, customers come to see the supplier. This provides organizations with a valuable opportunity to communicate with their customers and potential customers in a face-to-face situation.

These occasions take many forms.

Conferences

A conference may feature speakers from a number of different organizations who are experts in various fields, and attendees pay for the privilege of attending the conference. For example, a recent conference aimed at top decision-makers in NHS Trusts provided attendees with advice about taking advantage of a government scheme to allow Trusts to extend or improve their buildings. The speakers came from a variety of law firms, construction companies and architects. The conference also provided the speakers with an opportunity to promote their organization's expertise and to network with potential customers from the Trusts as well.

Seminars

Seminars are held by companies to provide customers with advice on developments in their market. At the same time, companies have the opportunity to extend their business relationship with attendees. For example, many of the larger accountancy firms provide breakfast budget briefings to discuss the implications of a new budget or taxation laws. Similarly, pharmaceutical firms arrange seminars for doctors to discuss new drugs that are available on the market.

Mobile road shows

These can be in the form of a mobile unit that goes around the country to promote goods/services. For example, the National Blood Transfusion Service attracts donors when its mobile units are placed at shopping centres or university buildings.

Trade fairs

Although there are some exhibitions that are aimed at the general public, such as The National Homes Exhibition, most exhibitions are directed at business-to-business activity.

Trade fairs are generally held in large exhibition halls where firms book a stand area and either hire a stand or pay for one to be designed. The stand and the corporate literature have to be presented in an eye-catching way to attract visitors to the stand.

Companies also have to cover the cost of staffing stands, pay for staff travel and accommodation costs and hospitality costs incurred when sales staff network with prospects and customers.

Exhibitions combine personal selling with non-personal communication activities and bring potential customers, at their expense, to a location that suits you. Nevertheless, many companies find that they usually need to undertake some pre-exhibition publicity to attract people to their stand.

Staff can make sales at exhibitions but they are usually used to generate leads that have to be followed up once the exhibition has finished.

Sponsorship

Sponsorship is another communications tool that can be used to put an organization's name across to a variety of publics and promote an image. Organizations can sponsor the arts, sporting events, individual sportsmen and women or even television programmes.

Organizations are usually interested in the type of sponsorship that either attracts publicity and media coverage or puts their name in front of their target audience in an interesting and maybe novel way. For sponsorship to work, it should be in keeping with the organization or its brand's image.

Sponsorship can be in the form of goods, for example, free football boots or financial reward to the sport or the individual. It could even be some kind of loss guarantee of the kind that occurs with some tennis events if they are rained off.

Sponsoring individuals can be risky if they attract bad publicity and are involved in some form of scandal. This could result in the organization's name being tainted by association. However, most organizations would withdraw sponsorship in the case of a scandal.

Public relations

The Institute of Public Relations has defined public relations as 'the planned and sustained effort to establish and maintain goodwill and mutual understanding between an organization and its publics'.

The above definition is a very broad one. It comprises a number of general activities, some of which you have already examined in previous units, and a number of specific activities that are devised to raise the profile of an organization or even a person representing an organization.

General PR activities generally relate to communicating with a variety of stakeholders and comprise corporate communications, community relations and customer care activities. In addition, there are a number of specific PR activities that relate to communicating with the media.

Corporate communications

- In house journals/newsletters.
- Annual reports.
- Gifts/incentives, for example calendars, key fobs, desk items, etc.
- Christmas cards.
- Business dinners/receptions.
- Corporate entertaining, e.g. golf tournaments.

Community relations

- Scholarships or bursaries.
- Charity support.
- Open days for the public – for example, the fire service often has open days.

Customer care

- Customer service departments.
- Complaints management.
- Customer advice and helplines.
- Ethical and environmental policies.

Specific PR activities
These are activities generally related to communicating with the media.

- Press conferences.
- Photocalls.
- Publicity stunts.
- Supplying feature articles.
- Open days/previews for the press – for example, some theatres have press nights.
- Product launch events.
- Advertorials/advertisement features (articles are written for the press but the space is paid for in the same way that an advertisement is paid for).
- Sending press releases.

Activity 9.3

Before you start reading the section on how to prepare a press release, read the following abstract taken from a press release that was sent to a local newspaper in a farming region in England. Ignore the format but explain why the content is not suitable and suggest how it could be improved.

PRESS RELEASE FROM XYZ FARMING LTD

Dear Editor

We believe that we can offer your readers an interesting news story and will be happy to provide fuller details if required.

A new concept in dairy cow feeding has been pioneered by XYZ Farming Ltd, which is specifically designed to meet the demand of consumers for milk of higher protein content and reduced fat levels.

These requirements are reflected in differential prices paid by most dairies to farmers with greater emphasis on protein content rather than butterfat: high butterfats also act as an effective constraint to the full use by the farmer of his quota allocation.

In the new Granary range of compound feeds the high levels of rumen bypass starch derived from rolled wheat, is pelletted in combination with high vegetable proteins . . .

Press releases

Most organizations have a PR policy, which means that press releases go through a rigorous checking and signing-off procedure whether they are produced in-house or by an agency. It is a specialized job, and one that you will not be involved with unless it is specified as part of your job role.

Nevertheless you should be able to produce a draft release to show that you understand how they should be written and presented, as it could become a task that is part of your job.

You should be aware that while organizations can pay to obtain advertising space, obtaining editorial space through press releases is subject to the editorial team finding the press release interesting and usable. Even if this is the case, they will probably be limited as to how much space is given to your press release and they will usually change it so that the angle suits their news purposes.

It is wrong to consider that press releases are 'free' advertising, as the time and effort put into writing a good press release has a cost associated with it.

The format of a press release

A press release format should:

- Feature your organization's logo at the top.
- Be entitled 'Press release'.
- Show the date the release was prepared or indicate when the news can be released (an embargo).
- Have a headline that sums up the story.
- Be typed with double spacing and have wide margins.
- Only use one side of the paper.
- Indicate that more 'copy' or text follows by using the abbreviation m/f at the end of each page.
- Clearly mark the end of the release with the word 'end'.
- Contain contact details for the media to make further enquiries.
- Contain additional notes in the form of 'background notes for the editor'.

The press release content should:

- Answer the questions who, what, when, where and how.
- Encapsulate the nub of the story in the first paragraph.
- Start with the key point at the top and add the 'bones' of the story in each succeeding paragraph.
- Contain interesting quotes that are attributed to a person relevant to the story.
- Be geared to the media, so you may have one version for the trade press and another for the local press.
- Use factual not flowery language.
- Be clear and concise.
- Relate to any accompanying photographs.
- Have a 'pic caption', i.e. a few sentences that explain the contents or name the people in a photograph.
- Usually be written as if the event has just happened (even if the presentation or the contract was won a few days ago), although some press releases inform of what will happen in the future.

See the question scenario in Activity 9.2.

(a) Assuming the event has taken place, prepare a press release for distribution to the relevant media. (12 marks possible for this part of the question.)

(b) State your objectives in preparing the release.

(c) Suggest which type of media you would send the release to.

Direct marketing

Types of direct marketing activity

- Direct mail (mailshots).
- Door drops (leaflets/coupons/vouchers posted through the door).
- Selling via catalogues/brochures (mail order selling).
- Direct response advertising in the press (off the page selling).
- Direct response advertising on the television (DRTV).
- Telemarketing (using the telephone to contact people to sell direct to them).

The most popular form of direct marketing in the UK for both consumer and business-to-business marketing is direct mail. Direct mail usually comprises a sales letter outlining the offer, a response mechanism and sometimes there is a separate piece which gives details of an incentive offer if you respond by a certain date.

How direct mail can be used

The principle is that organizations build a database of current customers' address details and their previous purchase history. By using this information the organization can target products/services that are tailored to suit the recipient's profile. For example, a bank will have all your financial details and could send you a mailshot promoting a gold status credit card if you fitted the income bracket and financial history for that product.

The same bank could rent a list of people with a gold card customer profile, from another organization, to send them a mailshot in the hope of recruiting additional gold card customers.

Direct marketing objectives

Direct marketing campaign objectives could be to:

- Generate sales.
- Build up sales leads.
- Invite recipients to visit a store.
- Build the company database.
- Remind people that an offer closes by a certain date.

Advantages of direct mail

- Response is measurable.
- You can test the copy in the letter or the design of mailshot components.
- You can target precisely and therefore it is cheaper than mass-market advertising.
- You can tailor messages to niche groups.
- You can time the campaign precisely.
- There can be short lead times in running a direct marketing campaign.
- Computer technology can mean sophisticated database management.

Disadvantages associated with direct mail

- Can be viewed as junk mail.
- Can be seen as intrusive.
- Investment costs for establishing and maintaining a database are high.

Exam/Revision Hints

You are unlikely to be asked theoretical questions that require you to regurgitate facts about various media or ones that ask you to differentiate between above- and below-the-line media. However, you will be expected to have an underlying knowledge of all areas of promotional activity, as they will often form the context of a question.

Be prepared to draft a press release, suggest copy for a simple advertisement/leaflet or propose simple layout instructions to a printer or in-house publishing department. You should also be prepared to be asked questions that relate to briefs and be able to suggest suitable media for communicating with customers in a variety of different circumstances.

See Question 6(d) on the specimen paper in Unit 11 for one example of the kind of question you could be asked that relates to this area of the indicative content.

Summary

In this unit you have examined a range of promotional activities that can be used to communicate with external customers.

Activity debrief

Activity 9.1

1 Calvin Klein fragrances are unisex and aimed at younger people. They are a highly branded product and are usually advertised using photogenic models in creative adverts on television. Consequently local press advertising does not seem to fit in with the image of the product.
2 A small hotel in Wales is unlikely to have the marketing budget to afford television advertising. Also, it would be rather wasteful as it is a mass-market medium. The hotel should specifically target holiday-makers who want to spend their holidays in Wales. They could consider the national press, perhaps a Sunday newspaper, that has a travel section and they should choose an edition when there is editorial coverage about holidays in Wales.
3 Harvey Goldsmith Entertainments are right to use radio as the 'product' fits the medium. They could advertise on national radio, specifically Classic FM, as that station appeals to opera fans. They may even use local radio to tie in with the locations of the concerts.
4 ASH has chosen a good mix of media to target young women. The cinema will be a good choice if they make sure their adverts appear before films that specifically appeal to young women. The magazines aimed at young women also seem an ideal choice for such a campaign.

Activity 9.2

See Figure 9.1.

See Figure 9.1.

Figure 9.1

> **Midchester Chamber of Commerce**
>
> LOGO
>
> in association with National Westminster Bank
>
> *Invite*
>
> ....
>
> to the e-commerce gala dinner
>
> *on*
>
> Friday 11th June 20XX
>
> *at*
>
> The Palace Hotel, Oxford Street, Midchester.
>
> 7.00pm for 7.30pm pre-dinner drinks will
> be served in the Hexagon bar.
>
> *RSVP by 30.5.XX to A. Candidate, Chamber of Commerce.*

The instructions to the printer might be as follows:

- Midchester logo to be inserted where it says 'logo' (see attached compliment slip and pantone references).
- 120 gsm white card with gilt edging.
- Black print.
- Typeface Arial.
- Typesize 12 point.
- Type to be centred as indicated on attached rough layout.
- Print run 250.

Activity 9.3

The two main criticisms are that the content is dull and the language is indecipherable.

Somewhere in the text there is possibly a news story but the way it is written makes it difficult to find.

The readers of a local newspaper want to read interesting human-interest stories that relate to the area they live in.

XYZ Farming Ltd is probably a local firm in the area covered by the newspaper, and the writer should make reference to this in the release.

The news story the writer could have developed is that XYZ Farming Ltd has introduced a new product that helps local farmers produce milk that is more popular with consumers and dairies pay higher prices for it.

To add some human interest to the story, the writer could have found a local farmer who actually had sold more milk to the dairies because of this new product. The writer could then have provided him with a suitable quote in the release, stating his delight with the new product. The firm could then have organized a photograph of the farmer, holding a bag of the miracle new product, standing beside one of his cows.

The press release could also have been improved even further if the writer had avoided jargon and used short, punchy sentences. It would also have been a useful tactic to get the name of the product (Granary) into the first few paragraphs of the release, as presumably the objective was to publicize the Granary feed and the fact that XYZ produced it.

Activity 9.4

(a)

MIDCHESTER CHAMBER OF COMMERCE

PRESS RELEASE

Date of release: 14 June 20XX

A gala dinner to launch the first e-commerce conference ever held in Midchester took place last night.

Celebrity guest speaker at the event, Bill Gates, said: 'It's great to see all the best minds involved in the internet business gathered in one place.

'This event certainly puts Midchester on the map as *the* place if you want to be involved in any aspect of e-commerce'.

Over 200 people attended the dinner and Andy Potts, the Chairman of the Chamber of Commerce, said: 'It's an unprecedented success and there's already talk about holding another dinner next year.

'It's a great opportunity for business people at the forefront of technology to get together to network and enjoy themselves at the same time. It will probably result in the region attracting lots more inward investment from this area of business.'

The dinner launched a two-day e-commerce conference, which will be held this week at the town hall and will be attended by business people from all over the world. It will feature a series of lectures and a number of workshops, some of which will be held online with other internet businesses in the United States and Japan.

Tickets are still available at £100 per person from the Midchester Chamber of Commerce.

For further information about the dinner or conference, please contact Sally Moss at Midchester Chamber of Commerce, Market Street, Midchester. 0161 234 7890. Fax 0161 245 8923. E-mail s.moss@ madeupnamenet.co.uk

— Ends —

(b) The objective in sending this press release was to promote the chamber of commerce and to publicize the conference. It could even be issued to attract inward investment from e-commerce businesses.

(c) The press release could be sent to the local newspaper and also to specialist Internet magazines.

Specimen examination question (June 1999)

Twenty marks possible.

You work for a charitable organization that has been established to promote health and safety issues in the workplace. You would like to run a marketing campaign highlighting health and safety hazards in the workplace and the potential financial damages that companies could incur. You also want to send a poster featuring health and safety hazards to a list of companies that are held on your database.

Draft a brief for your Marketing Officer that indicates the objectives of the campaign, target markets and any other details that you consider the Marketing Officer should have.

Specimen answer

SPA
The Society for the Prevention of Accidents

To: Ruth Arnold, Marketing Officer
From: Davina Darcy, Chief Executive
Date: 7 May 20XX
Subject: Brief for marketing campaign

Project details
Marketing campaign 8, summer 1999, highlighting health and safety issues in the workplace.

Background information
Government statistics show a rise of 25 per cent in the last two years in workplace accidents. A recent *Law Gazette* article has revealed a dramatic rise in employer negligent cases where damages have had to be awarded and in some cases the head of the company has been given a jail sentence.

SPA has a large database of companies that have requested information on accident prevention or have attended one of our training courses or have been added to our list through our own research into accidents.

Objectives
- To send out 3000 posters illustrating workplace health and safety hazards.
- To generate 1000 requests from personnel managers in industry for leaflets about accident prevention. This information to be added to our database.
- To generate 1000 requests from managers in the construction industry for leaflets about accident prevention. This information to be added to our database.

Target audience
- Companies on SPA's database.
- Personnel managers in industry.
- Managers in the construction industry.

Message to be conveyed

- Government statistics show a 25 per cent rise in workplace accidents over the last two years.
- That accidents can result in employers paying substantial damages and they can be held criminally negligent.
- That more accidents than ever before are happening in the construction industry.

Media

- Posters illustrating health and safety issues in the workplace to be sent to all the companies held on SPA's database. Each poster to be sent with a covering letter addressed to health and safety officers highlighting the penalties and pointing out methods of prevention. A copy of the letter should be provided so that the health and safety officer can give it to the company's Managing Director.
- Advertising and PR campaign in *People Management* with a direct response mechanism for personnel managers to request more information about accident prevention.
- Advertising and PR campaign in *Construction News* with a direct response mechanism for senior managers to request more information about accident prevention.

Timescale

Campaign should run from the beginning of September to the end of October 20XX.

Budget

A total budget of £8000 is available.

Objectives

In this unit you will:

❑ Examine technological developments in the field of communications.

❑ Look at the impact of the internet and e-commerce on customer communications.

By the end of this unit you should be able to:

❑ Explain how technological developments are affecting customer communications.

❑ Appreciate the principles of web site design.

❑ Understand how the internet can be used to build databases.

❑ Be aware of the steps involved in an on-line shopping transaction.

❑ Describe development in telecommunications and digital technology.

Study Guide

This unit covers indicative content areas 2.5.1, 2.5.2 and 2.5.3 of the syllabus. It provides an overview of technological developments and trends in communications.

It may only take you a couple of hours to read the unit but it should take you the duration of your course to build up an extensive knowledge of current technological developments in communications by accessing material outside of the textbook.

Study Tips

By the time this book is produced many areas of this unit will be outdated as the speed of technological change is so fast. Read this unit as a guide and as a signpost to topics that you can read more about in the quality press, specialist marketing magazines and specialist technical press. You should also use the Internet to experience how it can be used. Look up some web sites that are of particular interest to you and surf the web for more information about technological developments. One of many web sites that you could visit is www.net-profit.co.uk, which is in the form of an online magazine and provides information about technology developments affecting business.

In addition, look at how telecommunications equipment in your workplace has changed the way you and your colleagues do your jobs.

If you cannot access the internet at home or at work, you could find access at your college or local library or even visit an internet or cyber café where you can pay for access.

Interesting facts

Before you get started with this unit here are some facts and figures that you should be aware of.

Forty-four per cent of people in the UK have access to a personal computer at home. The most common use is playing games (73 per cent), with education a close second (72 per cent). About a quarter of the population uses a personal computer to do some work at home (27 per cent). Only 16 per cent can access the internet from home but this figure has quadrupled since 1996.

Technological developments in communications

Technological developments in communications are making massive changes to your personal and working life. They are changing the way you can shop, find out information, communicate with others inside and outside your organization, they are affecting the way that organizations promote their products/services and even changing the way organizations do business with suppliers and distributors.

E-mail, in particular, has become so predominant that for many it is their main way of staying in touch. The opportunities for developing highly sophisticated presentations using graphics, animation and sound are a long way from the handwritten overhead transparency or the scribbled notes on flip chart paper. The days of having to plough through a heavy brochure may be over for some as they click their way to the information they require on a CD-ROM.

And even the telephone has changed. The days seem numbered for those people who are able to sound as if they are at death's door when they ring in sick to work. Looking bright and cheerful on the end of a videophone will put a stop to that activity.

Most people already find that being away from the office no longer offers a break from colleagues and the boss because of the constant interruptions from their mobile telephone. And when they return to their office, they are probably met with a hefty number of voice-mail messages, faxes and e-mails before they can reach their in-tray. But for those of you who feel it is all too much, you could try going on-line to the vast number of company web sites to find another job.

The growth of the internet

The internet allows people from all over the world to communicate with each other via a global network of computers. Since 1991 restrictions were removed that enabled people to use the internet to make a profit. This has led to a massive growth in the number of web sites in the world and in the number of people connected to the internet.

Web sites

Internet software is required to access the internet and once you have gained access you can visit an address on the world wide web. A famous web site address is www.bbc.co.uk but you will see thousands of others on business cards, on product packaging and in advertising. Any organization or person can set up their own web site. A web site might contain information about the organization or about a person's particular interest or hobby. Information can be communicated using a combination of text, image and sound.

Web site design

In designing a web site you should consider what you are trying to achieve with it and consider who your audience are, what they will be interested in and what sort of equipment they are likely to have.

Although attractive design with sound and graphics can bring a site to life, you need to consider if your audience will have the latest equipment and a large screen to enable them to benefit from these facilities. One way to deal with this issue is to have an alternative version of your web site so that those not using a conventional desktop computer can still access it without the sound and graphic effects.

It should be easy for visitors to get around or navigate your web site. It also helps if it is easy to access and has a fast response.

The contents need to be designed in a non-linear format because unlike a book, where people start at the beginning, a web site can be accessed from any page. Books are also generally printed in a portrait format but web sites are in a landscape format, where the width of the screen is greater than its height. Consequently web sites should be designed with a landscape format in mind.

Good web design also creates a directory structure for the information and establishes links between every page throughout the web site. Hypertext will allow users to jump to other pieces of related information on the same site or to other sites anywhere in the world. It is also helpful if key words are highlighted and menus of information on the site are listed in bullet points for easy reading.

The content of a web site can start off quite simply with some company and product information. However, it is important that this is updated in terms of content and quality. The web site could then incorporate an organization's corporate video and music to make it more interesting.

Web sites are developing all the time, so the published word, the animated graphic, the broadcast picture, digital video clips and voiced messages can all be presented and interconnected.

Web sites should also be interactive and allow for an organization to build up a database of customers. One way to get people to register with their details is to restrict access to certain pages until details are registered. Another way is to build in some form of response such as a 'freebie' if visitors to the site leave their details. For example, one law firm allowed visitors to their web site to register their details if they wanted to receive an advent calendar highlighting areas of the law that companies could fall foul of. This allowed them to establish a list of firms interested in receiving legal advice that they could target with information.

So for many companies it is not just about the number of 'hits' on the site but the way a site can generate leads or actually convert people to business when visiting the site. For example, the Easyjet site is designed to allow people to make on-line bookings and the company measures the success of its web site by the level of sales.

Web site costs

These can vary from a very simple web site that would cost around £1000 to set up to those costing tens of thousands of pounds which can handle on-line shopping. An average brochure-type site currently costs around £5000 to design and set up.

One aspect that many organizations forget is that once the site is set up it needs to be monitored to measure response and maintained so that its contents are not outdated.

Electronic mail

Electronic mail or e-mail is a method of sending text files from one computer to another which allows you to send messages across the world in seconds. One way to send and receive messages is to set up an e-mail account with an internet service provider (ISP).

If someone named John Smith set up an e-mail account, his e-mail address could be jsmith@tesco.net.co.uk. To send him an e-mail message, you would connect to the internet and opt for the 'compose message' facility. You would then complete the various parts of the e-mail and compose your message. Your e-mail message to John Smith would then show who the message was from (your e-mail address so that the person could reply to you), the subject of the message and the message itself.

A company can have a corporate mailbox with each employee having private access to their own little part of it. For example, if you worked at Tiger Tours and your name was Mary Smith, your address might be msmith@tigertours.co.uk.

E-mail is like having a postman living inside your telephone who can deliver post anywhere in the world at the speed of lightning. However, it is more than a messaging service because text, graphics, video and sound can be sent and received across the internet.

The information is stored in the computer until the recipient retrieves it. It is usually cheaper than other forms of communication because it only incurs the cost of connection to the internet service provider.

Cost comparison of e-mail with other forms of communication
Table 10.1 shows the approximate cost of sending a 10-page document to a city in the USA:

Table 10.1

Cost	Communication method	Time taken to receive message
£1.56	First class post	5–7 days
£2.00	Fax	5 minutes
£30.00	Courier	2 working days
15p (cost of local call)	E-mail	Almost instant

E-mail etiquette
E-mail can revolutionize the way you communicate because it is so quick, easy and cost-effective. It is also paperless unless you decide to print out the message or the document attached to the message.

Because most e-mail messages are simply text files, the usual conventions connected with letter writing, such as letterheads, typesizes, typestyles, justification, layout, paper quality and signatures, are ignored. This lack of convention encourages people to be less formal than they would be if they were writing a memo or letter on headed paper.

The medium also encourages brevity, which can make you more productive in dealing with and sending messages. However, it can mean that messages sound curt to the extent of rudeness if you are not careful.

In addition, because it is easy to copy a message to everyone in your office with the click of a few buttons, it can encourage you and your colleagues to saturate people with more information than they really need.

You should also be aware that your employer owns e-mail messages sent from your workplace and employers have the right to monitor e-mail you send using their computers.

Advantages of e-mail

- Local call costs to anywhere in the world.
- Easy distribution to one recipient or many.
- Speedy delivery – almost instantaneous.
- No time zones to worry about – e-mail works while your recipients sleep.
- Can be addressed to a specific person.
- Will be delivered even if the recipient is out.
- No messy paperwork lying around.
- Messages sent and received can be stored for future reference.
- Security passwords restrict access to your mailbox to you.

Intranet

An intranet allows you to communicate on the internet in a local network that is not publicly accessible. Many organizations use intranets to distribute internal documents.

However, it can be used outside the organization to allow nominated people to share documents, expertise or opinions anywhere in the world. The network would be protected to ensure that only nominated people could access information, thus keeping the network secure.

The most common form of intranet is where corporate information is published on an internal web site, with hypertext links to related documents, enabling enormous amounts of time to be saved searching for information.

For example, in a law practice that merged with another firm in a town forty miles away, the intranet was used to create an internal 'who's who' of staff, including photographs. It then developed to include internal phone directories, which could be updated without continual re-printing costs, practice guides on word-processing house styles, the staff handbook, and even what was being served in the staff restaurant that week.

Eventually it went on to be used to produce practice-wide know-how material and legal precedents. In other words, it became a giant internal library with easy access to staff from inside the firm.

The benefits of intranets

- Reduced costs in printing and distributing documents.
- Publishing information without delay.
- No physical filing – saving time and space.
- Ability to find information quickly.

Extranet

An extranet is an extended intranet to key players involved in your everyday business processes in order to achieve total collaboration. This may include dealers, suppliers or business partners.

For example, when General Motors started using their extranet to enable purchase orders to be made by their dealers using an electronic form process, the cost of the transaction went down from £35 to less than 10p.

Look at the CIM web site www.cim.co.uk. As a student member you can access the private qualifications extranet area and see what information you can obtain there.

E-commerce

On-line shopping

Of course, you can visit web sites to do your on-line shopping for CDs, books and clothes. But for many people who like to shop for clothes and books in the centre of a big city where they can see and be seen, the idea of on-line shopping is unattractive.

However, those same people may not be so happy to make the same boring weekly shop for routine food items on a busy Saturday morning. So big retailers like Tesco and Sainsbury have grasped the opportunity e-commerce gives them to help their customers save time by enabling them to automate routine purchases (that are only changed by exception) and have the goods delivered as well.

How to shop on the internet

It is very easy to do your shopping on the internet. The most common way is to access a computer that connects to the internet through an internet service provider (ISP). This is usually done through a telephone cable using a modem. You would then access the online store through a web site browser, usually by the web site address (URL) of the on-line store. For example, you could connect to the online bookstore http://www.amazon.co.uk.

If, however, you wanted to purchase a pair of jeans and you connected to an online clothes shop, you would pull down the menu to choose the style or cut of jeans, the colour and the size of the item you require.

You would then complete an onscreen order form where you would provide payment and address details. You would then need to wait for credit card verification from your bank or credit card company. Once authorization was given you would just need to wait for dispatch of your order from the on-line store.

Other ways to use the internet

It is a mistake to think of the internet and e-commerce (doing business on the internet) as only using web sites to sell goods. E-commerce changes the way you interact with suppliers and organizations and the way they do business with you. For many organizations the key benefit from e-commerce is to use it to provide in-depth customer information. It can also be used to canvass feedback from customers.

Banks are using the internet to add value to the service they provide to current customers. With some banks you can transfer money from one account to another and find out your bank balance.

Your local doctor may soon be able to improve their service to you by allowing you to order repeat prescriptions via the internet. This will not only save you time but also free up busy receptionists to deal with people waiting in the surgery.

The internet is also a fantastic resource for obtaining information and so is an ideal tool to assist distance learning. You can access news and weather sites, and there are many that you can visit just for fun. If you are interested in helping your children find out about space exploration, then you could visit the NASA site.

Utilities and other large organizations with many customers will be able to save time and money by producing automated account and billing information and allowing customers to make on-line payment.

Some firms are using the internet to improve communications with potential staff. On-line recruitment information can enable people to have a virtual tour of offices with a 360-degree photograph and 'hot spots' can be clicked on to enable them to go into the still image in more detail.

Electronic data interchange (EDI)

For many organizations the internet will enable them to source parts, reduce waiting times for stock, cut the storage area they need for stock holding, and will mean cheaper distribution costs.

For example, a network of franchised garages had their purchasing organized centrally using the internet. This now means that if a franchise operator uses an exhaust from stock, this information is automatically communicated through EDI to the exhaust manufacturer, who can then re-stock the garage automatically. Business process and business communication is also transformed so that there are fewer telephone calls and less paperwork, which has a great impact on the efficiency of the organization.

EDI is also used to keep track of inventory. For example, FedEx have opened up the 'back room' to business customers so that they can order courier service and track a package. This adds real value to their business relationship with customers. It also means that staff are not tied up with routine queries about the whereabouts of a package but have more time to spend dealing with orders and more complex forms of enquiry.

EDI can therefore improve a company's ability to work with others in terms of sharing documents and other information, which improves strategic partnerships on a worldwide basis.

The internet as a promotional tool

A good example of a company using the internet as part of its promotional mix is Vauxhall. They have produced a lavish on-line brochure-type web site but have made it interactive with a live national traffic monitor to encourage car owners to visit the site. The site is also heavily promoted with banner ads on UK sites that appeal to car enthusiasts, such as *Top Gear* and the *New Scientist*.

A web site can be used to deliver detailed information prior to purchase and after-sales support, which is particularly useful for big purchases where people need to look around for information in their own time and at their own pace. To sell cars, it is very useful to be able to allow potential customers access to detailed information that they request in the comfort of their own home and then have the option to book a test drive. The flip side is that they can also shop around for the best price in an international market.

Brand building through web sites is still in its infancy but it could prove to be highly profitable in youth marketing. It is no coincidence that the soft drink manufacturers and sports goods suppliers have been pioneers in developing high quality interactive sites.

For web sites to work, it is essential that they are promoted by the following activities:

- Relevant advertising.
- Links to other sites.
- Sending details of sites to large search engines.
- Using web site address details on all stationery and advertising.

Data mining

'Push' technology means that marketers can post direct electronic mailings to potential customers' on-line mailboxes rather than paper mail through their front door. This technique has been used by Dell Computers but has been blasted by critics for its intrusive junk mail status. Dell say that they use it to target mail only at people who have requested information and it means that they can use their database to segment targets and send messages that are closely tailored to the recipients' needs.

Signposts for the future

The way people use the internet is opening up to all kinds of possibilities. You might study for a course using an interactive video tutor. If you are considering moving house, you could see if your current furniture would suit the new house without ever visiting it but by viewing it on-line. If you are fixing your car, you could access a DIY guide and then change sites to order parts online. If you find that this does not work, you could then access the services of an on-line mechanic.

Other developments include faster speeds for surfing web sites, improved safety for credit card transactions, improved graphics cards to view web sites and more use of firewalls to protect information from being grabbed by hackers.

Telecommunications

There have been massive developments in the field of telecommunications.

Automated switchboards are now within the reach of even the smallest firms. This enables customers to leave a message for a particular person or department through voice-mail. This facility also enables the organization to pre-select the response, so that if the customer requires information they are put through to department 1, for example, and if the customer wants to order goods, they are put through to department 2 and so on.

It will not be long before the videophone is in general use, where you will be able to see the person at the other end of the line.

Mobile phones are getting smaller and more powerful. They can be used to access e-mails. The newest Nokia Communicator is not much bigger than a mobile phone but opens up into a keyboard mode. It doubles as a mobile office with internet access, e-mail, telefax and can receive pictures from digital cameras.

ISDN

An ISDN line allows your computer to connect to other computers much quicker and enables much quicker transfer of large documents than if sent using a normal telephone line. This technology has been successfully used in *teleworking*, where homeworkers can source information from the office fast and effectively.

ISDN can also be used for:

- Sending information with graphics.
- Video conferencing.
- Broadcasting.
- Telemarketing/call centres.

Digital technology

Increased bandwidth for electronic communications is a general trend and has resulted in the introduction of digital radio and digital television.

Digital radio

The main benefits of digital radio will be improved sound quality and the ability to send additional data with radio signals. This means that text messages and even pictures could be sent as you listen to the radio. While the idea of having pictures on a radio might seem inherently daft, it could be simply used to have the name of the artist visible as a record is being played. Digital radio will probably be interactive, with 'tell me more'

159

buttons that can be used for people to find out more information if they want it. This will mean it can still retain the benefit of being a background medium (when required), so people can listen to it at the same time as doing other things.

Digital television

Digital television will allow for more channels and two-way communication. It means that information can be sent in the background and be accessed by choice. The implication is that you can find out more about an advert if it interests you. This will lead to television advertising becoming more direct response driven.

The technology involved in digital television will mean that people can view programmes in real time or not, as they prefer. If they do not view in real time, they will be able to filter out things they do not want to see, such as advertising. This may lead to more programme sponsorship.

The knock-on effect of the technology will be that viewers can programme the technology to tailor viewing to suit their TV habits which will result in a 'Channel You' type of programming. In my case that would mean hefty doses of *Coronation Street*, *The Bill*, *Friends*, *Frasier*, any period dramas that might be being shown, Manchester United matches, news updates and very little else.

The impact of more channels will lead to audience fragmentation, with more segmented channels. The implication will be that sports goods manufacturers like Adidas will advertise more on MUTV than on traditional television channels.

Other developments

Sending large amounts of information is becoming increasingly easy. Cheap CD printing and digital versatile disks (DVDs) allow the equivalent of thousands of books to be sent in a disposable medium.

This will mean that your college will not have to produce all its courses in a hefty prospectus. The prospectus could be produced on CD-ROM or DVD and a student could have immediate access to the pages required and move around the information in a more interesting way through the use of sound, graphics and animation.

Exam/Revision Hints	You will not be asked examination questions on how computers work or the history of the internet or about jargon connected with technological developments.
	You should be prepared to explain how technological changes are affecting the way that people and organizations do business and communicate.
	Be prepared to answer questions that are set in a context of new media and technology but test you on other areas of the syllabus.
	See Question 3 in Unit 11 for one example of the type of question that you could be asked.

Summary	This unit provides you with an overview of technological developments and how they are affecting communications. It also outlines the impact the internet and e-commerce are having on customer communications and signposts future developments in this and related areas.

Activity 10.1
You should have been able to:

- Check the Frequently Asked Questions section.
- Get access to past papers and examiner reports.
- Update your details, register for exams.
- Voice your view in the voting area.

Past examination question (June 1997)

20 marks possible

As part of a series of CIM branch meetings with the theme 'Impact of information technology developments on business communications', you have been invited to be a guest speaker and your subject is the internet. Prepare outline presentation notes which clearly show the key points you would make and the structure of your presentation.

Specimen answer

Outline presentation notes – The internet

Introduction
What is the internet and how can it help business communications?

Main body of presentation
What is the internet?

- Vast worldwide network of computers.

History of the internet

- US defence origins.
- Universities wanted to share information.
- Graphic capabilities developed in Switzerland.
- Development in the 1990s as people and companies see huge potential.

How does it work?

- Internet service providers needed to access network, e.g. CompuServe.

Trends

- Vast expansion of service, very competitive on price.

How can it help businesses communicate?

- Fast cheap communications – e-mail.
- Videophone and videoconferencing.
- Sales potential.
- Catalogues/product presentations.
- Advertising.
- Sales leads/database building.
- Purchasing.

Examples of business use

- Web pages for corporate information and product information.
- Job vacancies.
- Sales leads straight into database.

- Customer service.
- Online newspapers and magazines.
- Better for business to business than f.m.c.g.

Case study examples

- TNT parcels tracked online.
- Levi Jeans web page – lifestyle advertising.
- Rank Xerox generated £2m in sales leads.

NB This is an adapted answer written by a candidate in 1997.

Note: For this question there were 20 possible marks. These were apportioned as follows: 6 marks for the structure of the presentation and 14 marks for relevant content.

In the answer shown here there was a very clear structure and marks were awarded for the following: the title, headings, sub-headings, bullet points and a clear indication of an introduction. Unfortunately there was no conclusion section.

The content of the answer was generally satisfactory and showed an overall understanding of how the internet can benefit business communications. The content could have been more up to date and should have had less detail on the history of the internet.

Unit 11   Guidance on the examination paper

Examination paper format

The format of the Customer Communications examination paper does not differ from the previous Business Communications papers. You will have three hours in which to complete the paper. It will comprise a compulsory question in Part A, worth 40 marks out of a total 100 possible marks, and in Part B you will have to answer three questions, each worth 20 marks, from a choice of six.

The grading structure
The grading structure for the examination is as shown in Table 11.1.

Table 11.1

Marks achieved	Grade awarded
70 marks	A or Distinction
60–69	B or Credit
50–59	C or Pass
40–49	D or Marginal fail
30–39	E or Fail
01–29	F or Poor fail

Revision technique

In order to do your best in the examination you need to spend a sufficient period of time revising the whole syllabus. By limiting yourself to few topics, you may find yourself having to answer questions that you do not feel happy answering but have to, because they are the only ones that relate to the topics you have covered in your revision. The other problem you may come up against in the examination is that an individual question may cover a number of syllabus areas and that it is only by revising all the syllabus that you can answer all the sections in any one question. In addition, you may find that by restricting your revision and examination question practice, you are tempted to answer the question you would like to be asked rather than the one that is set.

Time management

Time management can be a problem, with many candidates not completing all the required questions. As it is unlikely that your answers will be so good that they merit full marks, it is better to attempt all the questions required rather than answering one or two very thoroughly.

163

By missing out a question from Part B, you will immediately lose 20 marks. You will then have to produce consistently high quality answers to all the questions answered, just to achieve the 50 marks required for a pass.

The problem is worse if you tackle the three questions from Part B in some detail but then run out of time to answer the compulsory question in Part A. By making this mistake you then have to achieve 50 marks out of a possible 60 available from Part B. This means consistently achieving 83 per cent of the 20 marks available on each question you answer. Candidates working under pressurized examination conditions rarely achieve this.

Consequently you need to practise working under examination conditions so that you know what you can write in the available time and how long you need to plan, and later review, your answers.

You need to allocate your time carefully. From the 180 minutes you have available, you will need, on average, at least 10 minutes to read through all the questions on the paper and to select three from Part B. Read the paper carefully and select questions that will enable you to obtain most marks.

You will also need at least 10 minutes to check through your answers at the end. By doing so you are less likely to make silly mistakes and omissions.

This leaves you with 160 minutes to actually answer each question. As the compulsory question in Part A is worth 40 per cent of the marks, you should allocate 40 per cent of your available 160 minutes (around 60 minutes) to answering this question. There may be two or three parts to this question. If this is the case, you need to see how the marks are allocated to determine how much time you can afford to spend on each section.

For instance, if you have to write a report that is worth 20 marks and draw a graph that is worth 5 marks, you should calculate that the report is worth half of the 40 marks available and should therefore be allotted at least half the time (around 30 minutes). You should then spend a much shorter time (around 7 minutes) on producing the graph.

For Part B, which is worth 60 per cent of the marks, you could allow around 96 minutes. If you divide this by three you will get an average time to allocate to each of the three questions you will need to answer. This leaves you with around 30 minutes per question.

Obviously, within the time allocation for each question, you need to allow time to plan the question in rough and leave enough time to actually write a structured and well-presented answer. If you do run out of time, it is better to use extended notes rather than leave an empty page for which you cannot be awarded any marks.

Examination technique

In most questions you will be required to assume a specific role. So, for instance, you could be provided with information about the frozen food market and, in the role of Marketing Assistant for XYZ Frozen Foods, be asked to write a report about market share for your Marketing Manager. The Marketing Manager for XYZ Frozen Foods would expect the report to be relevant to XYZ's market position and the contents of the report should be expressed in relation to XYZ Frozen Foods.

Furthermore, the context of the question will, in many cases, dictate the content of your answer. For instance, in drafting the agenda for the first meeting of a task group in your company, you should not include the agenda item 'Minutes of the last meeting' as it is the first meeting ever held.

You may also need to make reasonable assumptions as part of the context of a question. So, for instance, if you were asked to write about how improvements in your company's office telecommunications facilities could affect your business, you would need to state the current position and how the proposed changes would change and improve communications. You would therefore need to make assumptions about the current position to make the answer realistic.

Special care should be taken in answering Part A of the paper, which forms a mini-case based on an article from the marketing press or comprises a collection of marketing data. The questions may ask for a report, a letter, a press release or even structured notes for a presentation about some aspect of the data. Your comprehension ability and skill in selecting relevant data are important for the compulsory question. If asked to write a report, it is useful to remember that report writing skills are as much about what you leave out as what you put in. Avoid the temptation to reproduce all the data provided in the compulsory question.

Examiners will be looking for your ability to select relevant information and present it in an appropriate way that shows you have analysed and interpreted the information correctly. For instance, if the data in the question says '55 out of 100 UK holidaymakers prefer to spend their vacations outside the UK' and you are going to use this information in your report, you either need to present this information as a percentage or you could say 'More than half of the people surveyed preferred to spend their holidays abroad'. In addition, the information you do use should be grouped into relevant categories and presented under appropriate sub-headings within the 'Findings' section of the report.

Presentation

Presentation is an important aspect of all good scripts. Examiners find it difficult to award marks where a script is hard to read because the writing is illegible. In addition, candidates should clearly indicate the question being answered and use a separate sheet of paper to start each new answer to help examiners follow a script.

In presenting your answers you should leave about 25 per cent white space on a page and use underlining and highlighting to make your paper easy to read and examiner-friendly. When you are presenting visual information you should use relevant materials such as rulers, protractors or a compass and colour where appropriate. You should always use the graph paper that is supplied for any graphs or charts that you need to draw.

Finally, although marks are not deducted for every spelling or punctuation mistake, if your answers are so flawed with mistakes that the examiner considers that your letters, memos, reports, etc., could not be used in a real-life business context, then the examiner will be unable to award a pass mark for that question.

Summary

In this unit you have been given several tips for how to pass the examination:

- Revise all the areas on the syllabus and practise examination questions.
- Answer the question set, not the one you would like to be asked.
- Manage your time carefully.
- Read the paper carefully and select questions that will enable you to obtain most marks.
- Take time to plan and structure your answers.
- Be sure you take on the role of the question.
- Consider the context of the question.
- Make any reasonable assumptions in order to answer the question.
- Make your presentation examiner-friendly.
- Use appropriate equipment to draw diagrams.
- Take care with your use of English, spelling and punctuation.
- Take special care with the mini-case as it is worth 40 per cent of the total possible marks.

As there are no past examination papers that fully reflect the new syllabus, you should use the following sample examination paper to assist you in your revision and examination question practice.

Firstly, you should spend some of your revision and examination question practice identifying how you may be assessed in the examination. Take the table at the beginning of the specimen paper and use it to identify how the questions relate to the syllabus you have studied.

Secondly, having spent some time revising, you should attempt the specimen paper under examination conditions.

Thirdly, you should use the specimen paper marking criteria and the set of specimen answers that follow the examination paper to assess your performance.

This activity will enable you to see areas where you can improve upon your revision and examination question practice.

How the specimen paper relates to the new syllabus

Table 11.2

Question	Syllabus area
1	2.4.1, 2.3.5, 2.3.7
2	2.2.2, 2.2.3, 2.5.1
3	2.4.1, 2.5.3
4	2.1.6, 2.4.1
5	2.4.1, 2.1.5, 2.3.3, 2.3.4, 2.3.7
6	2.4.1, 2.3.7, 2.3.1, 2.4.2
7	2.1.1, 2.1.3, 2.1.6

Specimen examination paper

Customer Communications   3 Hours' Duration

Part A

Bambino
You work in the Marketing Department of Bambino, a small retail chain which sells clothing, accessories and toiletries for mothers, mothers-to-be and young children. The shops also sell larger nursery items, such as cots, nursery furniture, toys and prams. The chain comprises five shops located in London and various towns in the south of England. The directors of the company are keen to expand the operation into the rest of the country. One option being considered is the launch of a mail order service. Research has therefore been commissioned, to identify if there is a market for a mail order service.

The research
Research was conducted by a marketing research consultancy, First-Research, over a three-month period in 1999. The research was carried out via 250 telephone interviews with Bambino's customers. In addition, 500 postal questionnaires were sent to a rented database of women living in the Midlands and North-West of England. The women had the same customer profile as Bambino's current clientele. The postal survey had a 50 per cent

response rate. The incentive for returning the completed questionnaire was entry into a prize draw for £500 worth of Bambino clothing or nursery accessories.

The Bambino customer profile

- 80 per cent ABC1 women.
- 20 per cent C2DE women.
- 12 per cent aged between 20 and 24.
- 50 per cent aged between 25 and 35.
- 38 per cent aged over 35.

Survey results

150 out of the 500 women questioned in the postal survey said they would be interested in a Bambino home shopping service. 100 claimed they were not sure if they would be interested or not. The problems that women associated with home shopping were as follows: returning faulty goods, extra charges for delivery and packing, colours that did not match the images in the catalogue and uncertainty about the sizes of products.

A pilot project that involved placing a direct response advertisement for a boxed set of maternity clothes (comprising a skirt, sweatshirt and leggings) priced at £72.50 resulted in 1000 orders and only 23 returned items. The advertisement, in *Mother and Baby* magazine, cost £1750.

170 of those questioned in the telephone survey had used a catalogue to purchase maternity and child-related items. Tables 1 and 2 show a selection of their views on home shopping.

Table 1

Home shopping service used	Women who had used the service (%)
The previous catalogue	44
The Mumcare Catalogue	51
Foots the Chemist Home Shopping	24
The Tiny Tots Trading Company	7
Other	4

Table 2

Reasons for using home shopping	Women who agreed with this statement (%)
Live too far away from good shops	41
Like the idea of shopping at any time	10
Use catalogues as an information source about products	25
Can compare prices easily	10
Can purchase on credit	21
Like to shop in the comfort of own home	49
Difficult to visit shops with children	28
Too busy to visit shops	35
Other	3

A number of respondents were interested in looking at catalogues to find out about new products on the market. They were particularly interested in reading about new, innovative products, such as bath mats that showed the water temperature, baby monitor devices and 'toddler-proof' safety gadgets for the home.

The following are the results from women who expressed a preference about the product category they would most like to see featured in a

Bambino catalogue: toys 5 per cent; toiletries 11 per cent; children's clothing 29 per cent; nursery furniture 7 per cent; prams 9 per cent; clothing for mothers 36 per cent; and other items 3 per cent.

The respondents described the kind of home shopping service they wanted as follows: available 24 hours per day; can reach the service via a Freephone telephone number; can purchase goods by credit card payment over the phone; and will receive goods within one week of ordering.

Seventy-eight per cent of respondents said they would not buy off the internet. The most popular reasons for this included not having a computer, not trusting the internet, unsure of how to complete a transaction and concerns about returning faulty goods.

Question 1(a)
Based on the survey data obtained, write a formal report for the Marketing Director supporting the proposal to establish the mail order service.

(20 marks)

Question 1(b)
As an appendix to the report, draw a pie chart that shows preferences expressed by women about the product category they would most like to see featured in a Bambino catalogue.

(6 marks)

Question 1(c)
A number of regular customers often contact shops wanting to order goods over the telephone. Until the mail order service is fully operational, it has been agreed that staff will continue to respond to these requests. To ensure that all transactions and enquiries are handled in an efficient and effective manner, draft a script to assist staff in dealing with these enquiries.

(14 Marks)

Part B – Answer THREE questions only

Question 2
You have joined the Marketing Department at a firm of accountants. The firm has a large marketing database which features a list of the firm's current clients, organized in alphabetical order. The database contains either a client's home address and telephone number or, if the client is a business, the company's name, address and telephone details. No other information is contained in the database.

The firm's promotional activity is limited to the following:

1 Sending mailshots to clients and rented lists to promote seminars on various accounting issues, such as taxation for the self-employed, new tax laws affecting large firms and advice for companies in specific industry sectors.
2 Advertising in the town's local newspaper.
3 Developing a website.

(a) In a memo to the IT Manager, advise him of the marketing information that is required to improve the database.

(8 marks)

(b) Based on current promotional activity, in a memo to the Managing Partner, suggest how the database could be expanded with details of potential new clients.

(12 marks)

Question 3
You work in a public relations consultancy and handle the PR account for a company that designs websites and assists firms who want to do business over the Internet. A journalist contact on a regional business magazine has given you the opportunity to write an article on internet shopping.

Use no more than 500 words to write the article. In the article you should do the following:

(a) Outline the steps involved in an on-line shopping transaction.
(b) Explain the advantages of on-line shopping to both consumers and retailers.

(20 marks)

Question 4

You manage a successful city-centre coffee shop that has run a week-long sales promotion to celebrate its first year of trading. The promotion was advertised on the local radio station and allowed customers who bought a coffee to receive a free cake or pastry.

By the third day of the promotion your supply of cakes and pastries cannot keep up with demand. There are now a number of dissatisfied customers coming into the shop complaining about the promotion.

(a) Decide how you will provide a replacement to the current offer and put up a notice in the shop window that explains what customers can expect.

(6 marks)

(b) Before the city's newspaper writes an article about the sales promotion fiasco, draft a press release which explains what has happened and what the offer will be replaced by. You still feel you can use this opportunity to promote your business.

(14 marks)

Question 5

You are the manager of a residential care home for older people. A relative of one of the residents has written to head office complaining about missing laundry items. You investigate the complaint and find that the clothing did indeed go missing but was not labelled and was rather worn out.

You decide to write a letter in reply to the complaint but, before you have an opportunity to do this, you observe a member of your management team speaking to the relative. As you enter the office, the meeting degenerates into a loud argument about the missing laundry items and the relative storms out.

(a) Write a letter in reply to the complaint. **(10 marks)**

(b) For the next team briefing, produce a ten-point checklist of ways to handle customer complaints in face-to-face situations. Your list should contain information that relates to the following: body language, barriers to communication, tone of voice, effective listening skills and helpful phrases that can be used in difficult situations.

(10 marks)

Question 6

You work in the Planning Department of the regional health authority and report to the Chief Executive. You have just been asked to co-ordinate a recruitment day to minimize the staff shortages that exist in nursing, catering, cleaning and portering jobs within the authority.

(a) You have organized a task group to help you with the recruitment day. You decide to call a meeting in order to discuss the various tasks that will need to be undertaken. Draft the agenda for the task group's first meeting.

(6 marks)

(b) Managers from the nursing, catering, cleaning and portering departments will be undertaking first-stage interviews on the day. Provide them with a checklist outlining the five stages of the interview process. Briefly explain what each stage involves.

(5 Marks)

(c) In the form of a flow chart, identify the planning process that you will undertake in deciding the promotional campaign for the recruitment day.

(5 marks)

(d) List two relevant advertising media that you could use to advertise the recruitment day. Briefly explain your choice of media.

(4 marks)

Question 7

You have joined the Marketing Department of a company that produces genetically modified food. The company is located in an area of high unemployment and has recently undertaken an unsuccessful recruitment drive. In addition, people regularly jam the switchboard to ask questions about the potential dangers of eating genetically modified food. The whole issue of genetically modified food seems to attract controversy and as a result the company is currently attracting a great deal of negative publicity.

(a) Identify the company's stakeholders.

(8 marks)

(b) Draft out notes for a presentation to colleagues about 'Changing Customer Expectations'. In your presentation you should outline how customers and their expectations have changed in recent years and suggest ways in which bad publicity about the company and negative attitudes to genetically modified food can be counteracted.

(12 marks)

Marking criteria for the Customer Communications specimen paper

Question	Criteria	Possible marks
1(a) Report	Report headings	4
	Organization, structure and presentation	4
	Analysis of data and report content	12
1(b) Pie chart	Title, labels and source of information	3
	Accurate content	3
1(c) Script	Shows staff questions and caller answers	2
	Appropriate greeting	3
	Questions to elicit information relating to product, price, size, colour, payment method and caller details	6
	Appropriate close	3
2(a) Memo to IT Manager	Memo format	5
	Content relating to the following information: type of client (personal or company), client names, previous business transaction with firm by product (tax advice or audit, etc.), client billing, potential future business, size of company turnover/profit, industry sector	7
2(b) Memo to Managing Partner	Memo format	5
	Content relating to the following: using rented list response, direct response ads in local press and interactive website where enquirers register details	3

Question	Criteria	Possible marks
3 Article	Format including title, sub-headings, logical organization and presentation of information.	5
3(a) On-line shopping transaction	Content relating to the following: access to online store through website provider, pull-down menus to choose style, size, items required, complete order form, provide payment and address details, wait for credit card verification, await despatch.	5
3(b) On-line shopping advantages	Content relating to the following: for supplier – reduces overheads, expands reach of business, supply chains shortened, can offer price reductions, can build up customer profile/purchase behaviour, enables immediate response; and for consumer – offers global choice, price comparison and ease of shopping at home.	10
4(a) Notice	Layout, clear presentation, minimum text to convey message.	3
	Content of message that is a relevant and realistic solution, e.g. voucher for free second serving of coffee.	3
4(b) Press release	Format: title/heading, spacing, date and contact details.	4
	Key information in first paragraph.	2
	Content which provides a clear explanation and opportunity to promote the business.	4
	Appropriate tone.	4
5(a) Letter	Format to include two addresses, date, salutation and close.	5
	Content – thanks for information, uses apologetic tone, does not mention clothing was old, possibly offer of replacement/adjustment. To pass, the letter should be one that could be used in a business situation.	5
5(b) Checklist	Two examples of each of the following required, with one mark for each example of the following: body language, e.g. not hostile; barriers to communication, e.g. no interruptions; tone, e.g. empathic; listening, e.g. not interrupting; phrases, e.g. 'I'm sorry you're upset'.	10
6(a) Agenda	Apologies, realistic agenda to include items to be decided, such as location, date of event, staffing issues, promotion of event and date of next meeting.	6
6(b) Checklist	Content to include the following with explanation: preparation; opening; conducting; closing; and follow-up.	5
6(c) Flow chart	Content to include the following: purpose/objective; target audience; message; channel/media; and evaluation of objectives.	5
6(d) Media	Content could be two from the following list: local press, local radio, outdoor poster campaign, cinema or use of job centre, etc. Needs brief explanation to gain full marks.	4

Question	Criteria	Possible marks
7(a) Stakeholders	Content should include the following: local community near plant; media; current staff; potential staff; lobby groups, government; customers (current and potential) and retailers/distribution channel.	8
7(b) Presentation notes	Format to include heading and bullet points. Not essay-style answer.	2
	Content along the following lines: consumer may now have ethical concerns, be more sophisticated and litigious.	3
	To counteract the bad publicity the company should have a sustained PR campaign which could include any of the following: careline, produce leaflets/info; advertising; responding to press enquiries; have spokesperson to appear on broadcast media; lobbying the government, etc.	7

Specimen answers

Question 1(a)

To: Lisa Litmann, Marketing Director
From: Wendy Mok, Marketing Executive
Date: 29 July 20XX

Report on proposal to set up a mail order service for Bambino

1 Terms of reference
This report sets out to establish whether a mail order operation should be launched to enable Bambino to expand its market to the rest of England.

2 Procedure
FirstResearch conducted telephone interviews and a postal survey over a three-month period in 1999. The telephone survey was carried out via 250 interviews with Bambino's customers. The postal survey comprised 500 questionnaires being sent to a rented database of women in the Midlands and North-West of England who had the same customer profile as Bambino's customers.

3 Findings
3.1 Mail order demand for Bambino's products
A pilot project to assess demand involved placing a direct response advertisement for a boxed set of maternity clothes in *Mother and Baby* magazine. This resulted in 977 orders (not including returns) and brought in a profit of just over £69,000.

Of those who responded to the postal survey, 60 per cent said they would be interested in a mail order shopping service provided by Bambino and 40 per cent who were not sure if they would be interested or not.

The telephone survey revealed that 68 per cent of Bambino's customers had already used a catalogue to purchase maternity and child-related items, which confirms that the concept of home shopping is appealing to our customers and women with our customer profile.

The majority of respondents were not interested in conducting their home shopping via the internet. Seventy-eight per cent would not buy products off the internet and the most popular reasons for this are as follows: people do not have a computer; they do not trust the internet; they have concerns about returning faulty goods; or they are unsure of how to complete a transaction.

3.2 Home shopping preferences
Respondents described the kind of home shopping service that Bambino should provide:

- Available 24 hours per day.
- Accessible via a Freephone telephone number.
- Ability to purchase goods by credit card over the phone.
- Fast delivery (within one week of ordering).

Of those who expressed a preference, 36 per cent of women would prefer to see clothing for mothers in a Bambino catalogue, closely followed by 29 per cent wanting to see children's clothing; whereas only 11 per cent wanted to see toiletries, 9 per cent wanted to see prams and 7 per cent nursery furniture. (See Appendix)

A number of respondents were interested in looking at catalogues to find out about new, innovative products, such as bath mats that showed the water temperature, baby monitors and safety gadgets.

3.3 Perceived advantages of home shopping
The main reasons why women purchased items from a catalogue were because they liked to shop in the comfort of their own home (49 per cent) and because they lived too far away from good shops (41 per cent).

Thirty-five per cent of respondents were too busy to visit shops and 28 per cent considered it was too difficult to visit shops with children. Twenty-five per cent used catalogues as a source of information about products.

Other reasons cited were that they liked the idea of shopping at any time and of being able to compare prices easily.

3.4 Perceived disadvantages of home shopping
Respondents associated home shopping with certain problems: being able to return faulty goods; the extra charges associated with post and packaging; and uncertainty about the colours and sizes of products.

4 Conclusion
The research showed that a majority would be interested in purchasing products from a Bambino catalogue if one was available and it appears that many of Bambino's current customers have already bought products by mail order.

An initial direct response advertisement generated high demand for maternity clothes and made a substantial profit for the company, even after advertising costs had been taken into account.

The main demand appears to be for clothing for mothers and children. Respondents want to be able to order goods with a credit card, using a Freephone number, 24 hours a day and want quick delivery.

However, concerns were raised about returning goods, post and packing costs and the colours and sizes of clothing.

5 Recommendations
Based on the research data, the following recommendations are proposed:

- To establish mail order shopping to expand Bambino's market.
- The service should be designed to give quick delivery, easy returns procedure and post and packing costs that are below the market rate.
- Customers should be able to order products with a credit card, using a Freephone number, 24 hours a day.
- Products should be available via a catalogue and direct response advertising.
- The catalogue should mainly feature mothers' and children's clothing, with a section for innovative products and safety gadgets.
- The catalogue should include sizing information and should ensure that the colour of clothing in photographs in the catalogue is realistic.
- Further research needs to be carried out to identify the best way to promote and distribute the catalogues.

Question 1(b)
See Figure 1 for Appendix.

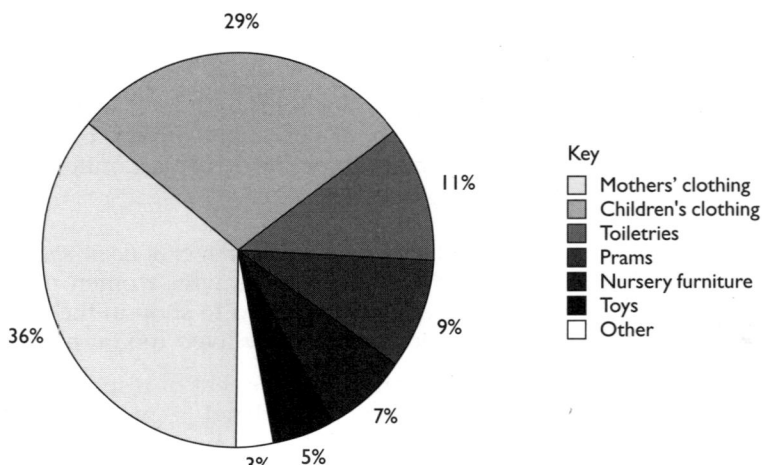

Figure 1
Appendix – Product category preferences
Source: FirstResearch 1999

Question 1(c)

MEMORANDUM

To: All staff
From: Marketing Manager
Date: 9 August 20XX

Re: Telephone transactions

As you know, we have a small number of regular customers who like to order goods over the telephone. Until the mail order service is fully operational, we will continue to respond to these requests.

To ensure that all transactions are handled in an efficient and effective way, I would be grateful if you would use the following guidelines for each telephone transaction that you deal with.

	Transaction stages	*Bambino staff response and action*
1	Customer rings.	Greeting, followed by shop name and location, your name and ask if you can help. For example, 'Good morning, Bambino in Chester, Helen speaking, how can I help you?'
2	Customer wants to order a product.	
3	Customer gives product details.	'Could you please tell me what the product is, size and colour (if appropriate) and how many you require?'
4		At this point check the product category number on the computer and input the order details into the system. Then double-check with the customer that you have the correct details.
5		'I'll just confirm the price with you, that's £x per x item and £y per y item.'
6		'Post and packing will be an extra £z, which will means there will be a total payment of £x.'
7		'Would you like to pay by credit card or switch/debit card?'
8	Customer states how they would like to pay.	
9		'Could you please give me your card number, expiry date and the name on the card.'
10	Customer gives card details.	
11		Ask which address they would like the goods delivered to.
12	Customer gives address details.	
13		Repeat the address details to the customer to check that you have the right information as you input the data onto the ordering system.
14		Give the customer a reference number in case they have to ring up to query the order in the future. Then ask them if there is anything else you can help them with. If the answer is no, then close the call by thanking them for their order and say goodbye.

Question 2(a)

Latham and Madison Accountants

Memorandum

To: A. Norak, IT Manager
From: Joop Staam, Marketing Manager
Date: 9 August 20XX
Subject: Marketing database

Currently we have a database that contains lists of clients and their personal details for clients who receive personal accountancy advice from us (as opposed to our firm working on their business accounts). In these cases we have no record of whether the individual actually has a business interest which could generate more work for us.

We also have a database that contains a list of company clients. For these we currently only have the business name and address/telephone details. We need to know who is our main contact within the company and we also need to know more information about the companies. We need to know the industry sector they are in, the size of business, their turnover and profit figures, the kind of accountancy work we are doing/have done for them and the value of their custom to us. Having this information should enable us to identify other areas of work that we may be able to do for them.

By adding this information to the database, we will be in a better position to target our mailshots to customers. We should be able to get most of this information simply by having staff from our firm undertake some formal and informal marketing research with their contacts within the various companies.

I should like to meet with you to discuss how this will affect the way the database is set up. My secretary will contact you to arrange a convenient meeting.

Thank you.

Question 2(b)

Memorandum

To: Petra Leeming, Managing Partner
From: Joop Staam, Marketing Manager
Date: 20 August 20XX
Subject: Expanding the database

Based on Latham and Madison's current promotional activity, there are a number of ways that the database could be expanded with details of new clients.

Mailshots
At the moment mailshots are sent to current clients and rented lists of companies to promote our seminars. We need to collate the replies from the people on rented lists who want to attend our seminars, as these people are strong prospects for new business who can be added to our database. From their choice of seminar topic, we can then send them information about a relevant area of accountancy advice tailored to their needs.

Local newspaper advertising
We need to incorporate a direct response mechanism in our local newspaper advertising. When people reply to an advertisement we can then obtain their full contact details so that we can send them targeted

mailshots about the specific areas on which they are interested in receiving advice, for example, tax, specific industry advice, business set-up, audit, etc.

Website development

We need to incorporate an incentive for people who visit our website to register their name, company name and contact details. This could be some form of free consultation offering a general accountancy health-check/advice session. This way we can use our website to add to our database.

Question 3

How would you go about shopping on the internet?

It is very easy to do your shopping on the internet. The most common way is to access a computer that connects to the internet through an internet service provider (ISP). This is usually done through a telephone cable using a modem. You would then access the online store through a website browser, usually via the website address (URL) of the online store. For example, you could connect to the on-line bookstore http://www.amazon.co.uk.

If, however, you wanted to purchase a pair of jeans and you connected to an online clothes shop, you would pull down the menu to choose the style or cut of jeans, the colour and the size of the item you require.

You would then complete an onscreen order form where you would provide payment and address details. You would then need to wait for credit card verification from your bank or credit card company. Once authorization was given, you would just need to wait for dispatch of your order from the online store.

Advantages to consumers

A firm's website provides a global presence not defined by national borders, only computer network coverage. So on-line shopping means customers have access to global choice. For example, a local bookshop may have thousands of books to choose from but the online bookshop can offer a choice of millions.

Some products are cheaper in other countries for a variety of reasons. It could be because there is greater competition which has brought prices down, or it could be that differences in taxation make the price at home more expensive. Examples of this are jeans and CDs.

It is certainly easier for consumers to shop around for cheaper prices without ever leaving their own home. Instead of paying for public transport to the shops or car parking fees, the cost of accessing the online store is only that of a telephone call.

Advantages to retailers

Suppliers can shorten supply chains so that goods no longer have to go through traditional warehouse and retailer distribution and services do not need to be sold through middlemen. This means that the cost of routine transactions can be reduced dramatically and in turn can be translated into price reductions for customers.

On-line shopping also means that suppliers can respond immediately to demand for goods and services. They can also become 'closer to the customer', tailoring products and services to individual needs as they obtain information about a customer's profile and purchase patterns.

Retailers need to have a professionally designed website and guarantee secure trading or they will lose, not gain customers. Retailers interested in finding out if online shopping could be relevant to them or wanting website advice should call WebMarketing on 0171 123 4567.

Question 4 (a)

COFFEE EXPRESS

CAKE PROMOTION

The free cake/pastry offer will be available on a first come first served basis.

If demand exceeds our supply of cakes/pastries, customers will be offered a free second cup of coffee as an alternative during the week of the promotion. (9 to 15 May inclusive.)

Thank you

The Manager

Question 4(b)

COFFEE EXPRESS PRESS RELEASE

Date of release: 11 May 20XX

City's sweet tooth hits coffee shop

Midchester's Coffee Express has been hit by an unprecedented demand for cakes and pastries during a sales promotion run this week to celebrate their first year in business.

Hordes of thirsty customers who were enjoying their usual cup of coffee also queued up for free cakes and pastries. By day three of the promotion, the shop's supply of cakes and pastries ran out.

Manager, Giles Sayner, said: 'I didn't realize Midchester people had such a sweet tooth. There have been queues all week and we just couldn't keep up with demand, so we can definitely say that the promotion has been a great success.

'But because our supplier couldn't deliver enough cakes and pastries, we have had to come up with another idea. Now and for the rest of the week (until 15 May) as an alternative, customers can have a second cup of coffee free.'

ENDS

Press enquiries:
Giles Sayner at Coffee Express 0161 889 1234

Question 5(a)

Green Gables Residential Care Home
2   Greengrass Way
Greenock
12 April 20XX

Dear Mrs Bryson

Your letter to our head office about your mother's missing clothes has been passed to me.

I have investigated the matter and have found that a blouse and skirt belonging to your mother did go missing after being sent to the laundry. They have now been recovered and returned to your mother.

I do hope you will accept my apology on behalf of Green Gables. I have spoken to staff, who have assured me that this incident will not be repeated.

To help ensure that your mother's clothes do not go missing again, I would like to ask you to label the clothes so that we can make sure that clothing items are always returned to their rightful owner.

Yours sincerely

Suresh Ghandi

Manager

Green Gables Residential Care Home

Question 5(b)

Checklist for dealing with customer complaints in face to face situations

Effective listening skills

- Do not interrupt customers when they are in the middle of making a complaint.
- Be open-minded and guard against stereotyping so that you do not 'tune out' from the complaint.

Body language

- Do not stare at the person complaining in a challenging way.
- Do not be tempted to give a bored sigh as if you are disinterested in what the person complaining has to say.

Barriers to communication

- Do not fold your arms as if you are creating a barrier between you and the person complaining.
- Do not allow any interruptions from colleagues to become a barrier to communication. Instead, try to take the person into another room or office where you can give your full attention to their complaint.

Tone of voice

- You should not raise your voice, sound angry or say things in a sarcastic tone of voice.
- Your tone of voice should not sound so cheerful that you sound as if you are making light of the complaint. You should therefore speak politely and confidently so that the customer feels reassured that you can do something about the complaint.

Helpful phrases

- You should show empathy to the customer by saying phrases such as 'mmm' or 'I understand'.
- You should apologize to the customer (this does not mean you are accepting full blame) for the fact that there has been a problem or use diplomatic phrases to calm an angry customer, for example, 'I'm sorry you're upset about this situation' or 'This is obviously an unsatisfactory situation'.

Question 6(a)

MIDSHIRE REGIONAL HEALTH AUTHORITY

NOTICE OF MEETING

A meeting of the recruitment task group will be held on 8 August 20XX in meeting room 2 at 3pm.

Meeting agenda

1 Apologies for absence.
2 Background to the decision to hold a recruitment day.
3 Briefing on vacant posts in the authority.
4 Decide on various tasks to be undertaken:
   (a) Job and person specifications to be written;
   (b) Job packs to be collated;
   (c) Agree a suitable venue;
   (d) Organize staff to interview candidates;
   (e) Decide how best to attract potential candidates to the event.
5 Allocate tasks.
6 Decide timescale.
7 Any other business.
8 Date of next meeting.

Question 6(b)

MEMORANDUM

To: All managers
From: Ann Candidate, Planning Department
Date: 11 August 20XX

Checklist outlining the five stages of the interview process:

1 Preparation. This includes preparing the content of the interview in terms of the information that needs to be given to candidates and the questions that need to be asked. In addition, some thought needs to be given to the logistics in terms of desk and chair arrangements, paperwork that is needed and identifying the staff who will conduct the interviews.
2 Opening. Interviewers must be prepared to set the tone and atmosphere of the interview with a friendly greeting and an outline of the structure of the interview.
3 Conducting. This refers to the main body of the interview when the interviewer will be asking questions, listening to answers and making any relevant notes.
4 Closure. It is appropriate for interviewers to make it clear when the interview is about to end, perhaps by saying, for example, 'And now a final question . . .' or perhaps asking the interviewee if they have any questions before the interview is completed.
5 Follow-up. The interviewer needs to collate the information obtained during the interview and decide on the follow-up action. This could be an appointment letter or one informing the candidate that they were not successful on this occasion.

Question 6(c)

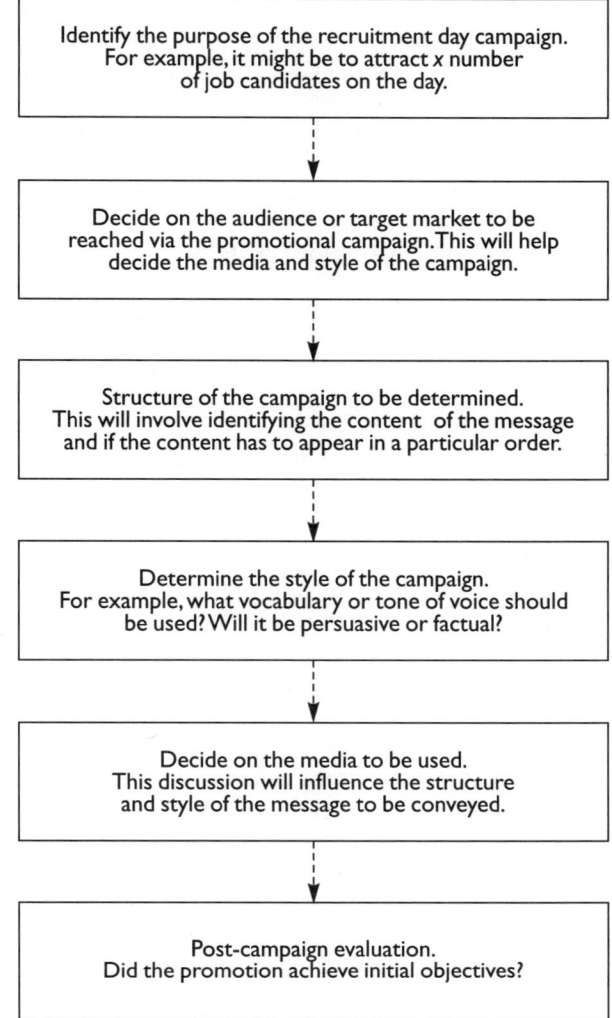

Identify the purpose of the recruitment day campaign. For example, it might be to attract *x* number of job candidates on the day.

Decide on the audience or target market to be reached via the promotional campaign. This will help decide the media and style of the campaign.

Structure of the campaign to be determined. This will involve identifying the content of the message and if the content has to appear in a particular order.

Determine the style of the campaign. For example, what vocabulary or tone of voice should be used? Will it be persuasive or factual?

Decide on the media to be used. This discussion will influence the structure and style of the message to be conveyed.

Post-campaign evaluation. Did the promotion achieve initial objectives?

Figure 1
Promotional campaign planning process

Question 6(d)

The media that will be used to advertise the recruitment day are local press and local radio.

Local press has been chosen because it has a wide circulation and is a known source of job advertisements. It also has a specific section for jobs in the health care sector.

Local radio has been chosen because it is possible to buy a package of advertising spots for a reasonable rate. It also covers a wider area than the local press and may attract younger people who listen to this medium. The other advantage is that it will give us a wide exposure to people who are not necessarily looking for a specific job, whereas people looking in the job section of a newspaper will be actively looking for a job. In this way we will be extending the number of people we reach with our campaign.

Question 7(a)

The company's stakeholders are as follows:

- Customers.
- Shareholders.
- Employees.
- Local community.
- The media.
- Suppliers.
- Distributors.

181

Question 7(b)

Presentation notes on

Changing Customer Expectations and the impact on XYZ Food Company

Introduction
The presentation will outline the following:

- How customers' expectations have changed.
- The current impact on our industry.
- How we can counteract the current bad publicity and negative attitudes to our products and XYZ Foods in particular.

Main body of presentation

Customer expectations

- Consumers are more assertive and willing to take action against companies.
- Action can be complaining, warning others away from the company to boycotting goods.
- Reasons are as follows: people are better educated/more knowledge-able, more widely travelled; there is more customer choice and customers are more aware that companies want to satisfy the market.

The current impact on our industry

- We are seen as unhealthy, unethical and even environmentally unsound.
- We have a recruitment problem.
- We have concerned people contacting us with questions about our products.
- We attract controversy and negative publicity.
- We have an image/PR problem.

How to counteract the image/PR problem

- Need to find out exactly what people are worried about and produce literature that answers these concerns with scientific findings using a fact not fiction approach.
- Need for general openness and information to various stakeholders.
- Need a positive PR and advertising campaign and establish a customer careline to deal with enquiries.
- Need to appoint a spokesperson to answer all queries from the press and to lobby government.

Conclusion
Summarize that customers have become more assertive, we are feeling the effects but we can counteract the current PR situation.

Approaching the module for continuous assessment*

In this appendix you will:

❏ Be introduced to a structure that will help you put together a Continuous Assessment Portfolio.

❏ Consider all issues that may arise as you work through the module.

❏ Consider aspects of team working which might apply to this module.

By the end of this appendix you will be able to:

❏ Put together a well-structured portfolio for assessment.

❏ Manage your time effectively in preparing for assessment.

❏ Work productively in a team to achieve results.

Study Guide

In this appendix you will be introduced to all you need to know and do to achieve a good result in the assessment of this module. There are no 'activities' in this appendix, as all the work it suggests relates to the assembling of your actual portfolio. In the introduction, we suggested that you read this appendix before you progress too far into your course of study, as much of the work can be done on an ongoing basis. If this is your first reading of this appendix, you will find that it makes more sense as you start to work on your assignments. You should return to this section as a final check before your folder is submitted for assessment.

Introduction

The Chartered Institute of Marketing has traditionally used professional externally set examinations as the means of assessment for the Certificate, Advanced Certificate and Postgraduate Diploma in Marketing. In 1995, at the request of industry, students and tutors it introduced a continuously assessed route to two modules, one at Certificate level, and one at Advanced Certificate.

*This appendix written by Gill Kelley.

With the revision of the syllabus for 1999/2000, the decision was taken to offer this route to assessment on four modules, two at each level.

Customer Communications is highly suited to assessment through projects and assignments, and this appendix is written to assist students whose tuition centres are running this means of assessment.

Carrying out a skills self-assessment

Students studying for the CIM Certificate in Marketing come from widely diverse backgrounds; some work in marketing, some are looking to move into marketing, some work in large organizations and carry out very focused roles, and some work in small organizations and carry out a wide range of activities. Some students are not currently working and are looking to acquire a new range of skills to help them find work in the future.

The 'Personal Development Assignment', which may be referred to as a 'Learning Log', gives you the opportunity to develop skills covered by the syllabus for this module which are very relevant to your personal situation.

You are encouraged to consider the following questions:

- *How important is this topic in my current work role? (or how important will it become in the future?)* You will have several sources of information to help you consider the answer to this question. If you are working, look at your job description, your last appraisal or performance review, and talk to your manager. You also have your own existing knowledge of your job to refer to – how is your role changing? Are you being asked to do certain things on a more regular basis? What is your organization doing? Is it introducing new products, or new computer systems or packages?
- If you are not working, look at advertisements for jobs that interest you and talk to other students about what their jobs involve.
- *How well do I do this aspect of the syllabus now?* It may be that you have not been involved with using this particular skill in the past, or perhaps it has just been introduced as part of your job.

A self-assessment checklist is shown in Figure A1. It consists of a list of marketing tasks which relate to the syllabus for Customer Communications. You should assess yourself against the list, marking (1) when the task is very important in your current role, or is likely to be in the near future, and along the scale to (5) where your job does not involve a particular task. You should then assess your current skill level in each area. It will help you arrive at a rating if you are able to talk to colleagues who you trust, as well as your own manager or tutor, and get their confirmation of your current skill level. When you have completed both columns you will find that the biggest 'skill gap' is shown by the widest gap between the numbers you have circled, e.g. an 'importance rating' of (1) and a 'skill level' of (5) is a key area for improvement.

Completing a Personal Development Log

When you have carried out your self-assessment tests and have arrived at an appropriate number of areas for improvement, your next step is to develop a plan to make these improvements. You may have come across the planning structure which follows in your earlier studies. It will also be useful in a personal development context:

Situation This is the result of your self-assessment.

Objectives Set some objectives for what you want to achieve, e.g. to improve my presentation skills with particular attention to structure, delivery and confidence within the next four months.

CIM Certificate – Customer Communications															
Task	Done now?	Important in current role*					Current skill level**								
Write direct mail letters	Y/N	1	2	3	4	5	1	2	3	4	5				
Write formal reports	Y/N	1	2	3	4	5	1	2	3	4	5				
Write briefs	Y/N	1	2	3	4	5	1	2	3	4	5				
Write press releases	Y/N	1	2	3	4	5	1	2	3	4	5				
Prepare tables	Y/N	1	2	3	4	5	1	2	3	4	5				
Prepare charts	Y/N	1	2	3	4	5	1	2	3	4	5				
Prepare diagrams	Y/N	1	2	3	4	5	1	2	3	4	5				
Use the telephone	Y/N	1	2	3	4	5	1	2	3	4	5				
Collect data	Y/N	1	2	3	4	5	1	2	3	4	5				
Present data	Y/N	1	2	3	4	5	1	2	3	4	5				
Plan presentations	Y/N	1	2	3	4	5	1	2	3	4	5				
Plan meetings	Y/N	1	2	3	4	5	1	2	3	4	5				
Plan discussions	Y/N	1	2	3	4	5	1	2	3	4	5				
Plan interviews	Y/N	1	2	3	4	5	1	2	3	4	5				
Lead meetings	Y/N	1	2	3	4	5	1	2	3	4	5				
Lead discussions	Y/N	1	2	3	4	5	1	2	3	4	5				
Lead interviews	Y/N	1	2	3	4	5	1	2	3	4	5				
Make presentations	Y/N	1	2	3	4	5	1	2	3	4	5				
Use e-mail	Y/N	1	2	3	4	5	1	2	3	4	5				
Use a computer database	Y/N	1	2	3	4	5	1	2	3	4	5				
Use computer accounts	Y/N	1	2	3	4	5	1	2	3	4	5				
Use video-conferencing	Y/N	1	2	3	4	5	1	2	3	4	5				
Create visual aids	Y/N	1	2	3	4	5	1	2	3	4	5				
Use graphics/colour	Y/N	1	2	3	4	5	1	2	3	4	5				
Use imagery/symbols	Y/N	1	2	3	4	5	1	2	3	4	5				
Use spreadsheets	Y/N	1	2	3	4	5	1	2	3	4	5				
Use the internet	Y/N	1	2	3	4	5	1	2	3	4	5				
Create a web page	Y/N	1	2	3	4	5	1	2	3	4	5				

Figure A1
Self-assessment checklist

*Where 1 = Very important and 5 = Of little importance
**Where 1 = Excellent and 5 = Poor

Strategy This is how you are going to meet your objectives. In the example given above you may decide that you have to improve your knowledge first, then practise and finally, ask a colleague for feedback.

Tactics The details involved in your strategy. Again, using the example given above you might decide to watch a training video which your own company uses, attend the session at college which covers 'presentation skills', and watch a colleague at work who has a good reputation for their presentations. Your next step may be to practise in front of a mirror, or, if you have the facilities, have your presentation recorded on video. You may also ask a colleague to watch your next presentation and complete a 'feedback' sheet so that you can measure your progress.

'Men' Who else is involved? The colleagues at work that you have identified to help you.

'Money' Do you need a budget? This is not necessary. You may decide to buy a book – but the library is also a useful source of information.

'Machines' If you decide to have your practice session recorded, then you need to find out how you can get access to the necessary equipment. Can your employer or the college help? Perhaps someone in your family has a camcorder you can borrow. Do you also need access to a computer to prepare the materials for your presentation? Does anything need to be photocopied?

'Materials' You may need to prepare slides or a PowerPoint presentation. You will need to prepare a 'feedback sheet' covering the areas you are looking to improve, so that your colleague knows what they are looking for.

'Minutes' When do you have to complete your assignment? It is useful to work backwards, in stages, from your deadline, allowing some time for contingencies.

'Measurement' Against what criteria will you measure your progress/ success? These will be detailed on the feedback sheet that you have provided for your colleague to use. You will make the decision when you have completed your background study – reading, training video, etc. Remember that you are looking to achieve, or make progress towards your objective, which should be SMART.

Now your plan is in place. Make a note of the 'milestones' it involves in your diary. By when do you need to have found an appropriate book to read (don't forget to write up your record of background reading!), and arranged to see the training video? By when do you need to have completed all of the preparation for your practice session? When will you arrange for your colleague to watch you present and give you feedback?

Now put your plan into action. There are too many plans that are lists of good intentions. You will achieve nothing unless you act on these intentions and see the plan through to the finish.

While you are completing this part of the exercise you should write up your Learning Log (an example is shown in Figure A2). Everything you do will form part of this 'log' – the plan itself, the notes you make about the reading you undertake and the video you watch, the notes for your presentation and other associated material, the feedback sheet from your colleague and, most importantly, your own reflective statement of what you have achieved and what you still need to work on. What was the most difficult part? How did you feel at the start of the exercise and how do you feel at the end? Did you achieve your objectives? If not, why not?

When you have made your plan for the first area for improvement, then you need to extend this to the other areas which you have identified and follow the above suggestions for each.

Working as a team on assignments

Working within a team on assignments can be an area of concern for many students who are being assessed in this way for the first time. However, many students who have gone through the process state that this has been the most useful area of learning for them. It is very relevant to today's workplace, as many of us now work in a team, or in more than one team, on a variety of projects. Areas of concern include – what if I can't keep up with the rest of the team? What if I let the others down? What if one of the others on the team lets us all down? Will it affect my marks if someone else does badly? In fact, most assignments are structured so that some of the marks are awarded for an individual's contribution and some awarded for the work of the team. Also, only one or two of the assignments are 'team' based – other assignments will be undertaken by you as an individual, and so the majority of marks you achieve are on your efforts alone.

Learning Log	**Date:**

Learning experience

Watching a formal presentation

What happened

I was invited to watch a presentation given by a potential supplier of new office equipment. I had attended similar presentations before, but was more interested this time because I have set myself a target to improve my own presentation skills.

The presenter was well prepared and brought his own computer and projector. The presentation was on PowerPoint and was very 'slick'. However, at the beginning I was following the content and only as it progressed did I start to concentrate on the presenter's style. At the beginning I found the presentation very professional, but when I focused on the way it was being put across I realised that he was sometimes just saying what was shown on the screen and, at other times, was not talking about what was showing on the slide at all.

Conclusions

When I make presentations, if I am confident in my approach and have everything on screen I will appear more professional than I feel.

It is important to be well prepared. It is also important to make sure that I both talk 'around' what is on the slide, and that I make sure what I am saying and what the slide is saying link together.

Actions

Arrange to make a practice presentation soon and get feedback from my colleagues. Make sure I am well prepared for this and that I rehearse beforehand.

When

Start straight away and make a firm date with my colleagues for two weeks' time.

Figure A2
Example learning log reflective statement

An important part of teamwork is working together to ensure that all are able to contribute on an equal basis – you will learn a lot about yourself and others through working closely on a piece of work which is to be assessed.

Dr Meredith Belbin, a British researcher, studied hundreds of managers working to solve exercises in teams.

He established that, in order to achieve their goals, individuals in teams have to recognize their differences. Imagine a football team made up of eleven strikers, or eleven goalkeepers! Many organizations think that by putting all their brightest people together, the team will consistently outperform other teams. This is not always the case, and Belbin realized that a successful team needed to be made up of a number of different 'roles' which related to different processes. For example, while there is a need for someone to take a strategic view, who is stable and controlled – there is equally a need for someone to pay attention to the detail of completing the task, and these people tend to be more anxious and introvert.

Belbin devised a questionnaire which identifies the role(s) which individuals are most comfortable in when working in a team. The roles are described as follows:

- *Implementer* – is stable and controlled and perceived by other team members as a practical organizer. They turn concepts and plans into practical working processes systematically. They can be thrown easily by sudden changes or too much uncertainty, and function through knowledge and expertise.

- *Coordinator* – controls the way in which a team moves towards the objectives using the team resources. They are intelligent without being intellectual, disciplined and have natural authority. They recognize the team's strengths and weaknesses and are good at setting priorities.
- *Shaper* – gets things done, is outgoing but can become anxious. They seek to impose some shape or pattern to group discussions. They have a high control need and can become impatient, impulsive and easily frustrated. Their outward confidence often conceals self-doubt.
- *Plant* – brings new ideas and strategies to the group through bright intellect. These ideas can inspire but a plant can sulk if these ideas are not accepted. The plant stays detached when team members get bogged down with problems and can then give a spark to move forwards.
- *Resource investigator* – is popular with team members and wonderful at networking outside the team. They build useful external contacts and resources for the team. They communicate, collect ideas, and adapt to find solutions from an outside view, preventing the team from stagnating.
- *Monitor evaluator* – analyses problems using their intellect. They can be perceived as cold, but their objectivity can prevent the team from making a mistake. They can be negative to change but their judgement is worth listening to.
- *Team worker* – cares about the team members as people and fosters team spirit. They are sensitive and loyal and don't like confrontation. The team worker likes harmony and works to develop this in team members.
- *Completer finisher* – is an anxious introvert who is particular about getting things done properly. They have personal discipline and give tasks more than the usual degree of attention. This can be perceived either as compulsive perfectionism or paying attention to detail. They also have a sense of urgency.
- *Specialist* – is someone who has a particular knowledge or skill. This individual is often more comfortable working alone than in a team. However, their contribution of specialist knowledge can often over-come a problem that is delaying progress.

You may not have the opportunity to identify your own team role, or those of others in your team. However, the key point to remember is that we are all different, and all have various strengths and weaknesses which can be used to best effect when working with others. It is up to everyone within a team to 'manage' the situation so that all are able to contribute, and that one person's strength is used to overcome another's weakness. Perhaps those of us who are most impatient with others when looking to make progress towards a goal have the most learning to do – it is part of everyone's role in a team to encourage, help and support the less experienced and less confident so that all achieve together.

There are a variety of issues that may arise when you are working with a team from your tuition centre. For example, most of you will be in demanding full-time employment which may involve working away from home from time to time. A member of your team may be ill, or have family commitments which make it difficult to attend meetings outside of tuition sessions. Again, it is part of teamworking to use the individual parts of the team to overcome such difficulties. Perhaps there are parts of the work that can be shared out and undertaken between meetings to minimize the time taken working as a group. How are you going to communicate? Is everyone on e-mail at work or home? Will contact be made by telephone or fax?

Teamworking can be very rewarding, and can forge strong bonds. Teams formed at Certificate level for continuous assessment work often stay together when they move on to the Advanced Certificate, and are still supporting each other when they tackle the case study at Diploma level.

Managing your time

What is time management? It's wisely using one of your most precious resources – *time* – to achieve your key goals. You need to be aware of how you spend your time each day, set priorities so you know what's important to you, and what isn't. You need to establish goals for your study, work and family life and plan to meet those goals. Through developing these habits you will be better able to achieve the things you want to achieve. When study becomes one of your key goals you may find that, temporarily, something has to be sacrificed in favour of time needed for reading, writing notes, writing up assignments, preparing for group assessment, etc. It will help to 'get people on your side'. Tell people that you are studying and ask for their support – these include direct family, close friends and colleagues at work.

Time can just slip through your fingers if you don't manage it – and that's wasteful! When you are trying to balance the needs of family, social life, working life and study there is a temptation to leave assignments until the deadline is near. Don't give in to this temptation! Many students have been heard to complain about the heavy workload towards the end of the course, when, in fact, they have had several months to work on assignments and they have created this heavy workload themselves.

By knowing how to manage your time wisely you can:

- Reduce pressure when you're faced with deadlines or a heavy schedule.
- Be more in control of your life by making better decisions about how to use your time.
- Feel better about yourself because you're using your full potential to achieve.
- Have more energy for things you want or need to accomplish.
- Succeed more easily because you'll know what you want to do and what you need to do to achieve it.

Putting together your portfolio for assessment

At last – you have finished all your assignments and your folder needs to be prepared for submission! A question often posed by students is 'How much should be in my portfolio?' There is no simple answer to this and it will depend on many things. Your tutor will have given you a 'Portfolio front sheet' which is shown in Figure A3.

This should be used as a checklist of your folder's contents and guide you through the process of putting it together. The first question you should ask yourself is 'Will this make sense to someone who has not met me?' The folder contents will be looked at by an 'internal moderator' – someone who works in your tuition centre, but has not taught you during this module, and may be looked at by one or more 'external moderators' – people whose job it is to ensure that all students on Chartered Institute of Marketing continuously assessed modules are marked fairly and consistently. This overview is taken as part of a quality control process that looks at the consistency of assessment within tuition centres and across the network of tuition centres.

So, when your folder is chosen, will the moderator get a true picture of who you are and all the hard work you have undertaken within this module? The first way you can help this process along is by including your CV and a brief description of your current work role. This will help the moderator put your work 'in context'.

The next thing which is asked for is an 'introductory page'. This again helps the moderator make sense of your portfolio. It does not have to be more than one page, and will be considered the 'starting point' in terms of the skills covered within this module.

For example, you might say:

> When I started this module I had just moved into my first marketing role. I was still uncertain of all that I would be expected to do within my new role, and this is why I decided to study for my CIM Certificate. When I

looked at the skills audit it was quite easy for me to identify my strengths and weaknesses. I was previously in a sales role and so my personal communication skills were a strength. I was used to gathering information from customers, in particular about what was going on in the marketplace and what they liked and disliked about my company's service. I also use the internet frequently – but only personally, not for business purposes. I have attended many tradeshows as part of the team which mans the stand, but have never been involved in arranging an event. I was used to working to achieve sales targets, and I had managed my own 'expense budget' in my previous role. My main weaknesses were going to be:

- Presenting information formally.
- Using databases and spreadsheets.

Once I had looked at this exercise I actually felt better about taking the module – but realized that I still had some way to go. Our tutor encouraged us to select topics from the list that would provide us with a challenge as well as being useful in our current and future work role, and this helped me pick the areas to work on in my 'Learning Log'.

Candidate name: _____   **CIM reg. no:** _____

Centre: _____

Section 1 (to be completed by the student)

Item	✓
CV and job description (if appropriate)	
Introductory page	
Learning Log	
Assignment 1	
Assignment 2	
Assignment 3 (if appropriate)	
Other relevant paperwork (not course notes)	
Final reflection	

This section to be removed before portfolio is returned to student

Section 2 (to be completed by tutor)

Item	Mark
Learning Log	
Assignment 1	
Assignment 2	
Assignment 3	
Total mark	

Tutor comments:

_____

_____

_____

_____

Figure A3
Portfolio front sheet

Your folder should now contain all the work you have done within your assignments. Again, it may be necessary to put a few introductory comments to each assignment, and a note of what your main learning points were from going through the exercise. If you have undertaken research for an assignment, then it may be appropriate to include this in the back of your folder as an Appendix. Your course notes should not be in this file.

After your assignment work you should include your 'Record of background reading' which is shown in Figure A4.

There is no limit to the number of sheets you include as a record of background reading – make your record as you are reading and don't leave it until the deadline for submission of your work. By then you will have forgotten where you found a particularly useful piece of information.

Your final reflection should conclude your portfolio and 'look forward'. Look back at your introductory page. What were your expectations at that point? Have they been met? Did the strengths you identified then turn out to be real strengths as you worked through your assignments? What have you learned about yourself as you have worked through the module? Did you dread making a formal presentation but, on the day, things went really well and you no longer fear being put into the situation at work? How much of your learning have you been able to apply at work? Have you been able to solve any real work problems through work you have done in your assignments? How much has your Manager been involved? What do they think?

This statement will be personal to you, and should look forward to points you have identified as needing work in the future. We never stop learning – keep up this process of continuous professional development as you go through your studies and you will have acquired the habit by the time you need to employ it to achieve chartered marketer status!

Candidate name: _____

This sheet should provide a record of reading you have undertaken in support of this module. It is not just a bibliography – you should list the key learning points from the chapter or article you read, and state whether you would recommend it to another student and why.

I	**Title/publication:**	**Author:**
	Chapter/article title:	**Publisher:**
	Key learning points:	
	Recommendation:	

2	**Title/publication:**	**Author:**
	Chapter/article title:	**Publisher:**
	Key learning points:	
	Recommendation:	

3	**Title/publication:**	**Author:**
	Chapter/article title:	**Publisher:**
	Key learning points:	
	Recommendation:	

Figure A4
Record of background reading

Summary

In this appendix we have looked at all the issues involved in tackling this module by 'continuous assessment'. Like life, you will get out of this process what you are prepared to put in. It is possible to achieve high grades, but you need to balance the work you are putting in to your examined modules with the work you are putting in here. Do not be tempted to neglect one in favour of the other as this will only lead to disappointment. One of the advantages of 'continuous assessment' is the feedback you are given on an ongoing basis to help you improve your practice. Remember, however, that your final 'grade' will be issued with your other examination results. Your tutor will be able to give an indication of how it may be graded, but final grades are awarded at 'moderation' and can be adjusted at this point.

Finally, remember that study and learning must be applied if it is not to be a waste of time, effort and money!

Appendix B Syllabus

Customer Communications

Aims and objectives
- To proide an overview of the communications process in the marketing context.
- To enable students to appreciate the importance of the customer when planning communications in marketing.
- To help students understand why effective communication is vital to all organizations.
- To ensure students can select and utilize a range of communication media across a variety of target audiences and business settings.
- To assist students in utilizing data to formulate effective customer communications.
- To explore the changing nature of customer dynamics and technological developments and their impact on customer communications.

Learning outcomes
Students will be able to:
- Utilize marketing research to improve customer communications.
- Analyse and interpret written, visual and graphical data.
- Formulate a range of communications to suit a variety of media and target audiences.
- Devise appropriate visual and graphical means to present marketing data.
- Select appropriate verbal and non-verbal communication in a variety of contexts.
- Apply customer care principles in designing customer communications.
- Demonstrate an understanding of customer behaviour and how that influences the use of various promotional methods.
- Appreciate the changing nature of the communications environment and explain how developments will impact upon organizations and customers.

Indicative content and weighting
2.1 Importance of the customer (25%)
2.1.1 Identifying different customer groups.
2.1.2 The importance of effective customer communications.
2.1.3 The changing context of customer needs and the impact of customer focus.
2.1.4 Building customer relationships and affecting client retention through communications.
2.1.5 Dealing with client feedback.
2.1.6 Managing customer care communications.

2.2 Finding out about the customer (10%)

2.2.1 Role of marketing research in communications.

2.2.2 Basic marketing research methods and sources of data.

2.2.3 Using data and identifying trends to improve customer communications.

2.3 The process of effective communication (25%)

2.3.1 The planning process – identifying the purpose, target audience, message, channel and evaluation of objectives.

2.3.2 The communication process.

2.3.3 The role of effective body language, tone, verbal and listening skills in communications.

2.3.4 Identifying and avoiding barriers to communication.

2.3.5 Interpreting, summarizing and presenting oral, written and graphical information.

2.3.6 Management of meetings and discussions.

2.3.7 The importance of effective oral communication – telephone, negotiation, interviewing and presentations.

2.4 Communication formats and media (25%)

2.4.1 Internal and external communication formats.

2.4.2 Using the promotional mix.

2.5 Technological developments and trends in communications (15%)

2.5.1 Using databases in customer communications.

2.5.2 The changing context of the communications environment.

2.5.3 The impact of the internet and e-commerce on customer communications.

Glossary

Above the line Any paid form of advertising on which commission is paid by the media to an advertising agency.

Advertising Any form of paid for media used to communicate messages to target audiences.

AIDA A useful principle for use in planning communications: acronym for Attention, Interest, Desire, Action.

Averages Measures of central tendency, used to find the number which is representativeof a group of numbers: the mean, median or mode.

Below the line Promotional activities not subject to commission being paid to an advertising or media agency.

Body language Medium for non-verbal communication: facial expression, gestures, postures, physical contact, providing clues as to our own and other people's behaviour and real feelings.

Claim or adjustment letters In marketing, letters dealing with faculty, mishandled or lost merchandise and other customer complaints.

Communication process Decoding – the message is received and meaning assigned by the recipient. Encoding – putting thought into symbolic or word form, ready for transmission. Feedback – the message is communicated back to the sender. Transmission – the process of sending the message, via a selected channel or medium, for example, telephone call or advertisement.

Customer A person one has dealings with.

Customer communications The process by which information is transferred and received from one individual or group to another both within and outside the organization.

Database A computer-based listing of names, addresses and other details of current and potential customers, which can be used for direct marketing.

Database management The process of maintaining and refining accurate customer information.

Decoding The means by which the recipient of a message transforms and interprets it.

Desk top publishing Allows a computer user to design and produce professional looking artwork.

DMU (decision making unit) Individuals who participate in the purchasing decision process.

DVD (digital video disk) Set to revolutionize the distribution of software. Looks similar to a compact disk but can contain more information.

Encoding The process of putting information into a symbolic form of words, pictures or images.

EDI (electronic data interchange) A network used to make an electronic link between an organization and its suppliers which enables paperless communications.

E-mail Electronic communications between users with e-mail addresses.

Graphs Visual representations which show the relationships between two variables by means of a straight line or curve.

Histograms Show a continuous distribution of data and can demonstrate the basic shape of the distribution with the display of columns/bars.

Internal market Those who are involved with the internal processes of a business organization, e.g. employees, shareholders, the board.
Intranet A private internet previously known as a network.
ISDN A digital telephone line that allows computers to send data and voice quickly.
IT The equipment, tools and systems used to create, produce, reproduce, distribute and store business communications.

Letters of recommendation Usually confidential, letters that convey information about people, their characteristics and suitability for a particular position.

Mean An average figure, found by totalling the sum of all the numbers in the group and then dividing by the number of numbers in that group.
Median The value of the middle number in a group; particularly useful when analysing extreme values in a distribution of numbers.
Memorandum Internal correspondence conveying short specific information.
Mode The most frequently occurring item in a list of numbers; useful wherein a frequency from a list can be commonly and easily identified.
Motions Proposals put to a meeting and which require a decision, usually through a vote.

Press releases Documents which convey topical and newsworthy information for the purposes of publicity and generating feelings of goodwill amongst the public.
Primary data Is collected specifically for the investigation or survey being carried out by using observation, experimental techniques, interviews and panel surveys or questionnaires.
Public relations All forms of planned communications between any organization and its publics with the purpose of establishing mutual understanding.

Reports Factual documents prepared to fulfil the needs of decision makers in organizations.

Sales promotion The use of short-term techniques to increase sales or achieve other sales objectives.
Secondary data Information that has already been collected and published elsewhere.
Stakeholders/publics Individuals or groups inside or outside the organization who come into contact with it or are affected by its activities.
Statistics A group of figures which relate to some important attribute or variable, presented in a manner which allows easy interpretation.

Table A matrix structure where data is placed in titled rows and columns.

Index

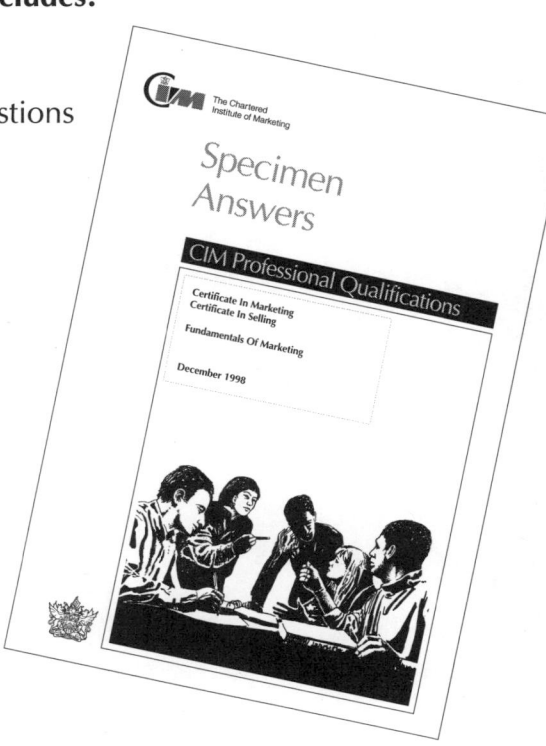